Gender, Branding, and the Modern Music Industry

Gender, Branding, and the Modern Music Industry combines interview data from music industry professionals with theoretical frameworks from sociology, mass communication, and marketing to explain and explore the gender differences female artists experience.

This book provides a rare lens on the rigid packaging process that transforms female artists of various genres into female pop stars. Stars—and the industry power brokers who make their fortunes—have learned to prioritize sexual attractiveness over talent as they fight a crowded field for movie deals, magazine covers, and fashion lines. This focus on the female pop star's body as her core asset has resigned many women to being "short-term brands," positioned to earn as much money as possible before burning out or aging ungracefully. This book is intended for use in undergraduate courses such as sociology of gender, media and society, and sociology of popular culture.

Dr Kristin J. Lieb is an assistant professor of marketing communication at Emerson College. She writes about branding in various industries, and has worked as a freelance writer for *Billboard and Rolling Stone*, a researcher for Harvard Business School, and a marketing and business development executive for several music-related companies.

Gender, Branding, and the Modern Music Industry

The Social Construction of Female Popular Music Stars

Kristin J. Lieb

Routledge
Taylor & Francis Group

NEW YORK AND LONDON

First published 2013
by Routledge
711 Third Avenue, New York, NY 10017

Simultaneously published in the UK
by Routledge
2 Park Square, Milton Park, Abingdon, Oxon OX14 4RN

Routledge is an imprint of the Taylor & Francis Group, an informa business

Library of Congress Cataloging-in-Publication Data
Lieb, Kristin.
Gender, branding, and the modern music industry : the social construction of
female popular music stars / Kristin Lieb. — 1st ed.
   p. cm.
Includes bibliographical references and index.
ISBN 978-0-415-89489-0 (hardback) — ISBN 978-0-415-89490-6 (pbk.)
— ISBN 978-0-203-07178-6 (ebook) 1. Women musicians. 2. Women in
music. 3. Feminism and music. 4. Popular music—History and criticism.
I. Title.
ML82.L54 2013
781.64082—dc23   2012029487

ISBN: 978-0-415-89489-0 (hbk)
ISBN: 978-0-415-89490-6 (pbk)
ISBN: 978-0-203-07178-6 (ebk)

Typeset in Adobe Caslon
by Cenveo Publisher Services

SFI Certified Sourcing
www.sfiprogram.org
SFI-00453

Printed and bound in the United States of America
by Edwards Brothers, Inc.

DEDICATION

This book is dedicated to women courageous enough to break the rules in the name of good, good music, or both—especially those WHO ROCK.

And to my extraordinary father, for being the strong, supportive feminist dad whom all girls and women deserve but few are lucky enough to have.

CONTENTS

ACKNOWLEDGMENTS   IX

LIST OF FIGURES AND TABLES   XIII

PREFACE   XV

CAST OF CHARACTERS INTERVIEWED FOR THIS BOOK   XXI

CHAPTER 1 CRITICAL FRAMEWORKS FOR CONSIDERING
           POP STARS   1

CHAPTER 2 FEMALE POPULAR MUSIC STARS AS BRANDS   31

CHAPTER 3 THE MODERN MUSIC INDUSTRY   67

CHAPTER 4 THE LIFECYCLE FOR FEMALE POPULAR
           MUSIC STARS   87

CHAPTER 5 THE LIFECYCLE MODEL CONTINUED   111

CHAPTER 6 THEORETICAL FOUNDATIONS FOR THE
           LIFECYCLE   136

CONTENTS

NOTES   169

REFERENCES   175

INDEX   185

ACKNOWLEDGMENTS

I offer my sincere gratitude to the village of people who helped make this book possible: Eileen Glanton Loftus, whose comments and suggestions throughout the writing and editing process helped immensely; Erica Schatle, whose wizardry in Emerson's Iwasaki Library helped me track down tricky stats and references efficiently; Amy Wicks, who should be inducted into the Graduate Assistant Hall of Fame for helping me with just about every dimension of the manuscript at one time or another; Mirena, Jay, and Brandon at Emerson Copy, who printed countless versions of this book at varying stages of development; Dr. Soo Yeon Hong, Dr. Angela Cooke-Jackson, Dr. Meghan O'Brien, Dr. Joseph P. Schwartz, Dr. Rebecca Ruquist, Dr. Kerry Herman, John A. Davis, L. B. Lieb, Lorraine Lieb, Katie Martell, Radka Zlatohlavkova, Samantha Barbaro, Andrea Service, Reanna Young, Danielle Hicks, and my favorite workaholics at Diesel, who each helped in various important ways as the project drew to a close.

I'd also like to acknowledge Tim Riley, who started as a critical interview source, became a valued Emerson College colleague and friend, and developed into my publishing mentor; Steve Rutter, my editor/publisher at Routledge, for "getting" my vision of my work and then pushing me and it much farther than that; and my excellent reviewers, Michael Borer at the University of Nevada, Las Vegas; Steve Groce at Western Kentucky University; Christine Hanlon at the University of Central Florida; Karen Sternheimer at the University of Southern

California; and Will Staw at McGill University, Montreal, for their constructive and instructive feedback, and the faculty and administrators of Emerson College for supporting my multidisciplinary work with both encouragement and a faculty advancement fund grant. I'd also like to thank everyone interviewed for this project, whether named in the book or not, for their candor, knowledge, insights, descriptions, explanations, and examples. Your contributions really brought the book to life.

Dr. Carol M. Liebler, my dissertation advisor and friend, and Dr. Carla V. Lloyd, the generous professor who first helped me to explore the ideas that led to my *Lifecycle Model*, deserve special thanks for being the earliest champions of this work. Susan M. Fournier, Douglas Holt, Jean Kilbourne and Grant McCracken also deserve thanks for inspiring me through their consistently creative, distinctive, and entertaining work.

Last, but not least, many thanks to my all-time favorite female artists, who don't often get the credit they deserve for making great music: Annie Holland, Justine Frischmann and Donna Matthews (Elastica); Carol Van Dyk (Bettie Serveert); Courtney Love (solo and with Hole); Exene Cervenka (X); Fiona Apple; Jenny Lewis (Rilo Kiley); Joan Jett (solo and with The Runaways and The Blackhearts); Kim Deal (with The Pixies and The Breeders); Kim Gordon (Sonic Youth); Liz Phair; Lucinda Williams; Neko Case (solo and with The New Pornographers); P. J. Harvey; and Tanya Donnelly (solo, with Belly, and with Throwing Muses).

And to so many others, for providing the songs and albums that turned into the soundtrack of much of my life: Adele; Aimee Mann; Alanis Morissette; Alison Mosshart (The Dead Weather and The Kills); Amanda Palmer; Amy Winehouse; Annie Lennox; Aretha Franklin; Kate Pierson and Cindy Wilson (The B-52s); Babes in Toyland; Belinda Carlisle, Charlotte Caffey, Gina Schock, Jane Wiedlin, Kathy Valentine (The Go-Go's); Beth Ditto (Gossip); Beyoncé; Bonnie Raitt; Bridget Cross (Unrest and Velocity Girl); Brittany Howard (Alabama Shakes); Carla Thomas; Carly Simon; Carrie Brownstein, Corrin Tucker and Janet Weiss (Sleater-Kinney); Cheryl "Salt" James, DJ Spinderella, Sandra "Pepa" Denton (Salt-N-Pepa);

Chrissie Hynde (The Pretenders); Correne Spero, Julie "Hesta Prynn" Potash, Robyn "Sprout" Goodmark (Northern State); Cyndi Lauper; Deborah Harry (Blondie); Diana Ross (solo and with The Supremes); Dionne Warwick; Dominique Durand (Ivy); Dusty Springfield; Etta James; Florence Welch (Florence + The Machine); Hilken Mancini and Chris Toppin (Fuzzy); Gillian Welch; Jill Cunniff and Vivian Trimble (Kostars and Luscious Jackson); Jo Stanli Walston and Cherilyn diMond (The Meat Purveyors); Jone Stebbins and Lynn Truell (Imperial Teen); Juliana Hatfield (solo and with Blake Babies); Kathleen Edwards; Kay Hanley (solo and with Letters to Cleo); k.d. lang; Kelly Clarkson; Kelly Willis; Kristin Hersh (solo and with Throwing Muses); Lady Gaga; Lauryn Hill (solo and with The Fugees); Leslie Day, Lori Yorkman, and Tina Cannellas (The Prissteens); Lily Allen; Linda Ronstadt; Lisa "Left Eye" Lopes, Rozonda "Chilli" Thomas, and Tionne "T-Boz" Watkins (TLC); Macy Gray; Madonna; Manda Rin (Bis); Mary Gauthier; Kori Gardner (Mates of State); Melissa Etheridge; Norah Jones; Peaches; Regina Spektor; Roberta Flack; Sade; Sheryl Crow; Shirley Manson (Garbage); Sia; Sinead O'Connor; Stevie Nicks (solo and with Fleetwood Mac); Susanna Hoffs (with The Bangles and with Matthew Sweet); Tina Turner; Tina Weymouth (Talking Heads); Toni Braxton; Tracy Bonham; Whitney Houston; Jenn Wasner (Wye Oak); Meg White (The White Stripes); and Poly Styrene and Lora Logic (X-Ray Spex).

List of Figures and Tables

Figures

1.1 The *Cultural Diamond* 3

3.1 Pre-production gatekeepers of popular music 82

3.2 Post-production gatekeepers of popular music 82

4.1 *Lifecycle Model for Female Popular Music Stars* 90

Tables

2.1 Sales typology for female pop stars 41

3.1 Gatekeepers 80

PREFACE

This interdisciplinary text focuses on issues of gender, branding, and the music industry that promise to ignite passionate conversations in sociology/women's studies/popular culture studies, mass communication/media studies, and marketing/branding courses. In it, I spotlight high-profile female popular music stars who rose to prominence between 1981, the year MTV debuted, and 2012, when this book was published.

More than any other cultural force, MTV made beauty and sexuality a primary factor in a musician's career. The advent of MTV in the early 1980s famously "killed the radio star," inverting the way in which fans, musicians, and executives experienced their favorite popular music. Prior to MTV, listeners heard music on the radio, and then saw the artist when they purchased an album, watched a television appearance, or attended a live show. MTV allowed audiences to see artists as they heard their music, forever linking the artist's image with her sound. Once audiences could see performers before buying their recordings, they began to have expectations about how their pop stars should look. For female artists, this presented a new conundrum, and a dual effect on their career potential. For some, such as Madonna and Tina Turner, these new rules created quick ascents and ubiquitous reaches, cross-capitalizing their success across various media platforms. But for dominant female artists of the 1970s who didn't have telegenic looks and charisma, new rules ensured their immediate repackaging (Heart)[1] or marginalization as behind-the-scenes players (Carly Simon). Talented but "unattractive" artists still existed, of course, but often at the margins of the industry if they did not succeed in repackaging themselves. New artists who were not camera-ready manufactured striking (and sometimes bizarre) looks or images for themselves or in their videos in hope of winning attention and exposure (Cyndi Lauper, Cher).

The video for Bonnie Tyler's "Total Eclipse of the Heart," a platinum single from 1983, provides a stellar example of an artist who didn't quite have MTV's definition of "looks" and responded by overcompensating with bizarre visuals and obfuscation techniques (e.g., shadows, long-distance shots, and short close-ups of the artist obstructed by seemingly random objects). This video is parodied as part of the Literal Video series on the *Funny or Die* web site.[2] Set in the context of Rod Stewart's "Hot Legs" video,[3] in which he and his bandmates are shot almost exclusively through the frame of a woman's legs, and Pat Benatar's "You Better Run" video,[4] in which the camera can't take its eyes off of her, Tyler's video offers a stark representational contrast.

While MTV changed the terms of success for many types of artists, including older men and black men, women, who already had a history of being objectified in popular culture, were arguably the group most affected by these changing expectations of what a performer should look like.

Despite this, the 1990s became a time of great optimism for women in the music industry. In 1996, for example, female solo artists outperformed male artists on *Billboard*'s Top 20 sales charts. Women also won the Record of the Year and Album of the Year Grammy Awards six out of ten times that decade, dominating the two most prestigious categories. Music industry books and trade articles announced a new feminist revolution. And with Shania Twain, Mariah Carey, Toni Braxton, Sheryl Crow, Alanis Morissette, Janet Jackson, and Madonna dominating the sales side of the popular music charts, the rise of the female pop star became a full-blown trend by the end of the decade.

But some feminist critics had their doubts about the long-term viability of this trend. As Susan McClary (2000, p1283) wrote: "despite the increasing prominence of women in contemporary popular music, periodicals such as *Rolling Stone* still tend to write about them in 'gee whiz!' articles that marvel at the sheer existence of such creatures, rather like the proverbial dancing dog." Others, such as James Dickerson (1998, p29), posited that these women had finally nailed the perfect formula for ongoing success: rebellious music that was directed at men and "expressed male fantasies about women," yet carried messages that resonated with women.

Many of the female artists who have since succeeded at the highest levels of the industry have adapted this formula to reflect contemporary cultural norms. Fergie, who has sold millions of singles and CDs as a solo artist and as part of the Black Eyed Peas, exemplifies this strategy in action. In "Fergalicious,"[5] she teases her presumed male audience repeatedly, telling them how "tasty," "delicious," and "hot, hot" she is. But she also tells her presumed female audience that she has her "reasons" for teasing the men (e.g., turning them on and taking their money), and declares that she "ain't promiscuous [...] all that shit is fictitious."

Female artists at the top of the industry continue to sell record-breaking numbers of units, even at a time when overall industry sales have withered. For example, with her debut album, *The Fame*, and its slightly reconfigured re-release, *The Fame Monster*, Lady Gaga has sold 20 million singles and 4 million albums (RIAA, 2012). Meanwhile, Madonna, who started releasing full-length CDs in 1983, has sold 18 million singles and 64 million albums (RIAA, 2012), and headlined the Super Bowl halftime show in 2012. For these *bona fide* superstars, possibilities abound, with concert tickets, clothing lines, fragrances, television and film opportunities, and magazine covers adding to their reach and success.

But precious few artists achieve such heights, and those who do increasingly rely on sex appeal. Music is a tertiary concern, behind the body and the star's ability to use it to maximum effect in videos, on magazine covers, in endorsement deals, and on stage while on tour. Media, in the form of cable channels, celebrity magazines, blogs and other web sites, have proliferated so much that these stars are on display 24 hours a day, and female artists who stay the "same" in the post-MTV era grow stale quickly and disappear from the limelight, if not the industry.

The MTV age also boosted the power of brands. Advertisers competed to win the buying power of young, trend-savvy viewers, and they did so by meeting viewers where they were—whether they were home watching MTV, in concert venues seeing bands, or, in more recent years, in popular online spaces. Those working behind the scenes to bring celebrity brands to life proliferated and became more influential, given the growth of distribution options, the promise of matching supply and demand more effectively through micro-marketing efforts, and the increased perception of artist accessibility (because you could see, hear, and read about them virtually everywhere). Yet, these new gatekeepers are underrepresented, if not entirely invisible, in our academic literature about the production of popular culture.

Pop artists have been studied through many lenses, but I only found two contemporary studies—Gamson's (1994) *Claims to Fame* and Ahlkvist and Faulkner's (2002) "Will this Record Work for Us?"—that used extensive data from interviews with industry gatekeepers to frame and explain their findings. The limited number of data-driven studies about gatekeepers, while unfortunate, represents an access problem—industry executives are busy and therefore unlikely to spend time helping with unpaid academic projects. They might also be reluctant to let outsiders see what's behind the curtain of pop star production for reasons that will become obvious later in the book. Given my prior experience in the music industry as a journalist and a marketing and business development executive, I had a unique opportunity to gain access to such people and learn about how female artists are branded and managed throughout their career lifecycles. I interviewed 21 industry professionals who had worked in the music industry or with music industry companies for 10 to 25 years, and worked in some capacity with gold- and platinum-selling female artists. I conducted in-depth interviews of 45 to 120 minutes with 21 respondents in 2006 and 2007, and then numerous follow-up interviews of varying lengths with many of the same respondents and several new ones from 2008 to 2012. These interviews served as the basis for Chapters 2, 4, and 5 of this book.[6] Interview sources included those who:

- managed female pop stars;
- promoted or marketed female pop stars;
- researched and wrote about female pop stars for industry publications;
- photographed female pop stars for CD and publicity shots;
- toured with female pop stars;
- served as personal assistants to female pop stars;
- wrote and executed marketing plans to help extend female pop star brands.

A list of those interviewed can be found in "Cast of Characters Interviewed for this Book." I have only included the names of those people who were willing to go on the record with their comments, though I have included some of the unnamed sources' commentary throughout the book.

This book uses popular music—something many students naturally enjoy, consume, and follow—to teach dimensions of sociology/women's studies/popular culture studies, mass communication/media studies, and marketing/branding in a relevant, contemporary way that resonates in their real lives. By offering students critical thinking frames through which to view the music industry and the artists/brands it produces, new dynamics emerge: the complex interplay between those who produce culture, those who consume it, the cultural objects that arise from cultural production, and the social world that sets the context for all of this negotiation and representation.

Throughout the book, I refer to these top-selling female artists as "pop stars." For the purposes of this book, a "pop star" is a female artist who has sold gold (500,000 units) or platinum (1 million units) across at least several releases and who has the capacity to extend her brand successfully into other entertainment verticals (TV, film, clothing, etc.). Women garnering this level of sales in the music industry are invariably positioned as "pop stars," whatever their genre of origin.

For example, we do not typically see platinum-selling female rock stars, and in the rare cases where we do (Melissa Etheridge),[7] they are often made over as pop stars once they achieve "crossover" levels of sales. Feminist music scholar Norma Coates (1997, pp52–53) explains why, even if women sound like rock artists, they are ultimately positioned as pop artists:

> In this schema, rock is metonymic with "authenticity" while "pop" is metonymic with artifice. Sliding even further down the metonymic slope, authentic becomes masculine, while artificial becomes feminine. Rock, therefore, is "masculine," pop is "feminine," and the two are set up in a binary relation to each other, with the masculine, of course, on top. The common-sense meaning of rock becomes "male," while "pop" is naturalised as "female." Real men aren't pop, and women, real or otherwise, don't rock.

Gender still constrains the types of musical roles available to contemporary female artists, further compromising their meanings. The gender constraints imposed upon female pop stars by society, industry handlers, audiences, and even female pop stars themselves will be considered in depth throughout the body of the book.

Cast of Characters
Interviewed for this Book

Peter Adams is a professional musician who has toured with Josh Groban, Rickie Lee Jones, Tracy Bonham, Juliana Hatfield, The Catherine Wheel, and numerous other artists and bands.

Janet Billig-Rich is a veteran artist manager and former Geffen Records executive who has worked with Nirvana, Courtney Love, and Lisa Loeb, among many others. She has also served as music supervisor for numerous film and television projects. In 2011, *Billboard* nominated her as one of the top 40 "Women in Music."

Lisa Cardoso ran Music and Lifestyle Marketing for Puma for two years, developing licensing and endorsement deals and branded events with major rap artists. Prior to joining Puma, Cardoso worked in a similar capacity for Converse on its Chuck Taylor line and for Reebok as a global marketing manager for lifestyle and entertainment. In 2012, Cardoso accepted a position building marketing campaigns and strategic music partnerships for Sonos, a company promising to "reinvent home audio for the digital age."

Anthony Colombo was a chart manager at *Billboard* for more than two decades, and is currently a music industry consultant.

Simon Glickman was a senior editor at the music industry trade publication *Hits*, and is currently a partner at Editorial Emergency, which specializes in copywriting and personal branding.

Kay Hanley is the former lead singer of major-label artist Letters to Cleo. More recently, she was a back-up singer for Miley Cyrus's Best of Both Worlds tour in 2007 to 2008. She currently works as a producer, composer, and artist manager.

Juliana Hatfield signed to Atlantic Records during the 1990s and performed with the first Lilith Fair tour in 1997. Once her deal ended, she began releasing her music through a variety of independent labels. She also made music and performed with her band, The Blake Babies.

Jorge Hinojosa has managed Ice-T for nearly three decades, successfully extending the Ice-T brand from music to documentary and feature film, reality television, fiction and non-fiction publishing, and gaming. In 2012, Hinojosa made his directorial debut with *Iceberg Slim: Portrait of a Pimp*.

Holly (Williamson) Hung is music director of Mob Scene Creative + Productions, which produces all manner of motion picture advertising. Prior to that, Hung was music supervisor for Mojo, LLC, a company that produced trailers for major motion picture companies, including Warner Brothers and Lion's Gate Films.

Elizabeth Lang is CEO and president of Muso Entertainment, a Los Angeles-based music marketing firm. Lang is a veteran publicist who worked with LeAnn Rimes, Woodstock 1999, and Rock the Vote prior to starting her own company.

Douglas Melville is chief diversity officer for TWBA, a Top 10 global advertising agency. In his previous executive-level marketing and advertising positions, Melville worked extensively with top celebrity brands in music, film, and sports. Past clients include multi-platinum-selling female pop stars.

Jamie Morris worked as a web marketer and database manager for a prominent independent music retailer (Newbury Comics), and a record label (Atomic Pop) before becoming manager of Interactive Marketing Systems for Paramount Pictures.

Lars Murray is vice president of digital for Sony Music. Prior to joining Sony, Murray held executive-level multi-media marketing positions with Virgin and Rykodisc.

Tim Riley is an author, music historian, and National Public Radio (NPR) critic who has written several biographies about prominent popular music stars, including Madonna, John Lennon, and Bob Dylan. He currently teaches journalism at Emerson College in Boston, Massachusetts.

Stephen Thompson was the *Onion*'s AV club editor for just under a decade, and is now an online music producer for NPR. Thompson also edits music-related columns for NPR.org, including Song of the Day, and participates regularly on NPR's *Pop Culture Happy Hour* podcast.

I also interviewed six other publicists, journalists, photographers, event marketers, artist assistants, and label executives throughout the process of writing this book. They agreed to speak candidly with me, but under the condition of anonymity, as in some cases they are contractually prohibited from making statements using their professional titles, and in others, participants simply felt vulnerable speaking so honestly about the workings of the industry.

1

CRITICAL FRAMEWORKS FOR CONSIDERING POP STARS

Lady Gaga exploded onto the popular music charts in 2008, selling millions of CDs, cycling through hundreds of dramatic and provocative costumes, and achieving a level of cultural resonance that made her ubiquitous by 2009. If you somehow missed her throaty "Ga ga oh la la" on the radio, there's little chance you missed the media coverage of her meat ensemble, her egg enclosure, or her Kermit the Frog dress.

Critics and fans have called her an original, a true game-changer for women in popular music. From a branding standpoint she is—her ability to forge meaningful relationships with fans using social media tools remains unparalleled and astonishing.[1] But when you peel off Gaga's meat suits, makeup, and wigs, what she really sells is the same old-school sexual fantasy offered by countless others—differentiated by a dash of modern freak, a heap of insecurity, and a series of exciting art installations. Her outfits arguably generate more discussion than her music.[2]

One of Gaga's signature rallying cries is "I'm a free bitch!" But her actions indicate how far from "free" she is. In theory, she can play the music business game however she wants; but if only one path—a path that emphasizes sex and shock value over musical talent—leads to stardom for female artists, so-called artist agency scarcely matters. "Bad Romance," which won MTV's Best Video Award in 2009, features

Gaga desperately changing clothes 15 times, and then being pawed by a group of women while men watch from a nearby couch.[3] As Gaga crawls toward the audience, she sings, "I want your love," and then dances in her bra and panties before ending up scorched in her bed by the video's end. If that's not an allegory for life as a contemporary female popular music star, it probably should be.[4]

The Cultural Diamond

Gaga's appeal reaches well beyond her music. Her success stems in large part from her audience connections, earned through her tireless and effective social media efforts. Wendy Griswold's *Cultural Diamond* (2008) provides a useful framework for considering the sociological forces that influence the construction and reception of female pop stars such as Gaga and their related product offerings. Griswold sets up four points of interaction: the *social world, cultural object, creator,* and *receivers.* These four points are critical for understanding *any* sociological process, as they are inextricably linked and mutually reinforcing. The *social world* covers all social interaction, including institutions such as families, schools or governments, and less organized social relation-ships. It represents all parts of our constructed social reality, including the aforementioned institutions, those who create symbols and messages, those who receive symbols and messages, and the symbols and messages themselves.

The *cultural object* point on the *Cultural Diamond* is, for the purposes of this book, the female pop star. (It could also be a specific CD or performance, but the artist serves as the dominant unit of inquiry throughout the text for consistency.) The *creator* point of the *Cultural Diamond* represents the people who create and distribute the messages and symbols that circulate throughout society. In the music industry, these roles are inhabited by publicists, artist managers, bloggers, photo-graphers, radio programmers, and retailers—basically anyone involved in assembling pop star symbols, images, messages, and narratives. One could also argue that modern artists such as Lady Gaga are *creators* as much as they are *cultural objects*, as long as we acknowledge that any pop star at or near Gaga's level has legions of people working on her behalf

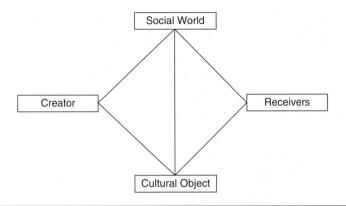

Figure 1.1 The *Cultural Diamond* (Wendy Griswold/Pine Forge Press).

to fastidiously create, maintain, and update her brand. Finally, the *receiver* point on the *Cultural Diamond* corresponds with music and pop culture audiences—fans of Lady Gaga who follow her for her music, her performances, her narratives, her fashion choices, her social agenda, or any combination of these things.

If we accept the relatively stable, mutually reinforcing societal forces presented in the *Cultural Diamond*, and acknowledge that there are constantly changing social dynamics among the individuals living within them, it makes sense to look for integrated explanations about individual behavior. This curiosity has led scholars from numerous fields to study how symbols, negotiated reality, and the social construction of society aids our general understanding of the *roles* that people play in society and the reasons for their role choices.

Sociological approaches to cultural production

For our purposes, the *Cultural Diamond* should be viewed as an umbrella or a container for the other theories presented throughout the book. Griswold notes that it is intended as a framework for all social interaction, and encourages the supplemental use of theories and models to explain more about the nature of the relationships between the points on the diamond.

Two schools of thought from the field of sociology prove useful in explaining the construction, maintenance, and reception of female popular music stars. Critical theory is a macro-level perspective that argues that popular culture arises from a top-down approach in which profit-motivated media companies sell the masses mindless entertainment to uphold dominant ideologies, thus controlling and profiting from audiences (Grazian, 2010). Those subscribing to the critical theory approach regard the media industries as able to "manufacture desires, perpetuate stereotypes, and mold human minds" (Grazian, 2010, p46) and to "reproduce social inequality by reinforcing degrading stereotypes of women" (Grazian, 2010, p57). This approach may sound somewhat anachronistic in that it often assumes a helpless audience unwilling or unable to resist the dominant messages of the culture industries. But progressive scholars within this tradition believe in the notion of polysemy, or the idea that a single sign (e.g., word, image, or, for our purposes here, pop star) can have multiple reasonable meanings or interpretations. But these words, images, and symbols exist in a broader production context, which helps to shape at least some of these meanings. Grazian (2010, p61) explained the process by which meanings can become powerful myths that act as cultural shorthand for those receiving them: "cultural hegemony operates at the level of common sense; it is a soft power that quietly engineers consensus around a set of myths we have come to take for granted." In the world of female pop stars, these myths center around youth, beauty, and sexuality, discussed in greater detail later in the book.

While the critical perspective provides a useful way of understanding the production of popular culture, we must dig deeper into symbolic interactionism and selected theories from sociology/women's studies/popular culture studies, communication/media studies, and marketing/branding to assemble all the parts necessary to study the way in which female pop stars are created, managed, and received by the various players on the *Cultural Diamond*.

Symbolic interactionism is a micro-level theory that suggests that neither the audience nor the media system singularly produces popular culture; rather, popular culture arises from the interactions between the various players and positions on the *Cultural Diamond*. In other words, audiences can resist dominant messages sent by producers, but they can also be influenced by them, as well as by other micro-level influences, such as friends and thought leaders in their given cultural circles.

Symbolic interactionism, named by Herbert Blumer in 1969, developed out of resistance to behaviorism, which held that all behaviors are acquired through conditioning, typically through reinforcement or punishment (Watson, 1913; Blumer, 1986). But the foundations of this type of interactionism, which informs contemporary thinking in communication and sociology, began as far back as 1902 when sociologist Charles Horton Cooley offered the concept of a "looking glass self," where a person's view of herself is a reflection of her expectation or imagination of other people's evaluations of her. In other words, we internalize how we *think* other people view us into our own self-image. "The imaginations people have of one another," Cooley (1902, pp26–27) wrote, "are the solid facts of society." Philosopher George Herbert Mead (1934, 1982)[5] used baseball as a way of showing how people learn to play various roles in society, offering that people don't learn from simple mimicry, but rather from interaction with and reinforcement from one another. (Mimicry wouldn't work in baseball, as we need pitchers, catchers, first basemen, and all of the other positions, and players need to adapt their behavior for the role/position they play.)

Sociologist/social psychologist Erving Goffman (1959) suggested that the roles people play are essentially scripted for various audiences and that as people act out such roles, they view themselves through the lens of their perceived audience. Returning to Lady Gaga, we can see how she acts or evolves based on her interpretation of her reception by the music industry, fans, and other artists alike. Goffman (1959) would likely classify Gaga as a master of "impression management" because while most people attempt to regulate their self-image to some extent, female pop stars arguably do so consciously and continuously, as their "self" is often a branded commodity. How these various audiences interpret or receive Gaga's actions, music, or narratives depends upon the meanings they ascribe to her, and this is a function of the ever-changing factors discussed above. Audiences also respond to Gaga based on their expectations of normative feminine behavior in contemporary society.[6] For example, Gaga's decision to wear a meat outfit[7] to the 2011 Video Music Awards (VMA) and immediately after on the *Ellen DeGeneres Show* was decidedly unladylike, as it shocked and disgusted vegans, vegetarians, and plenty of others, challenged norms of fashion and hygiene, and looked unattractive. At the same time, she drew interest for her bizarre and unprecedented fashion choice, and for what she said it represented—her support of individuality and gay rights.

Mead (1982) posited that human beings do not react directly to events, but rather to the interpreted meanings associated with those events. And given that these interpreted meanings are always in flux, so too are people's reactions to events. We can see this idea in action when we look at the range of interpretations of Gaga's meat outfit (e.g., she's crazy; she's disgusting; she'll do anything for attention; she's a visionary; she's making a political statement; she's challenging gender norms by being so brash; she's offending animal-rights activists; she's run out of tricks, etc.).

Consumer researcher Michael Solomon (1983) summarized Mead's work, offering that cultural symbols are learned through interaction and then mediate subsequent interactions—in other words, once a person learns a culture (e.g., the music industry), she should be able to predict the behaviors of others in it. A female pop star learns how to play her assumed "role" from her peers, her bosses, her audience, and their combined responses to her. Her definition of self comes from these evaluations, so it is a social process, not a personal one. Some pop stars create alternate identities (e.g., Lady Gaga, Pink, Beyoncé's "Sasha Fierce," and Nicki Minaj's various alter egos) presumably to separate the personal self from the public self. Berger and Luckmann (1966, p23) discussed the "ongoing correspondence between *my* meanings and *their* meanings in the world," acknowledging that there is a common *social world* between them, but it is highly subjective because it is socially constructed.[8]

As noted in the opening anecdote, it's not easy being a female pop star in contemporary times. The pace of communication, accelerated by 24-hour television news cycles and the 24-hour social cycle offered by the Internet and widely adopted social media platforms, has compelled celebrities to strategize *continuously* to remain culturally relevant. The celebrities have become dynamic brands that maintain overarching themes while adapting the specific communication of these themes through music, a mere subset of their larger, ongoing cable and online personalities. Meanwhile, audiences (*receivers*) scramble to make their own meanings as they react to *cultural objects*. The new pace of life has effectively amplified the inextricable links between and among the forces explained by the *Cultural Diamond*.

On the one hand, we have theory that supports *receivers/audiences* as having *agency*—that is, the ability to make their own discriminating choices based on the information they receive. But then we have stable social forces in our *social world* that effectively constrain those choices. The players represented on the *Cultural Diamond* can do numerous things that they rarely do in actuality. For example, record labels could sign more artists like Adele, Kelly Clarkson, or Beth Ditto (from Gossip)—powerful music-first singers who resonate deeply with their audiences, but aren't as hyper-sexualized as most contemporary female popular music stars. But based on the limits of our social system, our modern music industry, our country's gender norms and expectations, and our capitalist business ideals, we don't often make this gamble, opting instead to prioritize packaging over talent.[9]

In 2011, Gaga appeared in drag at the MTV Video Music Awards, dubbing herself "Jo Calderone."[10] Critics scratched their heads, audiences smelled desperation, and many dismissed the act as derivative of female artists from previous decades.[11] But for those watching closely, there was something ironic and shocking at play here. Had Lady Gaga burned through so many provocative female poses in so little time that all she had left to do was turn herself into a man? At one point, Jo, commenting on Gaga's artifice, pleaded, "I want her to be real!" Then, as if rehearsing for the "real," and with no elaborate outfits to upstage her music, Gaga sat down and sang her heart out on "You & I," demanding that audiences really *listen* to her for a change. These moves, more than any others, demonstrated Gaga's sophistication with respect to gender norms in the music industry.

As this book will demonstrate, female pop stars are held to rigid standards of appearance and beauty that box them into a small number of highly patterned types. For most, these types ring synthetic but unavoidable. Gaga plays that game expertly, but her transformation—into "Jo Calderone"—reads as an acknowledgment that this gender act has grown tiresome, and that sometimes it is easier to perform as a man than as a woman in the music industry. There are more artist types and positions available to men, and most of them prioritize music over their bodies and costumes. While performing as a man, Gaga wore a baggy t-shirt and jeans, which focused the camera's attention on her fierce vocal and musical performance—a refreshing change. Perhaps Gaga found her real "free bitch" while wearing men's clothes.

Gaga thrilled academics and those who view themselves outside of the hetero-normative gender dichotomy by "fail(ing) to do gender appropriately" (West and Zimmerman, 1987, p146) and by offering a (*reverse*) *gender display* (Goffman, 1967) by eschewing a conventional, idealized dramatization of how women are supposed to appear in favor of displaying dress and behavior more commonly associated with men.

As Gaga's Jo Calderone experiment unfolded, one could see the audience members making their own sense of the spectacle (Katy Perry giggling, Russell Brand staring blankly, and Britney Spears watching open-mouthed, all visible in the link in this chapter's note 10). Gaga counts on these negotiated and oppositional readings (Hall, 1980) of her performance to keep her image fresh and provocative. The more people talk about what she means, the more she is talked about, and the more she ultimately means. Of course, figuring out what she means may be too exhausting for some, so they just enjoy her various spectacles at face value, as entertainment.

If this situation were framed in *Cultural Diamond* terms, Gaga and her *creators/producers* offered a counter-normative or reverse *gender display*, and Gaga acted it out in her role as a *cultural object*. Gaga shocked and delighted her *audience/receivers*, who had different ideas about what her act meant and how effective it was, and talk of the event sent ripple effects throughout the greater *social world*.

Communication theory and pop star brands

Gaga and her handlers appear to understand that artists and audiences simultaneously send and receive messages, complicating old-school ideas about message creation, delivery, and reception offered by communication scholars. The communication process (Shannon and Weaver, 1949; Schramm, 1954; Berlo, 1960) is usually characterized as having a handful of distinct phases or parts. Although they have been refined in various ways to reflect cultural changes, they typically include a source or a sender, who encodes a message with intended meanings and then sends it through a distribution channel or channels to a receiver or a target, who decodes the message and derives meaning from it. While these models account for a good part of the communication process, they are less adept at explaining what happens when "noise" or competition interrupts the message as it is sent or received. Noise can be due to distribution issues—literal static or distribution errors—or due to a receiver's rejection of, resistance to, or misunderstanding of a message or an intended part of it. If the sender and receiver don't interpret the words and symbols used at all points in the process in exactly the same way, they are unlikely to end up in the same place at the end of it.

Human agency to deconstruct, resist, or negotiate the meaning of encoded messages was not given much consideration in early communication models, which focused mainly on the transmission of messages. The "mass society" communication models of the 1930s and 1940s claimed that the media had direct, immediate, and powerful effects on the audience. The magic bullet theory (also known as the hypodermic needle theory) argued that the public could be shot (or injected) with ideas, and were thus unable to resist them. But as time went on, scholars such as Paul Lazarsfeld challenged these notions, suggesting that sometimes other people interrupt or intervene in the communication process (Baran and Davis, 2003).

The two-step flow theory (Katz and Lazarsfeld, 1955), for example, posited that mass media efforts affected opinion leaders, who, in turn, influenced the thoughts and opinions of the audience. This theoretical development constructed opinion leaders as powerful in determining how audiences would process messages, so it was no longer a given that messages would be passively received by audiences as hoped or planned by the big media companies. Today, we might argue that Jon Stewart, Rachel Maddow, and Lady Gaga wield more influence over college-aged voters than, say, official government sources.

In contemporary times, alternate readings of and reactions to media messages are expected, especially as media literacy efforts[12] proliferate. So, at the end of the communication process, the source or sender often doesn't know whether the message has been received as intended due to a variety of complicated factors (such as family background, life experience, which opinion leaders one follows, profession, gender, class, race, or age). One's choice of opinion leaders is critical to one's understanding of a message: Just think, for example, about how *The Colbert Report*, Fox News, and PBS might handle the same story about gay marriage.

Rather than communication being strictly about information transmission or dissemination, it is now more comprehensively concerned with information-sharing, negotiation, and reciprocity (meaning the receiver can provide feedback or come away from an experience with negotiated meanings that sit somewhere between what was intended and what was received). Opinion leaders, particularly in the highly fragmented world of new media, help audiences to contextualize information or to frame it (Entman, 1993) in ways that make it easy for people to understand from their given social locations. Framing acts as cultural shorthand, emphasizing certain ideas while minimizing or ignoring others (Entman, 1993). This, in turn, privileges certain types of frames or stories, while ignoring others. In the world of female pop stars, this means that it is easier to market someone who looks and sounds like a past star because there's already a pre-existing frame for it.

Beginning with Berlo (1960), communication models allowed for the same person to simultaneously inhabit sender (*creator/producer*) and receiver (*audience*) roles. This is evidenced repeatedly in social media exchanges, such as on Facebook, where people post and receive posts on their respective walls. With new media, in particular, individuals are now seen as *creators/producers* and *receivers/consumers*, and opinion leaders and opinion followers simultaneously. The way in which people process messages is much more complex than originally thought: it changes with new technology, and communication theory continues to evolve with these inevitable changes.

More recent mass communication models, such as the Elaboration Likelihood Model (Petty and Cacioppo, 1986; Petty and Wegener, 1999), also contributed useful ideas about how consumers (in our case, music audiences) process marketing messages, indicating that some messages are processed centrally, using logic and problem solving, while others are processed peripherally, using auto-pilot and emotion. Processing also depends upon the individual's orientation to or feelings about the product or idea being pitched. Those impressions made while in the central mode are longer lasting; but those made peripherally can have strong short-term effects, especially if the same type of message is received repeatedly. This means that people may reject repetitively sexist marketing if it registers as such, or accept it passively if they are only half-alert or tuned in. This is where the aforementioned media literacy efforts come into play. If people have learned to critically consume media messages, they are more likely to know "what to look and listen for" as they read, watch, or hear such messages. In relation to this theory and its relevance to the *Cultural Diamond*, this means that better-informed *audiences/receivers* will likely spend more time in the central processing mode, where they can question the messages they receive.

Uses and gratifications theory (Blumler 1979; Ruggiero 2000) is also important to consider as we look at how and why audiences consume selected media. (e.g., entertainment, distraction, comfort, emotional support, reflection of self, inspiration, help navigating social situations, etc.). If you think about why you and your classmates are consuming this textbook, you will likely come up with different reasons, even in a small seminar. You might be reading it to learn, while someone else might be reading it so they won't be embarrassed if they are cold-called in class, while another person might read in the hope of earning a good score on a relevant assignment. Similarly, one person might watch MTV to learn songs or dance moves for the club that weekend, while another might watch it to be able to rag on *Jersey Shore* or *16 and Pregnant* at a party, while still another might watch to be mindlessly entertained or to make a significant other or roommate happy. A central idea behind uses and gratifications is that nobody can make anyone consume anything. People make consumption choices based on numerous personal and social factors, relevant cultural influences, and the choices they have at their disposal.

Popular culture studies

Emerging work in popular culture studies—especially the sociology of celebrity—also proves useful in understanding the content of this book. In her interdisciplinary literature review of celebrity research, Kerry Ferris (2007) determined that such research commonly focused on the "commodification" and "pathology" of celebrity construction and reception without considering how the cultural producers and the audience make their own meanings for and from celebrities. She argues that "meaning-making occurs on both sides of the celebrity-audience divide" (Ferris, 2007, p381) and that understanding the construction and reception of such meanings is "a necessary part of the full development and maturity of the field" (p380). In other words, celebrities are commodities, the audience is commodified, and celebrity culture likely has a range of negative effects on celebrities and audiences alike; but leaving the discussion at that level is overly simplistic, as stars and audiences are arguably both powerful and reactionary.

The New Republic editor Andrew Sullivan (1989, pp39–40) supported the notion that consumers aren't victims, or pawns, just consumers, stating that:

> Even within the captivity of consumerism, the consumer still has some room to maneuver: that she can choose this fantasy over another, this product over another; that she can outwit by mockery,

humor—or simply boredom—the schemes of an industry as much at war with itself as it is intent on capturing her.

These realities of modern celebrity lead marketers to pursue relevant strategies. Rein et al, authors of *High Visibility* (1987), write: "The ultimate selling strategy is to foster audience identification. Product marketers understand the process well: Measure consumers' self-images, demographics, and psychological needs, then provide them with products that embody characteristics which match and meet them" (p102).

So, in some sense, our celebrities help us to bridge the gap between who we are and who we want to be. Savvy marketers figure out the identity needs of various target markets and offer them solutions in the forms of physical products, services, and celebrities.

By linking ideas, models, and frameworks from sociology/women's studies/popular culture studies, mass communication/media studies, and marketing/branding, we get a sense of the context in which the modern music industry and the gender norms within it operate to produce branded female pop stars. Brand theory—which necessarily draws on all of the aforementioned literature bases to explain how people process and derive meaning from messages, consume products for their functional and symbolic value, and use brands in their daily lives to enhance their identities and project them to others—completes our framework for studying the social construction of female popular music stars.

The branding process

Pop stars are, indeed, brands, as familiar and aspirational as Coca-Cola or Oprah Winfrey. The construction of these brands may begin with a middle-aged music executive, or with a young teenager's dream, or with a magazine editor in search of a blockbuster cover. A pop star brand is built to capitalize on earnings potential, but also to resonate with the audience. This text argues how important parts of the music industry operate as gendered spaces, and how youth, beauty, and sex still anchor most female pop stars' careers. As Kotarba and Vannini (2009, p100) noted: "Despite the fact that there are multiple scripts available for performing one's gender, it seems that popular entertainment media (both in their magazine and television forms) are most intrigued with very few particular ways of doing femininity." The authors dubbed one of them a "postmodern Prima Donna" and described it as "mix of *diva* and 'girl next door,' of princess and pauper, of cosmopolitan jet setter and wholesome small town girl, of hypersexualized seductress and virgin" (Kotarba and Vannini, 2009, p100). Similarly, Connell (1987) speaks of *emphasized femininity*, or a way of *doing gender* that privileges the way in which men react to and reward such "feminine" performances.

In *Cultural Diamond* terms, brands are *cultural objects* produced by *creators*, with inputs from both the *social world* and the *audience* that ultimately receives them. Such brands thrive or wither based on how strongly they resonate with audiences. Increasingly, this means brands succeed or fail based on the effectiveness of their market narratives. And, as noted in the Preface, limited roles available for female musicians lead to limited meanings and, thus, redundant narratives. Brands take much of their strength from the stories they tell about themselves, leveraging important meanings into resonant narratives. Thus, limiting the role types of female pop stars limits the scope of many female pop star brands.

Brands rich in meaning have greater opportunities to be dynamic and to last—as long as they have an overarching theme to keep them "on brand," meaning consistent in ideas and ideology expressed. Having this overarching brand theme is critical so that audiences know what the brand stands for and so brand authors don't stray too far afield of their strategic intentions as opportunities present themselves. Audiences get bored quickly, but their chosen brands still need to possess memorable, meaningful strategic anchors. These anchors ensure that despite the multiple entry points and continuously changing articulations of the brand required to keep audiences engaged, the main idea of the brand will not be confused or diluted.

Gaga is a talented songwriter, vocalist, pianist, and performance artist. She's also a champion strategist and a master of delivering pitch-perfect brand narratives about self-acceptance that resonate far and wide. But she is by no means playing a new game, nor is she playing the old game much differently than her predecessors. Gaga often receives comparisons to Madonna, who also generated headlines with shocking costumes and ever-changing personalities more than two decades ago. We'll return to a discussion of these artists in Chapters 4 to 6, but for the meantime we can think of Gaga's overarching brand theme as "empowered deviance" and Madonna's as "sexual playfulness." Madonna could be called an "empowered deviant," while Gaga could be called "sexually playful," thus the overlap critics see between the brands.

Artist brands

This trend of artists and music industry handlers thinking about how to brand artists has intensified over time, such that the idea of an artist as a brand is beginning to work its way into academic discussions of branding. Social psychologist Jonathan Schroeder (2005, p1) argues that successful artists have embraced branding, no longer viewing it as antithetical to artistic integrity or authenticity:

> Artists offer exemplary instances of image creation in the service of building a recognizable look, name, and style—a brand, in other words. Successful artists can be thought of as brand managers, actively engaged in developing, nurturing, and promoting themselves as recognizable "products" in the competitive cultural sphere.

In Schroeder's (2005, p2) conceptualization, the artist plays a role in composing her public image, but indicates that however she may wish to be perceived, "neither managers nor consumers completely control branding processes—cultural codes contribute to, and constrain, how brands work to produce meaning." These codes, of course, are imposed by music industry norms, societal norms, and fan norms, which correspond to the *creator/(producer)*, *social world*, and *receiver/(audience)* points on the *Cultural Diamond*.

Indeed, Schroeder (2005, p3) identifies the "critical interaction" that occurs "between consumption and identity." This critical interaction reflects the remaining point on the *Cultural Diamond*: the *cultural object*.

Such objects are created in the *social world* by *creators* for *receivers*, who then consume the resulting *cultural object* in the form of the artists. When audience members engage with a brand, they try to determine its meanings by absorbing the messages that brand authors put into circulation and by adding their own creative interpretations. When the brands that audiences choose to engage with are people, the process can be even more complicated given that people are more dynamic than non-living products.

Person brands

Person brands differ from more traditional product brands because they have people, not static products, at their core. This makes them more difficult to manage given their dynamic nature and their self-within-a-self construction. Female popular music stars are also tricky to manage because they are person brands who are typically short term in nature, as will be discussed in depth in this and the next chapter. Shorter careers make female pop star brands more susceptible to cultural trends than their male counterparts. Therefore, they need to achieve cultural resonance quickly and deeply or risk fading into oblivion, thereby constraining their lifecycle and potential upside even further.

Given the heavy emphasis on their clothes, bodies, and representations, female pop stars must be expert at developing cultural trends or adapting to reflect cultural trends subtly but quickly. This has ramifications for the brand-building process; the market requires them to constantly make minute changes to their brands. Female popular music stars generally have a short window for success, and are increasingly constructed to be cross-capitalized empires who can generate vast amounts of revenue in a variety of entertainment verticals. Music appears to be a tertiary concern in the construction of such brands, behind the core asset of their bodies and their secondary ability to succeed in multiple revenue-generating capacities, such as fashion and cosmetics. I'm not suggesting that their music is not important—it is; but it often fails to reach the public unless the artist appears to satisfy the other conditions first. There are numerous explanations for this, including changing business models in the music industry and the knowledge that most female musicians have short careers and should thus capture all revenue possible before their window closes. As veteran music industry journalist and publicist Simon Glickman explained, these women are expected to be "all-purpose beautiful young things." They are constructed as such and positioned for the market by myriad experts in music, fashion, dance, film and television, and marketing, among other things.

Brand strength and brand equity

But still, these "all-purpose beautiful young things" need to stand for something meaningful in order to become strong brands that audiences can easily identify and recall. Traditional brand theorists say that brand strength relies on capturing desirable and distinctive images and associations in the minds of consumers and then carefully reinforcing them over time through marketing efforts, such as advertising and social media campaigns. This consistent approach is meant to establish brand strength, which is an indicator of how attached consumers are to a brand (Aaker, 1991, 1995). In the case of pop stars, this means there might be some signature part of the look designed to ensure that people instantly know who they are, wherever you see them.

In turn, *brand strength* is thought to be a predictor of *brand equity*, the positive differential effect that knowing a brand's name has on the consumer (Aaker, 1991). Just as customers pay more for Coca-Cola than a store brand because of its good name, customers will pay more (or pay at all in this day and age) for known artist brands. *Brand value* basically quantifies *brand equity*, indicating the financial value of the brand.

Some brand scholars, such as Susan Fournier, argue that *brand meaning* creates *brand strength and resonance*, which, in turn, enables firms to capture value from consumers.

According to Cravens and Guilding (1999), *brand value* can be calculated four ways, from a cost-based approach (which measures the costs associated with building a brand), to a market-based approach (which bases its estimation of value on how much a buyer would pay for it on the open market), to an income-based approach (which uses future

revenue potential directly attributable to a brand), to a more comprehensive formulary approach (which takes the weighted average profit
of a brand over three years and multiplies it by seven dimensions of
brand strength to get an estimate of a brand's financial worth). No
academic work to date has established the best way to value a celebrity
brand, presumably because there are too many variables to do it
effectively.

In other fields, scholars tend to rely on the market-based calculation,
as a market price is a literal indicator of value, and the formulary
approach because it was created by Interbrand, which ranks the world's
most valuable brands and is viewed as the most comprehensive measure
of brand value (Cravens and Guilding, 1999).

Brand meaning

Increasingly, the more progressive brand scholars, known as consumer
culture theorists (CCTs), argue that *brand meaning* drives *brand strength*
and creates resonance with customers. Susan Fournier (1998) argues
that *brand-meaning resonance* may be the most important measure of all
in assessing customer attachment, which, in turn, leads to more reliable
calculations of *brand equity*. (Entertainers and executives care deeply
about this because it's this brand attachment that keeps customers
interested in artists and coming back for more.) CCTs argue that brands
must continuously change over time to remain relevant and absorb
relevant cultural changes (Holt 2003, 2004; Wipperfurth 2005). This
approach would argue that artists should modify their brands regularly
in hope of setting, or at least closely following, cultural trends. That's
not to say that every CD release should signal a complete makeover. An
artist should adhere to her overarching theme, but remain flexible in her
interpretations of that theme. Let's return to Madonna, with her theme
of sexual playfulness. During the 1980s, Madonna played the role of a
virgin ("Like A Virgin"),[13] a pregnant teen ("Papa Don't Preach"),[14] and
a mercenary Marilyn Monroe-type seductress ("Material Girl").[15]
During the 1990s, she provoked audiences with images of sadomasoch-
ism and bondage ("Justify My Love"),[16] wrote a book called *Sex*,
and became a mother, walking the Madonna/whore line expertly.

From 2000 to 2010, she tried her hand representing a cowgirl ("Music"),[17] a club girl/dancer ("Hung Up"),[18] and a bisexual cougar (when she made out with Britney Spears and Christina Aguilera at the 2003 VMA).[19] Now in her 50s, Madonna is more limited in her expression of sexual playfulness, but she continues to push the boundaries. On June 11, 2012, Madonna exposed her breasts onstage during a concert and the footage went viral, dominating that night's entertainment news cycle with questions of whether she's too old for this kind of display.

So, who establishes this overarching theme, or, put differently, who determines what a brand means to fans? Traditional brand theorists would say the brand managers, but CCTs explain that everyone who interacts with the brand contributes something to its meanings. Current cultural brands, such as pop stars, are really *co-created* by consumers, professional handlers, and the cultural intermediaries who sit between them, such as journalists, bloggers, and critics. For that reason, the *brand's meaning*—its images, associations, narratives, personality, and what they collectively communicate to audiences—can be as diverse as those consuming it. For some brand managers, this is an unsettling thought, as the brand is always at least somewhat out of their control. In *The New Marketing Manifesto*, John Grant (2001) argues that the key to contemporary marketing is redesigning brands so that customers do more of the work and the company does less. "It's a paradox of New Marketing economics that the less you do, the more they participate, the more you are worth" (Grant, 2001, p134). In essence, brands have become as much what consumers make them as what companies intend them to be. Just think about the impact and power of Lady Gaga's legions of "little monsters" who help to build her narratives and spread her gospel far and wide.

Brand meaning and resonance

Fournier et al (2008, p39) posit that brand meanings resonate when they reverberate "within the contexts of the organization, the broader culture and the person's life. It is the echoing, playback, and refiguring of meanings that render them significant and relevant for purposes of communication, categorization and understanding."

Lady Gaga identified cultural shifts and voiced them to achieve meaning and authority among her ranks. She employed social media outlets extensively to meet her intended markets where she knew they would naturally be hanging out, and offered them something she suspected would be of interest to them. Then she spoke with them using their two-way communication platforms, and language, imagery, and ideals that resonated deeply. Dubbing her devout fans her "little monsters" was a clever double entendre, which played on the name of her first full-length release—*The Fame Monster*—and celebrated her fans for letting their freak flags fly proudly. She told them they were special and important exactly as they were, that all individual differences should be celebrated. This messaging, combined with the clear party ethic espoused in her dance hits and the artful repurposing of cultural trends in her fashion choices and videos, made her a perfect representative for the millennial generation and many outside of it who never felt they fit into society for their own reasons. By November 25, 2012, Gaga had 31,494,610 Twitter followers, and 53,835,491 likes on Facebook, staggering figures for each venue.

As Holt (2003, 2004) observes repeatedly in his work, dominant cultures are created, and most people do not actually fit into them. Many do not even want to. So, by interrupting staid narratives about what young people should want in this country, and replacing them with narratives about understanding, acceptance, and freedom, Lady Gaga addressed a major cultural tension and earned millions of eager followers who wanted to hear more about that.

Brands can make claims about themselves, but the marketplace will ultimately decide what feels credible and true. *Consumer culture theorists* believe in an active, meaning-making consumer, whereas the traditionalists' view assumes a more passive consumer who takes cues from paternalistic brand managers. The *Cultural Diamond* supports the CCT paradigm, indicating that however producers might encode their products for reception, there are numerous opportunities for interruption and negotiation by consumers, and the greater *social world* they inhabit. This thread will be picked up again in Chapter 5.

Sometimes, brand stewards learn that their brands carry meanings that were never intended for the product. For example, Susan Fournier's (1998) phenomenological study of women and their brands found that *brand meanings* are sometimes not present in products or even in the marketing of them. Rather, such meanings reside within the individual consumer at the intersection of identity themes, a theme carried on by Schroeder (2005) in his study of artists as brands. These identity themes might include feelings of inadequacy (which might lead one to buy something best-in-class) or a need for comfort (which might lead one to buy the brand that a loved one uses). In these cases, it's the customer, not the company, doing the positioning and figuring out the integration of the brand (Fournier, 1998). This work is consistent with the ideas presented in Chapter 6, in which media scholars (Hall, 1980; Fiske, 1992, 1994, 1997) argue that the audience plays an active role in accepting, negotiating, or opposing the intended/dominant meanings of cultural products, such as artists, songs, and videos.

Product symbolism and self-concept

Consumer researchers, such as Michael Solomon (1983), and brand theorists, such as Douglas Holt (2003, 2004), have argued that consumption behavior is social behavior, and that people consume products mainly for their symbolic value. This symbolism is created at the level of the *social world*, but is consumed at the individual level, as people try to figure out how to bridge the gap between who they are and who they want to look like or be. In this way, Solomon (1983) argues that products can actually be antecedents to related behaviors, as people purchase products because of how they and others will likely respond to their new appearance or role. Symbolically rich products are particularly important for those in the midst of transition—for example, a 12-year-old girl transitioning into her teenage years. She has no experience of being a teenager, only the impressions she has from watching and hearing the routinized scripts of others. So she cobbles together her new identity using a combination of representative products, scripts she's heard used by those in the desirable group to which she aspires to belong, and behaviors she associates with this new identity. She then tests how she's done based on how she and others react to her new look and attitude, and refines the process from there.

Boys and men engage in the same processes, of course, as they buy branded clothes (e.g., think sports or band t-shirts) to declare who they are to their new college classmates. In both cases, the consumers are establishing that they like something, that they want to emulate some-thing, or that they are a viable part of some group to which they desire affiliation, association, or membership.

Female pop stars do this, too, borrowing wardrobe, accessory, and hairstyle choices from stars who went before them to position them-selves among past successes in the minds of consumers. Lady Gaga has been accused many times of stealing from Madonna, Annie Lennox (a dominant female solo artist from the 1980s), and countless other pop cultural figures who succeeded before her. She uses commercial products and past pop star poses to indicate to audiences how to think about her.

Cultural resonance

Consumer culture theorist Douglas Holt focuses on the construct of cultural resonance, reasoning that resonance lasts longer and is more easily recalled than context-poor associations or claims about product functionality. Resonance develops within the *Cultural Diamond* as cultural products are developed to reflect the *social world*. Those that achieve resonance are those that best identify consumers' positions in the *social world*. Holt argues the consumers are most likely to remember effective stories or powerful myths offered by brands. Using this logic, the winning company or product—or pop star—is the one that creates the most compelling narrative constructions. Those with brand-specific details that stick in the minds of consumers build the greatest degree of resonance, and thus win the prize of increased loyalty and sales. Apple seems to take this approach, branding itself through specific memorable songs and design schemes. It's hard for many listeners to hear U2's "Vertigo," or Jet's "Are You Gonna Be My Girl"—which were both used in early iPod/iTunes television advertising campaigns[20]—without seeing the dancing silhouettes from the commercials play in their minds. Other examples of a pop star trying to achieve cultural resonance through narrative construction include handlers talking about Jewel living in a car—a story an executive who worked with her said was greatly exaggerated—and the rags-to-riches story of Tina Turner. More recently, it appears that Gaga's handlers are trying to change her narrative, featuring her "normal" side to dial down her flamboyance. Her 2011 television special *A Very Gaga Thanksgiving*,[21] run on ABC, featured Gaga visiting her elementary school, reflecting on deceased relatives, and generally showing her girl-next-door side.

For *CCTs* such as Holt, *brand equity* is a function of the quality of the stories told, provided, of course, that there is a competitive product to sell. According to Holt's (2003) model, if a brand's narratives have good historical fit, speak to tensions in society, create myths that lead culture, and speak with a rebel's voice, they will likely resonate with their intended audience and become successful, if not iconic. Equity becomes a function of staying culturally aware and changing with the times. According to Holt, Mountain Dew changed its central advertising character from an anti-yuppie hillbilly to a daredevil to a slacker due to cultural shifts—and succeeded by riding these changes and remaining relevant while still communicating its core values of rebelliousness and individuality. This openly defies the consistency-is-king mantra espoused by such traditionalists as David Aaker, and embraces the context-is-everything idea espoused by such cultural theorists as Holt and McCracken. At present, there are no solid metrics available for measuring *brand equity* in *consumer culture theory*, but execution metrics will likely emerge as this work is completed and people begin to operationalize their findings in new studies. Holt (2003, p8) predicts:

> Such knowledge doesn't come from focus groups or ethnography or trend reports—the marketer's usual means for "getting close to the customer." Rather, it comes from a cultural historian's understanding of ideology as it waxes and wanes, a sociologist's charting of the topography of contradictions the ideology produces, and a literary critic's expedition into the culture that engages these contradictions.

Holt's quote is instructive in its articulation of the multidisciplinary approach required of those conducting research within the more progressive areas of branding. His summary is also useful in assessing the strength of the Madonna brand. Borrowing from the traditionalists, let's assume that consistency in strategy is key, and drawing from the CCT researchers, let's assume culture dictates that our brand must change its tactics, and sometimes even its strategy, to remain historically relevant. Perhaps what Madonna's selling, at a strategic level, is not music, but rather female power, playfulness, and sexuality. Her music actually changes—it's the product, not the strategy. Maybe she's selling a sex book, or kissing Britney Spears at an award show, or peddling a video compilation—it's all supporting her core offering, her brand.

Multivocality

The *Cultural Diamond* is built on the idea that relationships between its four points (*creator/producer*, *receiver/consumer*, *cultural object*, and the *social world*) are linked in multiple ways, through myriad influences. It's no surprise, then, that brands come to mean different things to different people.

Fournier et al (2008, p46) call this quality "*multivocality*," meaning that a single brand can speak with many voices and have many different market interpretations. These multiple voices help a brand productively and efficiently address different target markets by tailoring communications with each. This quality enables brands to connect, and reconnect, with people over time as they change their self-perception. Thus, the way in which a brand (or a pop star) is presented to us in all its forms—through songs, videos, magazines, clothes, or fragrances—frames the way in which we see and experience it. But our own experiences and issues also provide a frame for how we make sense of such presentations. Fournier (1998) constructs brands as cultural resources that help people manage how they think about (or complete) themselves, and Belk (1988) argues that brands help people define themselves for themselves and others.

Star handlers must constantly monitor brand meanings in circulation and make honest efforts to respond to them in authentic ways.

Managing a star's image can be a full-time job for multiple people. A star's battery of handlers can put whatever spin they want on her behavior, but there's no guarantee the public will accept it as truth. In light of this, brand stewards might want to consider working with culture rather than against it in order to create resonant narratives. Wipperfurth (2005) argues that brand managers should be recast as brand facilitators. That's what effective celebrity handlers—especially managers and publicists—do, as we'll see in greater detail in the next chapter. They follow the artist's lead. Dynamic brands have to operate from open structures—the audience knows what the celebrity stands for, but not always how the brand will achieve its end. Lady Gaga again serves as a provocative illustration. She and her handlers might know where they intend for the brand to be in three years, but they can't reasonably anticipate all of the cultural opportunities and challenges that might arise in the interim to help or hinder their progress toward that end.

Celebrity endorsers and celebrity firms

The literature available for studying entertainment figures as brands is scant. However, two key published papers—Grant McCracken's (1989) work on celebrity endorsers and Rindova et al's (2006) work on celebrity firms and the social construction of popularity—and one unpublished work—Fournier and Herman's (2004, 2006) in-progress work on Martha Stewart—provide the framework for conceptualizing how to begin evaluating popular culture figures as living, breathing brands.

McCracken studied celebrity endorsers and their role in making or breaking marketing campaigns. He argued that the brand passes meaning on to the celebrity endorsing it, who then passes these meanings on to the consumer (McCracken, 1989). He specified that Bruce Willis is a great celebrity endorser, but indicated that Meryl Streep is not. Why? Bruce Willis is always Bruce Willis—we know what his "brand" means. Given her myriad dramatic roles and her well-documented acting ability, Streep disappears into each role, and does not have a consistent brand message. Stated simply, people do not know what to make of Streep in an endorsement setting (McCracken, 1989).

In today's terms, is she the witchy editor from *The Devil Wears Prada*, the free spirit from *Mamma Mia*, or the business-owning, handsome-man juggling entrepreneur from *It's Complicated*? This question begs another question, though: Does gender have anything to do with the decoding and understanding of celebrity brands? In other words, are men more likely to stand for something specific or uni-dimensional in the eyes of consumers than women? Are they expected to be consistent, eternally the same, growing from boy to man without fanfare? Are women meant to be dynamic but fluid, flowing from girl to wife to mother to grandmother? If women's roles are more multidimensional, shouldn't this lead them to a wider variety of opportunities?

In terms of career longevity, it's better to be like Willis—at least for those aspiring to build long-term careers in the music industry. Willis's musical counterpart might be someone like Bruce Springsteen (the working-class hero), Bob Dylan (the poet/rebel), Tom Petty (the Southern storyteller), or Keith Richards (the substance-abusing rock star with nine lives). People know what to expect from these artists— and it isn't centered on their bodies and outfits! While they've experimented sonically throughout the years, their basic brand identity has remained the same. This is wise in the long term because, as Lady Gaga is now learning, those who cycle through poses and identities at warp speed, relying on outrageous antics, provocation, and unpredictability, find themselves out of tricks in a hurry. Yet, she may be wise to realize that she is constrained by time and the clock is ticking. (This may explain why she is trying to reposition herself as the girl next door, as previously mentioned.)

Consumer culture theorists might embrace this ambiguity, however, saying that a culturally sophisticated brand manager could determine which elements of an artist to play up at given times to meet different ends. (In other words, these artists may have hundreds of '*brand meanings*' or '*brand associations*' or '*brand personality*' traits from which to select, and the key to nailing any given effort is to select the right fit for the given market or point in time). Female pop stars have many affiliations through their extensions, which give them the opportunity for *multivocality* and deeper *brand meaning*. But these opportunities are squandered repeatedly, as these stars are positioned as sex-first brands, remaining mostly undifferentiated with respect to important and enduring *brand meanings*. These missed opportunities for enrichment have consequences, as is clear from the theory discussed earlier in this chapter. If *brand meanings* drive *brand strength*, and *brand strength* drives *brand equity* and *brand value*, female pop star handlers need to focus more on building *brand meaning* so that their artists may, in turn, expect higher *brand value* and longer careers.

The major label structure and its component executive parts are notorious for looking in the rearview mirror to determine what will be successful, rather than looking ahead and taking a gamble on something genuinely different or creative. With this approach, they basically clone the same type of undifferentiated star over and over again. This leads to repetitive extensions that are almost meaningless because they're so similar they're forgettable. The only saving grace for those going through the motions is that there's always a new generation of teenagers to see these plays for the first time. If, instead, the artist's brand managers focused on genuine, meaningful points of difference, her audience would likely take notice and respond positively.

Constructing and maintaining a celebrity brand is an ongoing, ever-changing process. It requires flexibility, resourcefulness, and a commitment to changing with the culture so that the pop star/*cultural object*/brand remains dynamic and relevant. This means that rather than hiding unflattering stories about their artists, handlers might instead enhance their artists' brands by telling such stories to their respective publics in a compassionate manner before such stories break through less controllable channels.

The singer Fergie enjoyed a rising profile as a member of the Black-Eyed Peas, but she had a dark secret. Going solo in 2006 raised the stakes for her personal brand, and her handlers made a bold decision to proactively address her previous meth addiction as her first solo album, *The Dutchess*, climbed the *Billboard* popular music charts. This was smart on numerous levels as they were able to tell the story their way, rather than reacting when another source inevitably released the news. Fergie told *People* magazine that:

> Meth was the hardest boyfriend I ever had to break up with. I dug deep as to why I got there. It's the drug that's addicting. But it's why you start doing it that's interesting. A lot of it was being a child actor, I learned to suppress feelings.
>
> (Silverman, 2006, p1)

With this kind of positioning, who could be anything but sympathetic to this child-actor-turned-singer and addict, who kicked the habit and released one of the most successful female solo albums in history? But if she and her handlers had tried to hide or sanitize her past, making her out to be the "*good girl*," we'd have potentially had Whitney Houston's fall from grace all over again. (Three music industry professionals interviewed for this book noted that while Houston was positioned as the church-going angel, she was a party girl from the start, and that Bobby Brown was an obvious choice of partner for her, not a shocking departure that led to her demise). Tragically, Houston was found dead in her hotel room on February 11, 2012, having drowned under the influence of cocaine and prescription drugs (TMZ, 2012a, 2012b, 2012c; HNLtv Staff, 2012).

If negative *brand meanings* begin to circulate, and are not artfully and strategically monitored and managed by an artist or her handlers, they can cause considerable damage to the brand. This has happened at least twice, and arguably three times, with Christina Aguilera, who provides a cautionary tale when it comes to artists trying to differentiate themselves from the pack. Aguilera began her career as one of several former Mouseketeers who came to market in the 1990s. By 2002, Aguilera had taken her brand super-trashy—most famously with the song and video titled "Dirrty"—and the brand nearly imploded. Her short-term sales were strong—*Stripped* was one of her best-selling CDs—but her pornographic positioning began to tarnish her image among marketing and music professionals. It appeared that she may have had nowhere to go with her career.

Brandweek writer Phillip Van Munching (2002, p30) scolded RCA for being so negligent with such a powerful brand:

> I've seen the new Christina Aguilera video, "Dirrty," and I'm here to tell you that I'm shocked. Shocked. Not by Ms. Aguilera's wardrobe—essentially skimpy red panties and chaps. Nor by the subtle-as-a-brick-to-the-skull imagery, which features posters touting Thailand's underage sex trade, and dancers of both genders rubbing up against the chaps. Hell, I'm not even shocked that the song is terrible. No, what shocks me is that the folks at RCA records, Aguilera's label, would allow one of their biggest brands to implode.

Van Munching's backlash is brand specific, and he comes from a traditional branding point of view, which argues that a strong brand should be consistent, reputable, and have a long-term orientation. A strong brand should not do foolish things for short-term gains. But sometimes those managing brands do unwise things in the hope of reinvigorating them. As Van Munching observed: "We've seen this before, of course. Young woman, worried about her waning popularity, starts showing the goods" (Van Munching, 2002, p30). But he cautioned such stars against taking their images to "Skankville" and ending up in "self-imposed exile" (Van Munching, 2002, p30). Aguilera's handlers did not publicly respond to this article, but they did take her in a more wholesome, covered-up direction—until 2007, when they returned to a more sexual positioning, only to clean up her act yet again when she became a mother in 2008.

Then, when Aguilera botched the lyrics to the National Anthem while performing at the Super Bowl in 2011,[22] she and her handlers missed the opportunity to get out in front of the story. All she needed to do was apologize, say she was embarrassed, and make fun of her human self to make people remember that she's a person, too. She's done this over time, particularly in her nurturing role as a coach on *The Voice*; but this situation called for expert crisis management, and she simply did not get it. She and her handlers failed to acknowledge the blunder for so long that the story became much bigger than necessary as fans and commentators waited for a response. Now that Aguilera is riding high again based on the humanity she exhibits on *The Voice*, her handlers would do well to encourage her to maintain and cultivate her brand in its present incarnation.

Aguilera's trajectory proves instructive to aspiring pop stars and cultural observers alike. Aguilera has an undisputedly great voice, which has arguably given her more lives than most in the pop star arena. But the way in which she has used these lives provides interesting data for future pop stars to observe. She rose through the pop star ranks alongside Britney Spears, and for a time they competed to be the most sexually suggestive and, thus, the most differentiated. Both sold well during these times, but faced considerable backlash for their respective presentations and antics. Both became mothers and reined it in a bit. Spears then tried to go back to previous form, while Aguilera focused on being more likeable and more mature, which has served her well. Now Spears seems to be stealing a page from the Aguilera playbook, becoming a judge on *X Factor* in 2012.

Lady Gaga, Britney Spears, and Christina Aguilera provide fine examples of the way in which female pop stars are molded into brands that use sex appeal to catch the attention of the public. We have seen in this chapter that their success depends upon many factors other than music and talent. Their careers rise or fall based on a complex web of relationships between themselves and the listening—and viewing—public.

The sociological factors that influence the relationship between pop star and fan contribute significantly to the way in which these women are marketed to the public. In the next chapter, we will continue with a deeper examination of pop stars as powerful brands, and an exploration of the unique factors influencing the construction and maintenance of female pop star careers. Subsequent chapters will apply more specific literature from and about branding (Chapter 2), popular culture and the music industry (Chapter 3), and communication and women's studies (Chapters 4 to 6) to the branding of female popular music stars in order to explain the process more comprehensively.

2

FEMALE POPULAR MUSIC STARS AS BRANDS

As the *Cultural Diamond* suggests, society and popular culture are mutually reinforcing. As celebrities blur the line between the personal and the professional for attention, audiences themselves are blurring the lines between their personal and public selves via social networking sites such as Facebook and Twitter. At the same time, the lines between the content side of the entertainment business and the business side of the business (e.g., marketing and advertising) are collapsing, destroying the once-critical notion of artistic purity.[1]

As such boundaries collapse, and we can no longer distinguish a private person from her public representation of herself, we feel like we know her—especially if she is on Twitter, just like us. But what we really know is her constructed advertised brand. In the case of a celebrity, this brand is the end product of myriad professional authors, all struggling to select the *brand meanings* they presume will work best with her intended audiences. Selecting the right meanings and leaving the wrong ones behind is a difficult task—any one of us has thousands of possible meanings, and celebrities presumably have even more than that. But achieving resonance is all about selecting the right meanings for the right customer at the right time. Therein lies the "art" of managing a pop star brand. And the messiness.

In the first chapter, we saw how the *Cultural Diamond*, symbolic interactionism, and selected sender/receiver models of communication work together to establish the backdrop for the contemporary branding of female popular music stars. In this chapter, we'll apply some of the brand theory from the previous chapter to contemporary female pop stars. Chapter 2 relies on entertainment industry professionals, who play various roles in constructing or maintaining pop star brands, to explain the process. Those interviewed in this chapter (see the "Cast of Characters Interviewed for this Book" for detail) work or have worked as publicists, managers, journalists, photographers, label executives, marketing executives, web site executives, music supervisors, artists, and assistants. All have been in the entertainment business for more than a decade, and all of them have worked at close range with top-selling female popular music stars in various capacities.

Overall findings suggest that female popular music stars are objectified, productized brands who are considered high-risk investments given their relatively short-term careers and the tremendous amount of money it takes to market them successfully.

Numerous marketing books, most notably Holt's *How Brands Become Icons* (2004) and Christensen's *The Innovator's Dilemma* (1997), argue that many of the biggest hits come from producers who create narratives (in the first case) and technologies (in the second case) that revolutionize industries, not those that attempt to replicate past success stories. The lesson certainly holds on the technology side of the music business, where mp3.com, Napster, Amazon, and Apple's iTunes have revolutionized the way in which music is distributed, sold, stored, and accessed. The talent side of the industry, however, appears content to leave breakthrough innovation to the technologists, simply copying past musical successes. So there may be an economic imperative to innovate when it comes to technology, but to cling to tradition when it comes to the cultivation of celebrities.

Evolution and lifecycle of celebrity firms and person brands

In Rindova et al's (2006) work about celebrity firms, personification tactics are employed throughout the process of building a firm's celebrity.

Throughout the article, the authors indicate that when constructing firms for the public eye, those positioning them must make the firm appear to:

- be likable;
- have a voice;
- exhibit diversity;
- be memorable;
- experience conflict; and
- appear deviant, but not too deviant.

These component characteristics of celebrity help image, brand, and personify the firm for consumption, making it a legitimate cultural object within the *Cultural Diamond.*

Rindova et al (2006) isolate several characteristics required to achieve celebrity. In their study, they draw parallels between individual celebrities and celebrity firms. Firms, they argue, achieve their celebrity status through media attention, which increases their exposure and, subsequently, the number of people paying attention to them. Then, the nature of the attention must elicit "positive emotional responses" from the public and activate its needs for "gossip, fantasy, identification, status, affiliation, and attachment" (Rindova et al, 2006, p51). The authors do not concern themselves with whether this attention is warranted, but rather focus on the levers determining the prominence of celebrities. Firm celebrity is an intangible asset that is "created through the mass communication of carefully selected, prearranged, and oftentimes manipulated information about an individual's personality, talent, and style in order to create a persona that triggers positive emotional responses in audiences" (Rindova et al, 2006, p52, citing extensively from past literature).

After these celebrities or celebrity firms are put into wide circulation by their handlers, the authors suggest that journalists construct "dramatic narratives" to further entertain readers and give them reasons to care about the firm, or in the case of this study, the popular music star. Journalists focus on firms that "take bold or unusual actions and display distinctive identities" (Rindova et al, 2006, p52) as these firms make better dramatic actors. Deviance, novelty, non-conforming practices, and image management all play a role in the likelihood of achieving celebrity as a firm, but it must be controlled because when a celebrity firm is too deviant it will either not become a celebrity in the first place, or will cease being a celebrity due to this unwanted or unexpected behavior (Rindova et al, 2006). This tightrope-walking act is reminiscent of the virgin/whore act in that it's difficult to be both like everyone else and deviant, just as it's difficult to be both a virgin and a whore. But there is clearly a public demand for such seemingly contradictory displays, so we, as the audience, are left wondering which parts of the virgin/whore representation are real and which are constructed.

Fournier and Herman (2004, 2006) elaborate on these necessities in proposing a model chronicling the phases of person-brand evolution. In it, a person:

- births a brand;
- inserts himself or herself into the brand;
- becomes equal to the brand;
- becomes greater than the brand; and ultimately
- becomes less than the brand.

Using Martha Stewart as an example, they explained how, in the birthing phase of the brand, Martha infused it with her meanings (I'm a caterer, a decorator, your super mom, a humble-but-tasteful homemaker), and did so to the point where she became synonymous with the brand. Then, by extending her brand into cookbooks, television shows, Kmart clothing/home furnishing lines, and other realms (judge of Miss America, etc.), she became larger than the brand (Fournier and Herman, 2004). When Martha experienced legal difficulty, the Martha Stewart Living Omnimedia (MSO) firm wanted to separate from her, and product specialists came to take over different bits of her expertise. The authors commented that it was like building "mini-Marthas" across product lines (Fournier and Herman, 2004). Eventually, the brand became superior to, or larger than, Martha herself, as the brand shed its dependence on the person who birthed it (Fournier and Herman, 2004).

This model holds for artists such as Madonna and Cher, whose brand names are their given first names, and whose histories are known parts of their brand legacies. But for artists who establish their brand identities apart from their given names—such as Lady Gaga and Pink—this model might have to be revised somewhat to reflect the realities of this type of person brand or they might be unsuccessful brand mothers.

Stefani Germanotta, an unknown piano-rock artist who was dropped from her first major label deal, birthed the Lady Gaga brand during 2008 to 2009 in an attempt to save her career in recorded music. In the process of selecting her narratives, fashion accessories, and communication platforms, Germanotta breathed life into the brand, leaving herself, the person, out of it. Arguably, most fans did not—and still do not—even know of Stefani's existence. But Gaga became positively ubiquitous.

Ironically, the woman behind the manufactured Gaga brand, who was clearly not "born that way," is now in a place where she appears to be taking her constructed brand's advice about being one's genuine self. Now that there's nowhere to go in the shock-fest progression,[2] Gaga's flirtation with her original singer-songwriter persona could complete her evolution. Her new brand could thrive based on its authenticity, or fail miserably if people decided they do not care about what Stefani Germanotta has to say. Still, it would be a compelling brand experiment.

Celebrity brands are presumably more complicated to manage than product brands. Firms like to control their assets, and with person brands, this is out of the question. Traditional branding seeks to make everything consistent, and it is difficult to do this with people because all people have inconsistencies. As cultural studies scholar Stuart Hall (1980, 1981) notes, people should have the right to differ from themselves and not conform to type, regardless of social position. Whether such personal inconsistencies are exposed is simply a matter of how closely a celebrity is being watched, and how many people care about what she does. Publicity agents, and others involved in creating the public face of a celebrity, whether a pop star or a Martha Stewart, need to make a strategic decision about positioning the star as consistent (which, invariably, she is not) or human (which, invariably, she is). This is one of the major differences between marketing products and marketing people. While product brands and person brands both live in the public eye, product brands do not get plastic surgery or DUIs. They do not have public fights and break-ups, gain or lose weight, go to rehab, or announce that they're having a baby. Product brands do not get married or divorced, or mouth off to the wrong people. Celebrities do.

Contemporary notions of brand

Those interviewed used different words to describe the same phenomenon, and for good reason. To begin with, there are numerous definitions of brand. The traditionalist view is that a brand is a "name, term, sign, symbol, or design, or a combination of them, intended to identify the goods and services of one seller or a group of sellers and differentiate them from those of competitors" (Kotler and Armstrong, 2011, p231). The updated definition of brand, espoused by consumer culture theorists, is that a brand is more likely the sum total of what everyone who has experienced your brand in some way thinks about it (Keinan and Avery, 2008). In other words, you do not even have to drink a Starbucks coffee to have an opinion about Starbucks. This is true, in part, because of the influence of the *social world*.

Theoretical gaps: Person brands and short-term brands

Marketing and entertainment professionals have long been intimating that people can be brands. But academic scholarship is lagging behind practice (and trade publications) in this case, and academics are still debating the theoretical question of whether people can even be brands. This book provides data-driven evidence that female pop stars are *strategically constructed* to be products *and* brands in the music industry. Thus, academic literature needs to catch up quickly and reflect this reality of the modern marketing and music businesses.

In sociology and mass communication, for example, such work could help audiences to understand what goes into the marketing of pop stars so that they can use their increased understanding of the process to critically analyze marketing messages and the intentions of those sending them. It might also help such audiences to recognize the constraints female pop stars operate within and acknowledge the forces that lead so many of them to focus on sex and beauty in order to make the most of their short time in the spotlight. In marketing, discussing *short-term brands* and *person brands* is important because they clearly exist, and there is simply no formalized best- practice thinking available to practitioners that could help them more responsibly manage such people and product types.

As more *person-brand* work is published in academic venues, more scholars will become familiar with this meaningful term that practitioners have been using informally for years. This will help academics and practitioners to have more productive discussions about effective management strategies for such brand types, which may, in turn, improve the damaging, reductive way some of these women are currently managed. This treatment and the social effects of it will be chronicled in subsequent chapters.

Similarly, there is only one quasi-academic article exclusively dedicated to the study of *short-term brands*, which was written by Dan Herman, an Israeli consultant, in 2002. My data also clearly indicate that *brands can be classified as short term* and should thus be studied as such in greater depth. Given that many female pop stars are *short-term brands*, some effort should be made to establish how best to manage *short-term brands*, or how to change current strategies in order to build them for long-term success.

These theoretical gaps—the lack of theory about and definitions of *person brands* and *short-term brands*—create an interesting dilemma about how best to evaluate the management of aspiring pop star careers. An interested scholar or practitioner might read marketing literature or books about "fads" (Joel Best's *Flavor of the Month*) and "trends" (Malcolm Gladwell's *Tipping Point*), but would find that much of it is related to different industries—not popular culture and entertainment—which have different dynamics and rules. Most of the academic focus in the marketing/branding field is on building, maintaining, and revitalizing long-term or traditional brands, which, as I argue in this chapter, are few and far between when it comes to female popular music stars. With the exception of cultural branding discussions in which such scholars as Fournier and Herman (2004, 2006) and Holt (2003, 2004) describe the criticality of context and culture to brand strength, *short-term brands* are simply missing from the discussion.

The *short-term person brand* is a concept that is completely invisible in academic literature. But in today's celebrity-driven cultural environment, there is a great need for this unified conceptualization. Brand theory needs to be expanded to account for cultural phenomena, *short-term brands* among them, but codifying such instructions and guidelines is daunting given the messiness, and the openness, of the task at hand.

Traditional branding models are concerned with building brands that will last 50 or more years, and include mega-brands such as Coke, Pepsi, and McDonald's. Truly iconic entertainers, such as Elvis Presley, Marilyn Monroe, or even Whitney Houston, might also fall into this category, as their brands arguably became stronger after their respective deaths, and thus their brands have the capacity to live on indefinitely. In these cases, death conferred sainthood and strengthened the person brands; but many *person brands* never become iconic enough to get a brand bump from their death. The converted-sinner narrative, with its promise of redemption and recovery, is powerful in religious culture and popular culture. In the years just before her death, it seemed possible for Houston to rise from the ashes and redeem herself in the eyes of the public—America loves a comeback; but, tragically, she died before she could do so. The power and longevity of most *person brands*, whether they are musicians or celebrities, are constrained in the long term by three main factors: cultural changes, physical changes, and their biological lifecycle.

Given these considerations, what does managing a *short-term person brand* entail? Clearly, person brands should be managed differently than product or service brands; but few, if any, are addressing this issue in contemporary branding journals. Fournier and Herman (2006, p47) suggest that perhaps such theory should originate with the practitioners:

> As brand managers in effect become trend managers, academics may find more inspiration from industries such as movie making, music, and fashion than the packaged goods and durables forums that have historically informed our theories of the brand.

For that reason, I relied on those experts who are making and observing the judgment calls concerning female popular music stars, or *short-term person brands*, in the contemporary music industry, and built my definition and management consideration based on the data they provided me. Several guiding principles for *short-term person brands* emerged from my data and serve as the basis for this chapter.

Behind the scenes: Managing short-term person brands

Because there is precious little brand theory that speaks directly to managing *short-term brands*, much less *short-term person brands*, I asked those interviewed how managing such brands differs from managing more traditional products and services. My analysis of their responses led me to draft two organizing principles of female pop star management and five more specific tenets. Understanding these ideas should allow various audiences (including students) to view these celebrities with deeper comprehension and, as *receivers*, to bring a deeper sense of meaning to the pervasive messages the industry sends.

Two organizing principles:

- *There is a sales typology for female performers in the music business industry.*
- *In all but exceptional cases, female musicians are short-term person brands who must endeavor to protect their core brands, carefully managing art-versus-commerce considerations as they extend their brands into other entertainment realms.*

Five person-brand maintenance considerations:

- *Name is an important part of the brand equation.*
- *An artist's behavior and temperament can greatly change her management and publicity.*
- *Artist managers strive for an optimal level of artist accessibility and visibility, which maintains some separation between the personal and the professional.*
- *With female pop stars, the truth is often better than fiction.*
- *Artists and their brand managers cannot control culture, but they can work with it to get what they want.*

The remainder of the chapter will address these findings in sequence, discussing the organizing principles first, and then delving into the more specific strategic considerations.

Principle 1: Female pop-star brand typology, from *insignificant seller to career artist*

Organizing artists by sales potential sheds some light on the distance between the stars and the local heroes. Six major sales categories emerged from my data that provide a framework through which to view contemporary female musicians. They are the *insignificant seller*, the *road warrior*, the *indie rock star*, the *flash in the pan*, the *short-term brand*, and the *career artist* (see Table 2.1).

There is little doubt that different artist brand types exist for female artists in the music industry, but given the dearth of academic literature related to such performers, such types have not been named or characterized. The types offered here are admittedly broad categories that could be refined with more specific data and more time in a future book. But for the purposes of this book, it is simply important to note that there *are* different brand types, and that they exhibit different characteristics—especially with regard to market performance. It is important to note that my interviews with industry executives focused on artists who are or were capable of becoming *short-term brands* or *career artists* in order to see if there were similarities that could be established. The other sales types are represented here to

Table 2.1 Sales typology for female pop stars

Brand types	Sales range	Exemplar
Insignificant seller	<15,000	Eleanor Friedberger
Road warrior	<100,000	Sharon Van Etten, Ani DiFranco
Indie star	100,000–500,000	Regina Spektor, PJ Harvey, Neko Case
Flash in the pan	750,000–2 million (once)	KT Tunstall, Lauryn Hill
Short-term brand	500,000–3 million (multiple times)	Fantasia, Natasha Bedingfield
Career artist	500,000–5 million (four or more efforts)	Rihanna, Kelly Clarkson, Beyoncé

situate the studied stars in a wider industrial context. I defined these categories based on industry statistics, my own research, and prior music industry experience.

The *insignificant seller* is an artist who may be quite talented, but does not likely have the capacity to reach what major labels would consider to be an acceptable level of sales, or the potential for lucrative extensions, to justify continued marketing support. These artists, exemplified by artists such as Eleanor Friedberger, fall outside the scope of this project, but are mentioned here because they represent one end of the brand-type spectrum.

The *road warrior* is a performer who is known for her tireless touring and stage charisma. These artists often make their living on the stage, selling less than 100,000 units per CD release, but staying afloat through touring and merchandise revenue. Exemplars include Ani DiFranco, who at one time hovered closer to the indie star, but has settled comfortably into this category, and Sharon Van Etten, who finds herself in this position after three CDs.

The *indie star* is a critical darling and fan favorite among the cool kids, but her influence outpaces her sales, which typically fall between 100,000 and 500,000 per effort. Exemplars of this category include Regina Spektor, PJ Harvey, and Neko Case.

The *flash in the pan* is a musician who achieves explosive short-term sales because of her specific, contextual cultural resonance or one great song. But subsequent efforts aren't as culturally perfect, or the artist falters for a variety of professional or personal reasons and never matches the sales level of this one effort. Exemplars include KT Tunstall and Lauryn Hill, who caught on like wildfire and then virtually disappeared. It should be noted, however, that Hill is still regarded as widely influential, and recently returned to touring, playing small theaters during 2011 to 2012.

The *short-term brand* is an artist who, for various reasons, has greater longevity than a *flash in the pan*. She may have grown her audience organically by appearing in front of mass audiences for months as a reality show contestant, thus attracting huge audiences very rapidly, or been culturally resonant in a way that lasts longer than one effort. She has two or three CDs that sell well in major-label terms, which is at least "Gold" or 500,000 units per release. Exemplars include Fantasia and Natasha Bedingfield. If she continues to sell at this level, she becomes a *career artist*.

The *career artist* is an artist with four or more similarly defined "hit" CDs, whose label will invest in and manage her for the long term. Presumably, this means that her CD releases will be planned well, marketed extensively, and released to great anticipation and demand. Given her musical talent, she also has a range of musical options to keep her brand in circulation between CD releases, such as performing on Broadway. Exemplars in this category include Christina Aguilera, Kelly Clarkson, Beyoncé, and Shakira.

There are a few noteworthy career artists who persist for decades. Artists in this category include the best-selling female artist of all time, Barbra Streisand, who has sold 71 million units; Madonna, who has sold 64 million units; and Mariah Carey, who has sold 61.5 million units (RIAA, 2012). It is important to note that these women are truly exceptions, and that many of the top-selling female artists (e.g., Sade, Britney Spears, Shania Twain) got there on the strength of three to five mega-selling full-length CDs (RIAA, 2012). Artists in this category will undoubtedly have certain efforts that do better than others, but almost everything this kind of artist releases finds an audience of hard-core followers, and perhaps even attracts some newcomers.

Perhaps as important as defining brand types is speculating about why the categories are what they are. Not surprisingly, marketing appears to be the answer. The major record companies, in conjunction with other influential media, have the power and reach to manufacture quick hits. At the same time, the labels have a short-term investment and profitability horizon, so if the initial song or CD does not generate immediate "buzz" or interest, the artist is dismissed. If, however, the artist continues to resonate with culture, she can move into the *short-term brand* category. If the artist has the capacity to extend her brand through various means (clothing and fragrance lines, outside industry appearances in television, film, magazines, etc.) and continue to sell CDs, she may move into the *career artist* category or beyond.

Some label executives follow distinctly different portfolio management strategies for these different types of artists. Veteran music publicist and marketing executive Elizabeth Lang, who has workd with several multi-platinum selling female artists in different genres, explained:

> I feel so bad saying this, but when you've got an act that's not the priority or a career act, the label is just trying to make as much money as fast as they can and get them out there in any way, shape, or form. It's not about protecting an image—you wanna put them on a TV show where they get hit in the face with pies—sure! We'll do it! You'll get them an interview in the crappiest little publication. You just want mass, mass, mass, mass, mass. If somehow, they take off, then you can start cherry-picking what you would and wouldn't do.

Music historian and journalism professor Tim Riley, who has written several books about iconic pop stars such as Madonna, agreed, arguing that the promise of short-term upside potential often trumps thoughts of building a lasting performer or brand:

> The thinking, really, is so short term. It really is: "Can we squeeze a couple of hits out of them?" And if they turn around, and they want a career, we'll deal with that a few years down the road, but for right now, it's just like, "Let's just get the hits out, book them on the Super Bowl if we can, and get out."

In contrast, when a label executive determines an artist has longer-term potential, executives may adapt their strategies accordingly. Lang explained:

> RCA came out with Christina Aguilera and from the get-go said she is our Barbra Streisand. She's a career artist. I think they really can look at an artist and say this one has what it takes to go the long haul. If you're looking at a little pop tart, it's a completely different game. With a career artist, you are much more protective of their image in that you want it to be a slow burn. You want them on this TV show, on this cover, you want them in the right prestige publications. You want them visually looking like a star.

So, how do labels decide what separates a *career artist* from the others? In Aguilera's case, the label wagered that her powerful voice would carry her past her first couple of CDs and into a long-term career. Several respondents noted that if an artist has three successful albums under her belt she is on her way to becoming a *career artist*—the music industry equivalent of a long-term brand. However, several respondents also stated that if an artist does not score a hit on her first or second album, she will generally not succeed in the business, much less become a long-term brand. The business used to be organized around seven-record contracts between artists and labels, but these have become less common during recent years for a variety of reasons, including shifts in industry dynamics and anticipated longevity. "Remaining relevant for seven records is highly unlikely today," artist manager Jorge Hinojosa noted.

But deciding who's going to hit and who's going to flop can be a difficult call. And while some think stars can be identified right away, others are not so sure. Janet Billig-Rich, who has managed artists ranging from Nirvana to Courtney Love to Lisa Loeb, considered artists who looked promising initially but then more or less disappeared from the music scene:

> You don't know if you're a long-term brand, except in hindsight. Where'd KT Tunstall go? Where'd Lily Allen go? Where'd Nelly Furtado go? Where'd Missy Elliott go? Or Kylie Minogue?

Some wait for the marketplace to tell them who's a hit, and who's not. One former major label executive, who preferred not to be named, said:

> I wouldn't brand an artist as long term or short term. I would think of them as higher and lower profile. I would leverage a higher-profile artist to secure an opportunity for a lower-profile artist. If you can't get a B-level artist somewhere or something, you can offer the A artist to get your B artist coverage or attention.

There are also artists who exist between the stages mapped out above. Original *American Idol* winner Kelly Clarkson emerged from the pack of insignificant-selling colleagues by selling millions. Arguably, she made the transition from *flash in the pan* to *short-term brand* based on her talent and her hits, and is on her way to becoming a viable *career artist*. NPR online music producer and columnist Stephen Thompson explained:

> Kelly Clarkson is a talent-show winner who became a legitimate artist through a mixture of good fortune and hard work. She won *American Idol* more than ten years ago, and anyone who can sustain a hit-making career for ten years, particularly a young woman, is doing something right. At this point, her winning *Idol* is almost a footnote. I'm not sure whether she has even peaked yet.

Although Clarkson enjoys significant record sales, those interviewed were careful to point out that she's the exception, not the rule. They do not expect many others from *American Idol*-type backgrounds to experience similar success due to the way in which they are positioned in the public eye and come by their popularity.

Adele was cited by several industry veterans as a current example of someone who has the makings of a *career artist*, as long as her voice holds up. She underwent vocal surgery in 2011 to repair a vocal cord hemorrhage (Gottlieb, 2011). Even though she has only released two CDs, (dubbed *19* and *21* for her age during production), the power of her voice, her critical reception, impressive sales figures, and her highly differentiated artist-first positioning make her a strong candidate. Adele will be discussed in greater depth in Chapter 4.

At this point, having explored female pop stars as brands and proposed a basic typology of brand types by sales potential, I'd like to turn my focus to the more specific strategic considerations that emerged from my findings that could prove useful to scholars, students, brand managers, music industry professionals, and artists.

Principle 2: Managing female pop stars as short-term person brands

"Most artists recognize that they are brands," artist manager Jorge Hinojosa said. He explained that some artists would prefer *not* to be brands for fear of being viewed as too commercial, but noted that others hope to turn their brands into empires. "Madonna and Katy Perry embrace themselves as brands, and it shows," he said. Other respondents mentioned specific artist brand extensions by name—clothing lines, fragrances, and movie careers—and indicated that brand extensions help female performers to strategically change and update their images over time. Many cited this extension strategy as a vital element in staying relevant to a mass audience. Indeed, in Fournier and Herman's (2004, p12) study of the Martha Stewart person brand, they quote COO Shannon Patrick, who described the process of "making a business out of Martha's life." This is an interesting way to think about *person brands*, whether built for the short term or the long term. How many opportunities does an artist give a brand manager to "make a business of her life?"

Interestingly there are two portfolios in play in this scenario—the within-artist portfolio and the within-label portfolio. Both must be managed expertly in order to succeed. By leveraging different aspects of an artist's appeal (within-artist) and different kinds of artists (different genres and different brand types), labels create balance, and minimize risk, across their respective portfolios. Citing extensively from past literature, Fournier and Herman (2006, p44) encouraged this very approach, but pointed out the need for more innovative drivers: "Brand portfolios, for example, could be constructed to balance risks across

cultural contexts and time, as opposed to revenue-maximizing considerations of audience coverage and market reach."

Here "cultural context" and "time" become central considerations,
displacing, to some extent, the age-old marketing measures of "coverage"
and "market reach." Expanding the domain of brand theory in this way
calls for a new conceptualization of it. This likely means elaborating
upon past constructs and incorporating ideas from other disciplines that
better reflect the current cultural environment. With the relevant tools
and constructs available from marketing theory, communication theory,
and sociological theory, marketers and artists can expand their scope
beyond the producer-consumer dyad and into the broader *social world*,
which sets the context for everything they do and produce.

Fournier and Herman have articulated the need for the same kind of
interdisciplinary thinking, which prioritizes work that is culturally rich
and relevant over more rudimentary work that has historically been
easier to measure. In their words: "Marketers must shift their targeting
decisions to focus not on identifiable, reachable, and sizable consumer
segments but rather on those high potential brand meanings capable of
transcending segments and types" (Fournier and Herman, 2004, p33).
Douglas Melville, who ran brand initiatives for international pop stars
and professional athletes before joining his current advertising agency,
agreed, arguing that there has been a shift from a demographic-focused
marketing approach to a psychographic-based marketing approach to
managing celebrity:

> The psychographic is: What thought and vision do certain indi-
> viduals reflect regardless of age, creed, color, or race? A demographic
> is the opposite—what similarities exist between this select creed,
> color, and race. But with artists today, it's not about the demo-
> graphic, it's about the psychographic. In other words, you can find
> 18-year-olds, 30-year-olds, and 50-year-olds who love Britney for
> the meanings she's expressing, not the age they are.

Some who ready artists for the public eye seem to grasp this idea intui-
tively. Lang explained the painstaking detail required to effectively

bring an artist to market in today's cultural environment, focusing more on the look and the brand to communicate meaning than the music, especially as brand images are carried on smaller and smaller devices:

> If you look at Avril Lavigne, she was brought on the scene as "nice girl." It's almost as though a uniform is chosen for her. So you typically see her in a version of that outfit everywhere she goes. It's like creating a logo, a brand, a visual. And you see them dressing almost clone-like in the beginning because you need to reinforce who they are. If you see them at an awards show, they'll be wearing an outfit very similar to what they wore in the music video because that's the product they're promoting at that time. It'll be quite similar to the album cover art, too.

Glickman took the idea of the constructed homogeneous brand further, arguing that the music industry has moved away from artistry and toward commercialization since the late 1990s:

> Britney and others who broke at the end of the CD era very shrewdly got popularity based on diversification—they didn't just sell CDs, they sold toys, merchandise, movies, and what have you. So they were able to cross-capitalize their success. And at a certain point it kind of stopped them from being music artists in a sense; they were just sort of celebrities who occasionally made records— all-purpose, beautiful young things.

My informants explained that looks and marketability get artists seen and heard. Even extremely talented artists orchestrate attention-getting schemes to gain initial visibility in the industry. Once that brand forms, maintaining its viability can also be challenging. Perhaps we can call this the *Madonna effect*. My informants reported that she set the precedent for female pop star empire-building, but she may not have anticipated what followed. Now many artist handlers pursue empire-building from the get-go, before the marketplace has even decided on whether they like the artists as *musicians*.

Kay Hanley knows from her own experience how to extend a brand. Having tired of being a lead singer in a band where she had to "sell herself," she opted for a more lucrative career as a behind-the-scenes type. Since disbanding Letters to Cleo and becoming a mother, Hanley has created a production company (Art is War), written numerous television themes, including the *My Friends Tigger and Pooh* and *Generation O* theme songs, and penned songs for movie soundtracks *(Josie and The Pussycats)*. She's also performed music *in* films (*10 Things I Hate about You* and *Josie and The Pussycats*), composed and produced a series for Disney (*Doc McStuffins*) and toured as a Miley Cyrus back-up singer in the Best of Both Worlds tour in 2007 to 2008. She also managed, published, and produced a band (Shut Up Stella) that got a major label record deal. She still makes solo CDs and plays live, but "out of pure love," not economic hope or necessity. "I am much happier working behind the scenes and not having to sell myself," she said. "I needed to figure out ways to take advantage of what I've accomplished in the past to help support my family. I've had some great opportunities, and I've been able to capitalize on them."

One of Billig-Rich's clients, Lisa Loeb, has followed a similar extension strategy, but with different products. She launched an eyewear line, published two children's books, wrote a musical, and starred in two reality shows. Billig-Rich plays the role of brand facilitator, helping to make these extensions work so that Loeb becomes better known and more accessible to fans. "Being on TV helps sell music and helps create a brand that helps sell other things, whether it's books or eyeglasses," she said. "Being on TV as herself lets people get to know and trust her in a way they didn't before."

Brand extensions

Every executive interviewed mentioned that these stars' commercial value comes from the possible extensions of their respective star "brands." Today the strength of a celebrity brand is a function of the diversity of appeal that person possesses. The stronger the star's position in the *social world*, the more likely she is to parlay her musical talent into other entertainment realms such as film or television. As the star creates various branded products, which spread across different parts of the entertainment world, she keeps herself in circulation in between musical releases and tours, and lengthens her time in the limelight. Increasingly, female pop stars are extending their brands into fashion and cosmetics, too. Such a star effectively cross-capitalizes her successes and manages the risk of any one of her involvements going south by practicing sound "portfolio management" (Negus, 1999, p14). By making sure she has widespread appeal, and with different audiences, the star can insulate herself from a unified backlash against her for any reason. She may fall out of favor with one camp, but still be cool in the eyes of the others. Additionally, she may attract new fans with each endeavor to make up for the natural loss of other fans. As an artist ages, for example, she can make the decision to grow up with her current target market or continue to make music for younger generations. Either decision would make her appeal to one group while losing appeal with the other.

These days, in order to remain relevant and sell competitively, a female popular music star must extend her brand into non-music realms, effectively becoming a brand portfolio. Every brand gets tired and periodically needs revitalization. One way to revitalize is through brand extensions. Extensions present a natural opportunity for popular music stars in that people want to dress like them, smell like them, live like them, and look like them. That's why Madonna, Jennifer Lopez, Gwen Stefani, Beyoncé, and Jessica Simpson have clothing lines; Britney Spears, Christina Aguilera, Jennifer Lopez, Mariah Carey, and Celine Dion have signature fragrances; and Whitney Houston (*Being Bobby Brown*), Britney Spears (*Chaotic*), and Jessica Simpson (*Newlyweds*) all had reality shows.

When extending a brand, it is best to do so in a timely fashion, in an appropriate manner, so that artists do not stretch their brands or miss their window of opportunity. Many pop music careers are short-lived, so creating extensions before they end may be what allows a pop star to retire comfortably. Consumer culture theory might call this approach appreciative of inevitable cultural changes. There's no reason a pop star shouldn't *try* to develop brand extensions. But she should not stray too far from her natural core, or she will damage the very brand that makes extensions possible.

The field of marketing offers extensive research about brand and product extensions, and the factors leading them to succeed or fail. Scholars suggest that balanced brands that score high on familiarity and appeal tend to work best as extension bases, as long as the extensions are similar to the core offering (Lane, 1998). The continuity between the original brand and its extensions enables consumers to transfer their attitudes from the parent brand to the new extensions, which is critical for the new product's success, and the long-term health of the core brand (Lane, 1998).

Extending brands via licensing deals

Among the smartest and most efficient revenue-generating opportunities for artists today is licensing their music for use in TV shows, films, and commercials. British alt-rock sensation Florence + The Machine has worked this method all the way to the bank, placing its first single ("Kiss With a Fist") from its debut CD, *Lungs*, on *90210* and several lesser-known programs; and its second single, "Dog Days Are Over," on *Gossip Girl*, *Community*, *Glee*, and in the trailer for the theatrical release of *Eat, Pray, Love*. Another single from *Lungs*, "Cosmic Love," appeared in everything from prime-time dramas (*Grey's Anatomy*), to vampire-thrillers (*The Vampire Diaries*), to top-rated reality programs (*So You Think You Can Dance*). The licensing strategy appears to have worked well, earning the band near-ubiquitous levels of exposure and critical acclaim—it was nominated for "Best New Artist" at the 53rd Annual Grammys in 2011.

The band's sophomore release, *Ceremonials*, was released in October 2011 and had already placed a track, "Heartlines," on *Gossip Girl* by December 5, 2011. The band had also garnered numerous high-profile live performances, appearing on *Saturday Night Live* ("Shake It Out" and "No Light, No Light"), *X Factor* ("Shake It Out" and "Spectrum"), and *Good Morning America* ("Shake It Out"), among others. If executed well, these live performances create demand for the songs performed, making licensing opportunities more likely as the album matures and the songs grow in popularity.

Collaborations as extensions

As pop stars progress through their lifecycles, they often try to borrow *brand strength* from others in order to maintain dominance, making guest appearances in others' songs and videos. Close associations with other prominent artists can provide leverage, contribute positively to *brand meaning*, and protect against suddenly becoming dismissed as uncool. (Think the Madonna–Britney make-out session at the 2003 Video Music Awards. It was quite likely engineered and executed to update the Madonna brand with younger audiences, while validating the Britney brand with older audiences and younger haters.) More recently, in 2011, Jennifer Lopez (J-Lo) invited rising rapper Pit Bull to guest on her song "On the Floor" and more established rapper Lil Wayne to join her on "I'm Into You," presumably to update her image and make her relatable to contemporary club-goers.

Beyoncé and Shakira had both experienced multi-platinum market success—in different generic realms—when they collaborated on the "Beautiful Liar" song and video.[3] They likely did not "need" each other to maintain market resonance; but one could reasonably speculate that this was done to make Beyoncé a hit with Latin audiences and Shakira a hit with black audiences.

Collaborations as extensions in rap

It's important to note that some artists, particularly rap artists, collaborate early on, strategically building their own brand identity by borrowing equity from existing stars. These collaborative efforts often, but not always, stem from the same label or the same conglomerate music company. Rapper Nicki Minaj's mix-tapes, made and circulated from 2007 to 2009, put her on the map with other rappers, who apparently liked what they heard. When she signed to Young Money for her major label debut, she inherited its stable of prominent artists as potential collaborators, as the label has an interest in pairing its prominent artists with its rising stars to refresh the former and bolster the latter. By the end of 2011, Minaj had collaborated with David Guetta, Drake, Diddy, Eminem, Usher, Kanye West, Ludacris, Robin Thicke, Britney Spears and Ke$ha, and that was only one year after her major label debut—2010's smash hit *Pink Friday*. By February 2012, Minaj's brand was so strong she was collaborating with Madonna, appearing alongside her and M.I.A. at the Super Bowl, where they performed "Give Me All Your Luvin'."

Unlikely extensions

The *Cultural Diamond* reminds us that every action and every product takes place within the greater *social world*. One could argue that every time an artist gets married or divorced, has a child, enters a rehabilitation facility, discovers religion, or experiences a public tragedy, she extends her brand in some meaningful way, which shifts her position in the *social world*. Dr. Kerry Herman, assistant director of the Global Research Group at Harvard Business School, explained it this way: "It captures more markets, more audience. It takes these celebrities from being one dimensional to being three dimensional." Such tabloid appearances do not typically sum to increased sales, but do enhance the star's visibility, which can be difficult to generate between projects. It also has the potential to make people who do not follow the star's music consider her for other reasons. Examples include when Beyoncé and Jay-Z had their baby (Blue Ivy Carter), when J-Lo and Marc Anthony got divorced, and when Whitney Houston struggled with drug addiction.

Given the increasingly blurring lines between entertainment content and advertising—now called "branded entertainment"—these pop stars become *cultural objects* who are not only dynamic entertainment content, but also ever-circulating advertisements for themselves. In other words, every time they appear anywhere, in any capacity, they reinforce or extend the meanings of their own brands in some way.

Journalist-turned-brand-consultant Simon Glickman dubbed this phenomenon "popularity based on diversification." What he is describing is the process of extending an artist's brand and reach into non-music products and industries in order to bolster her success while it lasts.

"Saying you're in the music business is like saying you're in the rotary phone business," said artist manager and former label executive Janet Billig-Rich. "You really have to expand out." Billig-Rich went on to say that a healthy revenue portfolio for an artist today is a 70/30 split—70 percent coming from "everything else" and 30 percent coming from the music. "It's hard to make a full living on just music," she said. "But music drives everything else. Unless you do the music, all the other things don't come." Hanley and Loeb learned this through time and practice. Now in their 40s, both singers/entertainers work on projects that will likely appeal to the women who listened to them 15 years ago *and* their small children. This is a perfect example of growing up with one's audience and succeeding through extension (as opposed to continuously courting the youth market despite personal and cultural changes).

Brand marketer and advertising executive Douglas Melville, thinks modern-day demands placed on musicians to be shrewd, savvy businesspeople have become unreasonable, if not impossible. Melville recalled the following about the video for Shakira's World Cup song, "Waka Waka":[4]

> Four hundred million people voluntarily logged on to a web site, searched her name, typed in her name, and watched a video—for at least 30 seconds for it to count—and she didn't even get paid for that? The video was just used as a way to make money in other avenues. That's what you're telling artists. You made a really good song, and it's amazing that 400 million people listened to it. But in order for you to make money, you've got to figure out how to lever-age that into new businesses.

In Melville's view, that just shouldn't be the musician's job—they should focus on creating and performing music. But, increasingly, branding and sales responsibilities have become things that artists have to actively think about, not to sell out, but to make a living.

In addition to the two organizing guidelines for managing *short-term person brands*, there were five other strategic ideas generated through discussions with industry professionals about maintaining the integrity of such brands while extending them to maintain resonance throughout time.

Five ways in which pop stars can update while still trying to keep it real

One:
What's in a name: Keep it real or adopt a pseudonym?
According to my participants, one of the first big decisions *person brands* need to make is whether to use their real name, to adopt a pseudonym for the marketplace, or to do both at different times to represent the full range of their character(s). Some argue that using one's own name guarantees authenticity and integrity, while others argue that using one's own name is a recipe for disaster. Melville explained the tricky balance of deciding how to brand a celebrity in today's media environment:

> Nowadays, if you start a business, you call it Google, or you call it Microsoft. You don't call it Bill Gates. People have stopped using their name as the landmark for their business. It's reality versus fantasy. When people name something after themselves, that's too real for people.

He argued that there are good reasons for this trend, but suggested that there are also drawbacks:

> If you have a pseudonym as a name, you market that differently than if it's your birth name. You have to look at the integrity of the name. If it's your real birth name, you market it in a completely different way because if the company goes down, you as an individual go down regardless. There are very few people willing to use their actual birth name now. Everybody's coming up with stage names and pseudonyms. That's a big deal because they don't take the same pride in their work.

This suggests that for artists not expecting to have long careers, as is the case with most female popular music artists, the best thing to do might be to create a differently named brand, infuse it with some mystery, and ride it until it goes down in flames. In this scenario, if Pink missteps, Alecia Moore will still be able to survive and prosper in a different life. Beyoncé inhabits the middle ground, adopting her given first name as her stage name, but trading it in periodically to become other characters, such as "Sasha Fierce."[5] Lady Gaga may use the fact that audiences do not know much about Stefani Germanotta as an opportunity to introduce more of her genuine self later. She could borrow a trick from Kiss and show us Gaga unmasked or un-costumed, just a talented musician playing a piano or guitar. Or she could remain Gaga, but strip down her show, once her *schtick* wears thin.

"Who's not gonna tune in for Gaga Unplugged?" Billig-Rich asked.

Two:
Suggest what your brand means, but seek your audience's (receiver's) contributions to make it complete, then control what you can
Unlike traditional brand authors who encode brands with meaning with the intention of having them decoded by customers, some people who manage *person brands* realize they cannot strictly control artists or the public's response to them. Billig-Rich said she always tried to "let the artist lead." She explained:

> I think that they're the ones who are going to know how to promote themselves the best. They sort of know who they are, and, again, artists really watch pop culture. As a manager, even as a publicist, I always saw myself as a facilitator.

She speculated that more traditional unidirectional brand authorship probably "happens more in the teenybopper market," when, due to their youth and inexperience, artists "need people to sort of figure it out for them."

In a 20-year career, Hanley has both led and learned to follow an artist's lead. Formerly the lead singer of major-label artist Letters to Cleo, Hanley is now a producer, composer, and sometimes artist manager. She says that no matter who is defining the artist's brand, it needs to ring authentic with audiences. "People can smell bullshit from a mile away," she said. "Conversely, people can spot a real deal from a mile away and people love a real deal. The key is to figure out a way to be exactly who you are and express that as clearly as possible," she said.

Traditional brand theorists claim that consistency and reinforcement are vital to maintaining a brand. If people do not know a brand, or can't remember it, it does not have much value—or much meaning—in the marketplace. But creative people tend to rebel against the very idea of consistency—why is it necessarily better than change and evolution? For some, maintaining a brand image feels like an intrusion. Hanley explained her initial feeling about the subject from an artist's perspective:

> Our first big video was for our first single. It was like our only hit. We made the video for the song, and then, much to my surprise and horror, it got on Buzz Bin on MTV, and all of a sudden people were recognizing me wherever we went. So I immediately dyed my hair fire engine red and cut it all off, so that people wouldn't know who I was. And the label was just like, what the fuck is wrong with you? Every time after that that we would make a video, I would change the color of my hair and change the clothes that I wore just so that I wouldn't be recognized as that girl from the video. And the label was just like, what the fuck is wrong with you? How are we ever supposed to sell this band if you refuse to be recognized, if you refuse to create—I guess they wouldn't have put it in these terms back then, but if you refuse to create a brand?
>
> Then Kool-Aid tried to license one of the songs from our second CD for a commercial, and I was like, no fucking way. Not in a million years. And they offered us $25,000 to license it, and we were like, fuck you, no way, we will not do it.

Hanley said that was the right move for her at the time, but that she has backed off of this position somewhat, as the music industry and the concept of what constitutes a "sell out" has changed. She explained:

> I've come to believe that what I do for work has value. I was confused about that when I was younger. I was doing something that I happily would have done for free.
>
> Advertisers need it. People who are sad need it. People who want to listen on headphones stoned need it. People who need a song to dance to at their wedding need it. I do something that not many people are able to do and that I love. I shouldn't confuse that for "it should be free." I should be paid. It is my job. And the only job I have.
>
> My friend has a song in a Yoplait commercial, and she's making bank for it. She could probably buy a house for what she made from one national commercial. I would happily take a national commercial at this point.

Hanley noted that times have changed so much that the younger artists she has managed and advised, such as Shut Up Stella, a band that was signed to Epic Records but has since disbanded, did not have any of these art-versus-commerce conflicts. "They wanted to be famous, they wanted to be stars," she said. Each member of the trio is now pursuing her own solo career. One of them opened for Britney Spears in her summer 2011 tour.

Three:
Artist "accessibility" is important—but have some boundaries, some self-awareness, and some graciousness
My informants all mentioned artist accessibility as a vital part of most highly successful female artists' marketing package. But where and how they draw their lines about what's public and what's private differed by person. Some were fine with fans knowing about stars' boyfriends and babies, viewing them as opportunities to humanize the star. Others viewed these so-called "opportunities" as a mixed blessing. They may keep an artist in the limelight, but they may also compromise her

privacy and cause others to objectify or mock her. This, in turn, makes it harder to maintain a positive brand image. Several of those interviewed commented on numerous ways in which artists can compromise their "longevity" through "overexposure"—or the wrong kind of exposure. Others argued that as artists become popular, they often lose their sense of this line. Handlers may not rein them in because they have to become "yes" men and women to keep their jobs or because they believe the extra accessibility to be beneficial to an artist's career. Hanley explained: "The thing that I've come to learn or have come to see is that anything that gets people to care about you again, or in the first place, is a way to extend your brand." Melville argued that overexposure and scrutiny will naturally happen to women because the public feels entitled to know everything about where they go, what they do, and who they do it with. This is because women and men come to market differently. Respondents reported that women come to market instructed to overshare, while men come to market coached to say as little as possible and remain mysterious. Melville observed that while a judge on *American Idol*, Paula Abdul was "dissected to the point of uncomfortability" in a way that Randy Jackson and Simon Cowell were not. This problem was exacerbated by Abdul's 2007 reality show on Bravo, *Hey Paula*, in which she appeared overly emotional, self-obsessed, and delusional. (In one episode she complained: "I'm tired of people not treating me like the gift that I am.")

Nevertheless, Melville noted that he believes celebrity stalking has gone too far and has begun to erode the potential for long-term brands. For those reasons, he argued that artists and managers have to decide how to keep the artist's privacy a little more genuinely private. Others echoed this idea, and suggested that the root of the problem is that celebrities are held up like "prizes" in our culture. Accordingly, audiences look to pop star behavior as a roadmap for similar success. The personal assistant to a platinum-selling rap artist noted: "These pop stars, these movie stars—they are the prize. I think things like *American Idol*, the Pussycat Dolls, and the Spice Girls make the common person think that they could have that. Isn't that what we're taught?"

Others are disgusted by the whole practice—especially when one seemingly uses one's own personal life *willingly* to garner professional attention. NPR's Thompson argued:

> I think my biggest pet peeve is the singer who uses her personal life in ugly ways [...] who writes the song about how he or she was sexually abused and then goes on *Entertainment Tonight* to promote the song about how he or she was sexually abused. I think it may be the most disgusting thing ever; I hate it beyond words. You're like exploiting yourself all over again.

But such personal disclosures are not always the artist's idea. Sometimes, an artist's backstory, or personal history, is even changed to be more palatable to audiences. My participants indicated that many working in marketing capacities in the music industry attempt to sanitize artist images in order to make them more desirable to the public, such as in the aforementioned case of Whitney Houston.

But how much of an artist's real personal life should be available for public consumption? Fournier and Herman (2006, p23) suggested that *person-brand* managers consider the following set of questions in planning such strategies:

> Effective person-brand development required ongoing consideration of a host of person-brand boundary questions: What person meanings were needed to (re)build the brand; what person meanings were leaking inadvertently onto the brand that deserved (re)consideration, dilution, or change; what person meanings should be transferred away to other meaning makers. MSO [Martha Stewart] failed to appreciate that the management of the person face was neither an opportunistic nor a crisis-induced activity; it was an integral, comprehensive, and ever-present responsibility for effectively managing the person-brand.

Their framework suggests that monitoring an artist's meaning on a daily, and perhaps even hourly, basis is key if artists and artist handlers wish to stay apprised of an artist's myriad meanings. Such a person should have the vigilance of a crisis manager even in non-crisis times. Waiting until an undesirable meaning enters wide public circulation is unacceptable, and can create irreversible damage to an artist and her career. Whitney Houston's downfall exemplified the risk of unmanaged meanings. According to several respondents, her positioning of *good girl* ran contrary to her party-girl personality. Houston's handlers swept her "bad side" under the carpet repeatedly. Had her issues been acknowledged, embraced, and managed, it's possible she may not have struggled as much as she did over the tension between her public persona and private life.

Four:
The truth is better than fiction

Just as Houston's handlers might have been wise to represent her a bit more compassionately and honestly, other stars would be advised to tone down their honesty, particularly if someone else is writing it for them. The idea of a hyper-confessional song not even written by the artist is hilarious, but such songs do exist. Thompson mused: "My favorite song is called 'What It's Like to Be Me,' which Britney Spears performed but didn't write." In fact, Britney's ex-boyfriend Justin Timberlake wrote it with Wade Robson. The irony was not lost on *Rolling Stone* reviewer Barry Walters, who reviewed Britney's third album, *Britney*, in the November 22, 2001, issue of the magazine. He wrote:

> Britney Spears is now so high-concept, such a distillation of what made pop singers like Paula Abdul, Janet Jackson and Madonna so fabulously marketable, that her third record, Britney, is a concept album about herself. She's "Overprotected." She's "Lonely." She's "Not a Girl, Not Yet a Woman." Britney just wants to be Britney, this self-reflexive CD reasons, even as everyone around her is feverishly constructing "Britney" the product.

Again, the interactions among Britney-the-person, Britney-the-construction, and Britney-the-brand are difficult to disentangle. What's real and what's constructed is open to speculation, and audience meaning-making, as Fiske (1992, 1997), Hall (1980, 1993), and others explain. But sometimes my informants felt that they could see the wheels of strategy turning as particularly contrived events unfolded. Riley, the music author, isolated and discussed several stunts from the Britney Spears arsenal:

> It's like, "Well, what do we do to make this shocking, bold, and provocative? Well, we'll kiss Madonna on the mouth, let the snakes loose in Vegas." How do you one up yourself after that? But you're still just a fuck doll. It's all very cynical. It's very short range. I think it's much more marketing-oriented now, like "How many niches can we plug into with this product?" And the aesthetics are trailing way, way behind.

And while such thinking has surely created more opportunities for female artists, my respondents speculated that it has also forced homogenization in the industry. One industry professional who preferred not to named explained:

> Everyone has incorporated themselves. It's a factory. That is something that has hit me between the eyeballs in Los Angeles. It's one of the reasons that I'm actually working my way out of the industry. It really is about commodifying a person. And how far can you take it?

In today's cultural environment, most things, including integrity, appear to be available for sale. My informants told me they believe they can tell when someone's feigning an interest in a product line or an event in the name of sales and publicity. Those built-to-last career artists always ring genuine, and informants indicated that this quality distinguishes *short-term brands* from those who endure in the long term. The personal assistant to the female rap star explained:

> I think there are two tracks. There's a track where an artist is very heavily involved and creative, and [their extensions] are really

grounded in something that is real. And there's the track of just trying to make as much money as possible because time is running out. And you can tell the difference.

Billig-Rich argued that an ounce of prevention in such cases can positively influence artist outcomes by minimizing the shock value of exposed imperfections. She shared her strategy:

> I've also worked with artists, like Jewel, who were great at owning their differences. Like work the negative, before people point out that you have terrible teeth. Put it out there—smile with your big giant snaggletooth, you know? Or like whatever the negative is, you just put it out there.

Billig-Rich thought that Jewel's offbeat approach and personality actually ingratiated her to her audiences and allowed her to celebrate her differences before they could be noticed and interpreted as liabilities. In some cases, however, Billig-Rich argued that handlers must simply react to a situation because there's no opportunity to be proactive. She recalled:

> I think you're always just chasing the ball. Shit happens, and then you figure out how to spin it. Jail happens, and then the cabal gets together, and it's like "OK, how are we going to handle this jail situation? What are we going to say?" The artist is going to be asked about it, and [she or he] needs to be comfortable with what the spin is. You can't create the spin and not have the artist be party to it. Everyone comes up with what's the most believable story and puts the client in the best light. Or sometimes it is just a big lie and, yes, we're going to rehab for exhaustion.

Lang stated that by 2006, Whitney Houston, who had already been constructed and reconstructed by her handlers, seemingly without her buy-in or involvement, was officially a brand liability. She was behaving like herself, not her constructed image, and Lang detailed how a label would likely look at handling her situation:

I'm sure any business manager at a record company could tell you, there's a point of diminishing returns with an artist. If she's too difficult, too costly, too much of a liability, they'll let her go. At the point of diminishing returns, maybe they're only into us for another two records, we can chuck a greatest hits record against the wall, write off the other one, buy them out—whatever we have to do. We will do it.

Risk management is taken seriously, and in the music business, there are not many second chances. Sometimes if an artist is as extraordinary as Whitney Houston, she's lucky enough to get a second chance. But even in those cases, artists may not be able to convert on such opportunities due to personal issues. So the labels play it conservatively, doling out second chances only when they believe they will generate substantial revenue more or less immediately.

Lang stated:

It's a business. There's a perception that the music industry sells the markets originality, but it doesn't. It's a high-risk investment. It's super-high risk. The label is the bank, and they've essentially loaned the artist all the money and the resources to achieve a means to an end. If they feel as though their investment is being mishandled, they will come back in. Just like a bank would with a hotel.

Artists should know this history up front and learn from the case studies of artists who came before them. That way, if they find themselves in a tough position, they know that they're not alone and have some ideas about where to turn for advice. For example, Miley Cyrus and her handlers could take a page from Christina Aguilera's successful comebacks. After debuting as a talented ex-Mouseketeer, Aguilera became too sexually risqué (when she released *Stripped*). She came back from that as a glamorous *diva* and a new mother, thus setting herself up for a longer-term career. Then she faltered again with the Super Bowl debacle, only to come back as a champion of aspiring female artists on *The Voice*. It is important to note that Aguilera only got these chances because of her exceptional talent and the fact that her label had invested in her as a *career artist*.

Five:
You can't control culture, so work with it to get what you want

While all of my informants said that the only way for a female performer who is not conventionally attractive to sell millions in today's environment is to sell her song(s), one of them believes industry insiders have the ability to change public perceptions of what's beautiful and, in so doing, give great artists with different looks a fighting chance of succeeding with their own songs.

Hanley mentioned a major label artist who is very heavy, but has what it takes to be part of such a change:

> It's all about selling it and believing in yourself. She's like, "I'm a fat fucking bitch, and I don't care. You're going to love me, you're going to love my voice. I'm going to wear tank tops and knee-highs, and you're going to fucking love me. And you're going to want to fuck me, too." You've got to act the same way that Courtney Love does or Chrissie Hynde (of The Pretenders) does. Because that's really what rock and roll is all about, or what music is all about, it's confidence and bravado and selling it, and "Fuck you, and you love me, you know it." That's what rock and roll is all about, just as much as it is about the music. It's about persona.

Further, she argued that if one is "300 pounds" and "willing to put [oneself] out there," she may have a better chance of success because she's differentiated. "That's when it comes back to branding," Hanley said. "Nobody's going to confuse you with anybody else—you've got one up over a lot of people." Hanley also suggested that the time is right to effect such changes in the music industry, with respect to types and presentations of artists. She noted that there are ways of marketing fuller-figured artists without selling them out to "Pizza Hut" for commercials, and she actively wants to play a role in figuring out how best to do so. "I would take those people and help them be a giant 'fuck you' to popular culture," Hanley concluded.

Summary

This chapter has examined the female popular music artist as a brand, and argued that many handlers err in applying outdated, one-size-fits-all methods to their artists regardless of the unique differences. Two organizing principles and five recommendations were presented to help readers understand the branded context in which these stars operate. To recap briefly, the organizing principles were that female pop stars can be organized by sales typology, and that they are typically *short-term person brands* who must continuously update their brands while preserving their essential values. The five lower-level strategic necessities were: considering whether an artist uses her given name; knowing what artists and managers can and can't control with regard to branding; weighing the pros and cons of accessibility and making brand-appropriate decisions; focusing on the truth of personal narratives, preferably before they enter circulation; and appreciating that culture cannot be controlled, but must be regularly monitored and addressed.

But who are the specific music industry players who ready these pop star brands for the public eye? Who are the gatekeepers who determine what music is ultimately released to the public? The following chapter explores the component parts of the modern music industry and how they work together to produce pop stars.

3

THE MODERN MUSIC INDUSTRY

Most academic work in popular culture clusters around three points of the *Cultural Diamond*—the *social world*, the *cultural object*, and the *receiver* (sometimes referred to synonymously in this text as the *audience* or the *consumer*). This leaves the *producer* point relatively understudied, and given the access problems associated with interviewing gatekeepers, those studies are often theoretical (not data-driven) in nature. Previous chapters attempted to fill in some of the blanks caused by this imbalance by providing interview data with music industry experts (*creators*, sometimes interchangeably called *producers* in this book). This chapter addresses the structural, industrial norms at play within the music industry as a way of providing context for how such producers do their work. Certainly, such producers feel pressure from the *social world* and audiences, but they are also bounded by the norms of their profession, by the imperative to make money, and how those around them have historically done their jobs.

The music industry has experienced a wealth of drama and revolution in the past 15 years, from the advent of .mp3 files, to the creation and ubiquity of Napster, to the ascent of Apple as the country's top music retailer. The relevant industry gatekeepers, those people who decide what audiences will see and hear, have changed to some extent. In addition to traditional gatekeepers, such as traditional radio station owners, there are newcomers—for example, Spotify and Songza—which operate as new-form gatekeepers in the same general space. Despite the new competition from online and mobile competitors, traditional radio continues to hold relatively steady in power and influence for big artists. At the same time, *cultural intermediaries*, those who negotiate between *creators*/musicians and audiences, have arguably grown in importance, stripping at least some of the power from more traditional gatekeepers.

This chapter explores the component parts of the modern music industry; the gatekeepers who police content; some of the industry's core assumptions about artists and audiences; and some of the industry's issues and opportunities related to gender and branding.

Music industry structure

A look at the structure of the music industry and its key associated parts—record labels, radio stations, retailers, and distributors—reveals volumes about how pop stars have been created historically. But that is likely to change as CD sales drop precipitously and other products or assets in a pop star's portfolio become more important. One high-profile artist manager quoted in a 2007 *Wall Street Journal* article explained: "Sales are so down and so off that, as a manager, I look at the CD as part of the marketing of an artist, more than as an income stream" (Smith, 2007, p2).

That's a pretty damning statement, but the numbers bear it out. The precipitous decline is attributable to numerous factors, including the rise of file sharing, the decline of specialty music retail, and the advent of digital purchasing options such as iTunes. The impact has gone from being a threat to a promise, as music sales just declined for the 11th consecutive year. The Recording Industry Association of America (RIAA) reported that CD sales fell 19 percent nationwide in 2010 (Wills, 2011).

The silver lining, if there is one, is that sales in the legal digital music market grew astronomically, exceeding $3 billion in 2010 in the United States (Wills, 2011). Using Soundscan data, *Billboard* (Christman, 2010) reported that physical CD sales accounted for approximately 51.8 percent of total music sales in 2010, while digital tracks and albums made up the remaining 48.2 percent. Furthermore, a recent report from Strategy Analytics Digital Media Strategies predicts that "U.S. consumers will spend more on online music than CDs for the first time in 2012" (*Telecommunications Weekly*, 2011, p1105).

iTunes, in particular, has revolutionized and redistributed music sales. It was launched in 2003, became a Top 10 music retailer in 2005, and had sold 2 billion songs and 90 million iPods to play them on by the end of 2006 (Jobs, 2007). By February 2010, iTunes had sold 10 billion songs; by July 2011, 15 billion songs (McNeil, 2011). By June 2012, iTunes had sold 30 billion apps and generated $7.14 billion, or about $0.24 per application (Van Buskirk, 2012). *The Financial Times* reported that iTunes had 69 percent of the digital music market in the United States in 2011, with Amazon following in second place at 12 percent (Edgecliffe-Johnson and Nuttall, 2011).

Ironically, the world's biggest music retailer is actually a hardware company that understood consumers—an interesting application of the relationship between the *Cultural Diamond*'s *creator* and *receiver*, or, in laymen's terms, the content producer and the audience. Apple has the luxury of pricing music low and making its profits on higher-margin items, such as its operating systems, hardware, downloads (e.g., books), and applications. This means that iTunes puts pressure on record labels to sell single tracks for between $0.99 and $1.29, while making most of its own profits elsewhere (Fried, 2003; Christman, 2008). Apple's App Store, launched in July 2008, also helps it keep its music prices low and its content fresh and dynamic. Application offerings range from stripr, a comic book aggregation app, to iTrailers, which provides movie trailers and reviews, (McNeill, 2011). The app store simultaneously generates revenue *and* loyalty, as consumers are less likely to switch providers once they've purchased critical apps for their current platform and devices.

Apple was also ahead of the curve in recognizing the power of music to sell related products. By using catchy licensed music in commercials for its iPods, Apple simultaneously generated excitement for the featured songs, which people Googled and bought, often from iTunes, and for its hardware products, which had the capacity to play these exciting songs anywhere users cared to listen to them. This, in turn, led to more companies thinking about how to give their brands meaning through the use of music, and to musicians thinking about how to generate revenue as recorded music sales declined.

Licensing and sponsorship

As noted in Chapter 2, music (published in traditional CD or online file form) no longer serves as the artist's primary product. CDs (and digital music files sold as downloads via iTunes and other online retailers) are instead used as brand pieces, or calling cards for artists to use as they pursue more profitable sales channels. Licensing, touring, and the sale of merchandise have become increasingly important parts of the artist's profit portfolio. As noted earlier, many female pop stars extend beyond these realms into fashion, fragrance, television, and film to generate as much revenue as possible in the relatively short time they have.

Lisa Cardoso, who ran Music and Lifestyle Marketing for Puma, said that artists can make money from sponsorship deals in numerous ways, from wearing the brand for a certain length of time, to appearing at brand-sponsored events, to licensing their songs for use in Puma commercials, to lending their style, inspiration, and name to product lines. The level of involvement and payment varies with the caliber of the artist. Major sponsorship deals can generate millions for the artist and the Puma brand, while smaller endorsement deals run from about $50,000 to $300,000. These high payouts are a major reason that female pop stars have become willing to leverage their looks to secure sponsorship deals. In such scenarios, the brand benefits by absorbing some of the artist's brand meanings (McCracken, 1986, 1989), thus helping them to connect with audiences who value those meanings. The artist wins by earning a large payday, and through the extra exposure she experiences when the sponsoring company advertises their affiliation with her via expensive marketing communication efforts. Cardoso said that companies are willing to pay artists well because the arrangements are exclusive; in other words, an artist working with Puma cannot represent competing brands during the length of their deal, and thus can't earn additional revenue from competing companies. "At the end of the day, we want to be relevant to that younger consumer," Cardoso said. "The way to do that is through key touch points in their life, and music is the No. 1 thing."

Holly Hung, music director of Mob Scene Creative + Productions, which produces motion picture advertising, said that the best way for contemporary musicians to generate considerable revenue is by licensing their music to ads, television, and film. Hung shared that developing artists might be paid a one-time fee of $50,000 for use of their licensed music, while a well-known hit-maker might command $1 million because their brand is already valuable and therefore actually helps to brand the lesser-known film as it is promoted.

Labels

The methods of getting music to consumers have changed considerably since 2000. New and alternative distribution channels have proliferated, and already they are beginning to impact the economics and dynamics of the traditional music business. Perhaps the party most affected by these changes is the record label.

As the industry contracted, so did the major record companies. By 2004, there were only four major music conglomerates—BMG Music Entertainment, Vivendi Universal, EMI Group PLC, and Warner Music—which, between them, controlled more than 70 percent of global recorded music sales. Independent labels accounted for most of the remainder of recorded music sales.

In 2011, Universal Music Group captured 31.4 percent market share in albums and ten-song album equivalents. Sony Music Entertainment followed with 27.4 percent of the market, while Warner Music Group earned 19.8 percent of the market (Christman, 2011c). EMI finished fourth among major-label conglomerates with 9.6 percent, and independent labels collectively took 11.6 percent of the market. *Billboard*, noted, however, that the 11.6 percent figure did not include "independent labels that are distributed by major-label-owned indie distributors" (Christman, 2011c).

By 2012, there were only three major music companies—Universal Music Group, Sony Music Entertainment, and Warner Music Group. (During 2011, Universal acquired EMI, and Sony acquired EMI Publishing. Warner Music Group was acquired by Access Industries, but continues to operate under the Warner Music Group name). Reliable sources disagree about current market share—mostly a function of calculation methodology—though most rank Universal first, Sony a close second, and Warner a distant third (Christman, 2012).

This consolidation affects popular musicians, who may now find competition within their own music company or within their own label. Given limited resources, major labels cannot invest heavily in all of their bands; as a result, they have to manage their portfolios. Often they will pursue one-of-a-kind strategies, where they will support one female singer-songwriter, but not a second because they are better served spreading the risk and investing in a hip–hop musician or a male rock band. So artist brands need to have unique selling propositions because the more positively differentiated brand will win in such cases, and the other(s) will receive minimal support or be dropped from the label entirely.

Increasingly, labels are using social media vehicles to attract and retain audiences for developing and established acts. Three platforms outperform the others consistently, according to Lars Murray, vice president of digital for Sony Music. "As far as social nets go, Facebook, Twitter, and YouTube stand above all the others, and then you fill in the blanks from there," he said. These tools all aid in developing brand personality, which can be the basis of relationships that artists have with their fans. Such relationships are valuable because they keep people interested in the artist or band even when there is not a new CD or a tour. Lady Gaga, Katy Perry, Rihanna, Britney Spears, Shakira, and Taylor Swift are particularly adept at these relationship maintenance skills, as all are consistently ranked toward the top of Twitter's Top 10 Most Followed List.

While social media platforms undeniably provide new opportunities for artists, handlers, and fans, some industry veterans caution against overestimating their relative impact upon the success of artist brands.

"New media is not nearly as important as people think it is," said Jorge Hinojosa, who has managed Ice T for nearly 30 years. "If they think it's a 10, it's probably a 1."

Radio

These days, radio, long known for playing a limited set of songs repeatedly while they are popular, is facing competition from every direction. Industry experts anticipate a day when terrestrial radio will be displaced as the great industry hit maker—but not too soon, as radio is still far and away the most common way for people to discover or learn about new music.

According to *Radio Dimensions* (2010), there were 30 commercial stations in 1922 and 11,213 commercial radio stations in 2008. As terrestrial radio grew, so too did Internet radio, adding another 30,000+ stations to the mix, and satellite radio, now an option in many cars and homes, adding several hundred more.

As of 2007, terrestrial radio had 282.8 million listeners; Internet radio had 29 million; podcasting had 7.1 million; mobile audio streaming had 4.1 million; and high-definition radio had 300,000 listeners (Miller, 2008). In 2010, approximately 6 percent of Americans subscribed to satellite radio (*Radio Dimensions*, 2010).

"I am firmly convicted and continually disappointed that terrestrial radio is still the difference in making most breakout hits," said Sony's Murray. "If you have a radio hit, it takes you into a different league. You can have a complete viral hit on YouTube that just sweeps the world. And that's still not enough to get the song played on the radio." Artist manager Jorge Hinojosa echoed Murray's sentiments, asserting: "Radio, unequivocally, is still the most powerful driver of recognition and record sales."

Internet radio, which offers potentially limitless stations for free as long as you have high-speed Internet access, has also become compelling as more and more Americans go online. A recent Arbitron/Edison Media Research study indicated that in 2009, 17 percent of people aged 12 and up listened to Internet radio during the previous week, up from 2 percent in 2000. Podcasting, user-generated arrangements of digital audio files uploaded to the Internet for other users to retrieve and play, is also becoming more popular as people access their "radio" content through diverse and emerging channels (*Radio Dimensions*, 2010).

Business Wire reports that more than 50 percent of US broadband households prefer the computer as their digital music access point; but now even that is changing as smart phones and cloud-based delivery models are bringing music to increasingly portable and consumer-friendly devices (*Radio Dimensions*, 2010). In 2010, 34 percent of US broadband consumers used their mobile phone as a music player, up from 9 percent in 2007. Digital music providers such as Pandora, Spotify, and Songza have responded in kind, working to make their services accessible through numerous devices and thus more portable (*Business Wire*, 2011). This has made radio's stranglehold on popular music diminish somewhat, but it is still an incredibly powerful medium.

For decades, radio station managers played important roles as gate-keepers, but as the *social world* and entertainment distribution have changed, so too have related gatekeepers. The rise of on-demand ser-vices, which enable audiences to be their own deejays, and the glut of music that has become available via social media channels have only intensified the need for gatekeepers and filters because audiences do not have time to sift through endless content options themselves. The location of these gatekeepers, and their respective roles in the music industry, is changing radically, though.

Retail

In 2006 alone, approximately 800 music stores (nearly one-third of those previously in existence in the United States) went out of business (Smith, 2007). Closures have been attributed frequently to the rise of online retail giants, such as Amazon, which have simultaneously offered convenience, selection, and competitive pricing, and the narrow margins commonly associated with CD sales. At the same time, big box retailers such as Best Buy and discount chains such as Walmart have been chal-lenging traditional music retail stores and online music retailers by sell-ing CDs incredibly cheaply—sometimes below cost—in order to attract young people to their stores. This practice of using music as a loss leader, and making up retail margins on other products, was unsustainable to many music retailers, including Strawberries, Musicland Holding Corp., which filed for bankruptcy in January 2006, and Tower Records, arguably the best-known traditional music retailer, which began liquidation proceedings in October 2006 (Semuels, 2006).

New England-based independent retailer Newbury Comics strategically adapted its product mix to include higher-margin popular culture merchandise—and recordable media such as blank compact disc recordables (CDRs)—to preserve its overall profit margin.[1] But even though independent retailers maintain a more diverse mix of music than the big box and discount retailers, they cannot compete with the selection offered by an online retailer such as Amazon, given limited shelf space and inventory cost. The large retailers do not compete on selection, choosing instead to carry only "blockbuster" hits at low prices because music is not their core business. Established brands become critical at this point as retailers expect their few selected titles to be instantly recognizable to audiences and sell aggressively. As a reference point, music represents "one-tenth of 1 percent of Walmart's gross revenues," but 50 percent of RCA Music Group sales (Kirk, 2004). In fact, by March 2007, big box retailers were "quietly reducing" the floor space allocated to music (Smith, 2007). As less space is available for selling music, the power of brands increases: retailers don't want to carry anything that isn't recognizable and doesn't sell.

For at least a decade, music industry observers have been declaring that physical retail is dead. In 2004, Mike Dreese, founder and co-owner of Newbury Comics, declared that physical music chains would be dead by 2014 (Segal, 2004), and he appears to be fairly close in his prediction. The number of US independent music retailers declined 40 percent between 2004 and 2010, according to Almighty Music Marketing. Chain stores have not been immune to consolidation and closures; in July 2011, Borders announced it was closing its doors because it was "bleed(ing) cash" and unable to find a buyer to save the company (Specter and Trachtenberg, 2011, p1).

In 2012, *Billboard* reported that only 31.3 percent of music sold was through mass merchants such as Walmart; 31.2 percent of music sold was through digital retailers such as iTunes; 19.5 percent of music sold was through chain music stores; 10.7 percent was sold through non-traditional channels (excluding digital); and 7.2 percent was sold through indie music stores.

If we look at the music industry through the lens of the *Cultural Diamond*, perhaps the greatest change has been on the part of the audience. Dramatic changes in the way in which customers buy music have forced the *creators/producers* and the *cultural objects*/products made by the music industry to change quickly. The *receiver/audience* now calls the shots to a degree it has not before, and those selling music products have had to adapt to meet new consumer expectations. As traditional retail faltered, non-traditional merchants—including digital download stores, online CD retailers, concert venues, mail-order outlets and non-traditional, non-music retail stores such as Starbucks—gained momentum as they gave customers the flexibility and customization they had come to expect. *Billboard* reported that such retailers posted "an 8.2 percent gain in album sales to 118.3 million units, accounting for 36.3 percent of all U.S. album sales in 2010" (Christman, 2011a). Further, it noted that this non-traditional merchant category "displaced mass merchants, like Wal-Mart and Target, which suffered a nearly 20 percent decline in sales to 107.7 million units." Chain retailers suffered the steepest drop in sales, posting a 30.6 percent drop to 73.8 million units. *Billboard* attributed the losses to major chain closures (Trans World Entertainment) and shrinking shelf space for music (Best Buy). Also during this period, SoundScan recategorized some independent chains such as Newbury Comics as indie stores, resulting in a statistical bump in that category. "Partly as a result of that realignment, the indie sector posted a 10.6 percent gain as album sales totaled 26.2 million" (Christman, 2011a).

These days, retail sales may come primarily from older audiences. In 2008, 10.9 percent of recorded music was bought by shoppers between the ages of 15 and 19 (down from approximately 12.3 percent the previous year) and approximately 10 percent was purchased by 20- to 24-year-olds. During the same time, people 45 and older purchased 33.7 percent of all recorded music, which was a dramatic jump from the previous year's 24.8 percent (RIAA, 2008). This suggests that while the young end of the market may be pirating music, the older set may be buying more of it given new opportunities to do so, such as iTunes and other innovative retail offerings and environments. The same data may also suggest that sellers are more successfully targeting older audiences now that they have more distribution venues and consumer data available to them.

Distribution

Electronic distribution of music, enabled by new technology, more users with broadband Internet access, and a willing public, has revolutionized the way in which music is sold. Increasingly, non-music companies, such as Apple and even McDonald's, are promoting or selling music.

Distribution changes have also led to the return of the single. Although singles were sold regularly in the 1940s and 1950s—and to a lesser extent from the 1970s to the 1990s—the format was practically dead when new web sites such as Napster and mp3.com came along and changed consumer expectations. Now, rather than expecting to pay $15 to $20 for a traditional full-length album, a consumer can cherry-pick favorite songs—for free—by visiting a download site. If the illegality of such "shopping," which reached its peak in 2002, bothered potential consumers, they would only need to wait a couple of years until legitimate download sites, such as Apple's iTunes and Real Networks' Rhapsody, became available and offered competitive, unbundled single pricing. After years of failed attempts by record labels to cut out the middleman and sell music directly to the public, start-ups that put the customer first won the distribution battle. By the end of 2004, illegal downloading, or peer-to-peer file sharing as it was sometimes euphemistically called, was waning as high-profile court cases made examples of those participating. But still in 2012, illegal downloading remains a problem, despite concerted efforts to stop it. As former music industry executive and digital media consultant Jim Griffin asserted many times throughout his Sunday Pho lunches in Los Angeles in the late 1990s: "The genie is out of the bottle, and it's difficult to compete with 'free.'"

Importance of non-musical factors in new music sales

As consumers migrate to digital formats, music industry economics are changing, as are the retailers. Apple and Amazon were among the first companies to grasp and accommodate the needs of a modern buying public whose idea of how music can be purchased, and for what price, has changed considerably over the past decade. This may mean that hits have shorter lifecycles, and marketing efforts will have to become more extreme, or "in-your-face," so as to rise above the clutter and gain recognition. This has implications for female popular music stars, who already sell their audiences more than music, in that their musical offerings may be further eclipsed by quick song- and CD-cycle times. Truly differentiated brands provide the obvious solution. In this accelerated environment, new gatekeepers will emerge to separate the wheat from the chaff, or, less optimistically, the music that sounds like it has the potential to be popular from music that does not. Whether these changes work for female popular music stars by diversifying what can and will become popular, or against them by making music even less central to their overall marketplace offering, remains to be seen.

Artist manager Jorge Hinojosa said that labels now prefer to sign all-inclusive, 360-degree deals with artists because "if the artist makes any money off his or her brand, the label does too." (This is in contrast to the label only making money off of more traditional record sales.) In Hinojosa's view, "the pendulum has swung in the artist's direction" in that artists are now free to experiment with different types of projects in various entertainment verticals which can help them build, strengthen, diversify, or reinvigorate their brands. Labels also benefit because they take a cut of any sales generated by the artist, even in non-music realms.

"In general, record companies are the critical catalyst in an artist brand becoming successful in music, which, in turn, attracts non-music companies," Hinojosa said. "The record companies' financial investment combined with their powerful connections and expertise at radio, retail, and with the media set the artist up for success as a more generalized commercial brand."

Gatekeeping

The process by which music industry power brokers select which messages they will release into culture is called *gatekeeping*, a term coined by sociologist Kurt Lewin (1947) to explain social changes in communities. This definition was adapted by Shoemaker (1991, p1) for application to media practices: "Simply put, gatekeeping is the process by which the billions of messages that are available in the world get cut down and transformed into the hundreds of messages that reach a given person on a given day."

There is simply too much content available on a daily basis to share all of it with the general public. The addition of niche *gatekeepers*, in the form of bloggers, podcasters, Facebook friends, and song and album recommenders on iTunes and Amazon, is promising, however, in that now people can select their own gatekeepers to more accurately reflect their own tastes. For female artists, this may be a powerful development, suggesting that it is possible to create niche hits outside of the system by using contemporary marketing vehicles to build brand awareness, and then brand relationships. For example, as of November 25, 2012, six of the ten most followed people on Twitter (Lady Gaga, Katy Perry, Taylor Swift, Britney Spears, Shakira, and Rihanna) were female pop stars. This indicates that these stars and their handlers have mastered the art of relationship maintenance via this platform. In contrast, Justin Bieber is the only male pop star, and the only man other than Barack Obama, to appear on this list (see Table 3.1 for a list of traditional music industry *gatekeepers* and emerging popular music *gatekeepers*). Interestingly, the *gatekeepers* are changing, but at the point of consumption, not production. And while the roles are changing, *gatekeepers* remain as powerful as ever. In other words, the music industry structure hasn't changed as quickly or as profoundly as consumer demands (in large part enabled by innovative technology companies focused on customer solutions) for more compelling ways of finding, exploring, and purchasing music.

Conventional music industry *gatekeepers* are still abundant and powerful in the role of building and popularizing artists and music. They contribute to brand-building in traditional ways by making audiences aware of artists and artists' products via conventional channels. On the production side, gatekeepers are record-label presidents and vice-presidents, artist and repertoire (A&R) representatives, and publicists.

Table 3.1 Gatekeepers

Traditional music industry gatekeepers	Emerging popular music gatekeepers
Record labels	Apple/iTunes
Consumer music magazines (e.g., *Rolling Stone*)	Prominent digital music sites (e.g., eMusic)
Radio stations	Podcasters
Billboard	Bloggers
Physical music retailers (e.g., Tower Records)	Online retail (e.g., Amazon)
Concert promoters (e.g., Ticketmaster)	Celebrity-driven magazines (e.g., *People*) Prime-time television (e.g., *American Idol, The Voice, Glee,* popular shows that incorporate music)

In the cultural intermediary role are journalists, music critics, chart managers from *Billboard*, and merchandisers for iTunes. On the consumption side, there are radio station owners and programmers, and, increasingly, television station and film owners and producers—and that's just the tip of the iceberg. Collectively, these *gatekeepers* influence what people hear and do not hear by making decisions that support the dominant culture and refusing most efforts that lack the promise of immediate commercial success. But as stated above, this appears to be changing as consumers find reliable gatekeepers on their own, through social networking sites, music sites, and a multitude of other means. This has implications for how modern brands are built. This new niche of *gatekeepers* has the potential to dilute the power of the traditional *gatekeepers* by showing artists that there are new ways of attracting a following and becoming popular without them. But still, those interviewed could not come up with examples of significant artists who had broken big without the support of traditional *gatekeepers*, which itself is telling data.

Independent labels

Traditional processes leave commercial music standardized, homogenized, and what becomes popular tomorrow often resembles what is popular today. Genuine departures from industry norms are rare because the existing industry "system," which pursues the "blockbuster model," does not know how to accommodate originality. Independent labels play a vital role in filling in where the majors leave off. There are plenty of audiences interested in the "art" side of art versus commerce, and the independent labels serve them. Independent labels (or "indies") are concerned with diversifying music, enabling new voices, and reflecting the wider culture through their choice of artists and their support of creativity. Female artists who don't fit the cookie-cutter molds of the major labels may find success on independent labels, as they develop large enough fan bases to justify their continued support and invest-ment. Indies are generally more "ear to the street" than major labels, and as such they understand the cheaper but often more difficult forms of marketing they need to employ in order to "break" an artist to the public. Often, when an independent label does support the early development of an act, a major label then sees the appeal. The major label then signs the act, cuts a deal with the indie label, and often succeeds with the act, given the indie's hard work in the artist's early career. This is how much of the creative or "groundbreaking" music we hear makes it through the gates. It is also how some unconventional-looking female artists some-times find major-label homes. The irony, or the marketplace reality, depending upon your perspective, is that when this happens, these inde-pendent labels often become major labels and leave the next generation of creative musicians for the new independent labels.

Pre-production gatekeepers of popular music

At the artist level, labels provide the first filter or gate (see Figure 3.1 for examples of pre-production gatekeepers in the music industry). If they won't sign an act, that act has little chance of selling 500,000 units, much less millions in today's media environment. An act can easily record and release its own CD, but if the gatekeepers are not fighting for its cause, the musicians are resigned to picking up listeners one by one. This can be a lengthy, and potentially costly, pursuit. If one is signed to an independent label, she may have small or even modest amounts of money spent on her, but can therefore expect only modest gains.

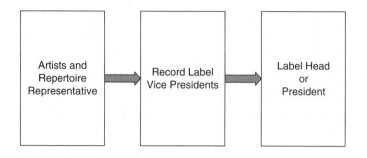

Figure 3.1 Pre-production gatekeepers of popular music.

(There are not many middle-class musicians. Artists are generally rich, poor, or working a bill-paying day job. But changes in production costs and sales expectations are making it possible for more artists to become viable middle-class musicians who can make a modest living selling their music through various channels.)

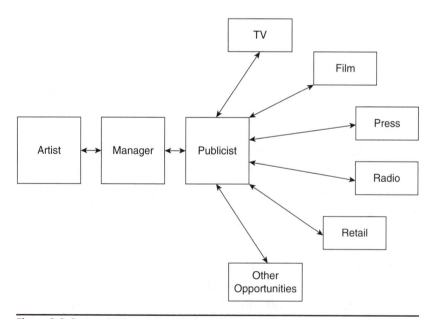

Figure 3.2 Post-production gatekeepers of popular music.

The blockbuster model

Music industry scholar Keith Negus (1999) calls "portfolio management" a good analogy for the music industry, which releases approximately 30,000 albums per year. By the Recording Industry Association of America's count, there have been 16,251 gold (500,000+ units) or platinum (1 million units or more) albums since 1958, or approximately 340 titles per year (RIAA, 2006). In an effort to diversify one's portfolio, one "spreads the risk" over multiple investments in the hope that those that "hit" will cover those that do not. It is commonly accepted in the industry that one in ten CDs issued by a major label will resonate with audiences and "hit," or achieve profitability. Another one of these ten will break even, thus covering its own costs. This means the one "hit" must achieve monstrous sales to cover the accumulated losses of the remaining eight CDs. In short, the required magnitude of the hit predicts its necessary characteristics. In other words, as Elberse (2008) and others have argued, it's easier to make a blockbuster from an already-established brand. This blockbuster management model is not uncommon in the cultural industries or elsewhere, as both the film industry and the pharmaceutical industry pursue similar management strategies. So, what incentive do the producers of the other nine CDs, or films, or drugs have for staying in the existing game?

If an artist is signed to a major record label, she competes with other acts for marketing dollars. An act is most likely to be supported if the label believes it will be successful enough to be a blockbuster. This is often based on how similar it is to something that has succeeded before. Similarly, an act will likely be dropped from the label if its first CD fails to sell well. In fact, the act may be dropped if its first single—should it be so lucky to have one—does not "explode" or "blow up" on the radio. This brings us to perhaps the greatest historical post-production gatekeeper of all in the music industry—the radio station owner and/or programmer. These people decide what goes on the air and, therefore, what people hear (see Figure 3.2 for examples of post-production gatekeepers).

Radio programming decisions are made in a variety of ways—from gut instinct in some cases to payola (now called pay-for-play) in others

(Ahlkvist and Faulkner, 2002). But mostly, the major radio conglomerates, such as Infinity and Clear Channel, control the airwaves by virtue of how many outlets they own. According to one *Billboard* chart manager, some stations make none of their own programming decisions. Rather, such decisions are made by a "suit" in a far-flung location who is statistically analyzing trends to create playlists. Such suits are unlikely to take chances on female artists who do not conform to type, as they look instead to replicate previous blockbusters. As noted in the Preface, female artist types are artificially constrained, so this practice is even more punishing for women. Simply put, there is no real love of music in these contexts, but rather a love of money and, in some sense, a love of industry tradition.

Labels act as pre-production gatekeepers for the music industry, but that's only the beginning. There are also opinion leaders—the journalists and the chart managers of the world who tell the intended audience of popular music what they should pay attention to and what they should disregard. Not surprisingly, charts consist of simple formulas: generally sales + airplay = chart position. Some charts rely simply on sales or radio play. Radio programmers, then, are king in the traditional music industry world. If an artist wants to sell records to a mass audience, she has to force her records on the air by any means necessary. If she does not, she won't get played on the radio, sell volumes, or rank on *Billboard*, the conventional industry standard of popularity in the music business. These entities are all interconnected. Without these external measures of market validity, journalists won't likely care about her or cover her, and yet another channel of communication closes in front of the artist. Then again, *Billboard* is now competing with new charts measuring different types of popularity (e.g., non-revenue-generating downloads), so it is no doubt losing some of its influence as hit measurement becomes more democratized.

Historically, recording artists, and those who support them, worked tirelessly to get noticed and to receive the prize of Top 40 airplay. But now that numerous other channels for exposure exist—many of them through visual media sources—it's no wonder that so many female artists have opted to emphasize their looks as a marketing and survival strategy despite the inherent perils chronicled in earlier chapters of this book.

Men may elect to emphasize other dimensions of themselves, such as their musicianship, as there is a longer tradition of that type of positioning for male artists. But as noted in Chapter 2, female artist brands tend to make beauty and sex central elements, thus downplaying their musical talent.

These days the industry, and the televised contest shows that now continuously supply it with new talent, seeks more of the same, according to Juliana Hatfield, an artist who was signed to Atlantic Records during the 1990s. "The whole *American Idol* thing is so baffling and horrible to me. They're celebrating a lack of originality, and a lack of individuality," she observed. "People know that the winner is going to be someone who is the most like everything else."

Branded music shows, such as *American Idol*, produce branded commodities in the form of contest winners, so Hatfield's argument makes sense in music industry/blockbuster terms and brand terms alike.

Summary

This chapter has examined the key parts of the music industry, providing an inside look at the processes and conventions of labels, radio, retail, and distribution. It has discussed the structure of the industry, and its gatekeepers, and how they work independently, but regularly produce similar products as they pursue blockbuster hits. Technological innovation has changed the way in which music is bought and sold (through online retailers, digitally, and increasingly in singles form), consumed (on mobile devices and online), and experienced (via social media and biographical films, such as Katy Perry's *Part of Me*). As these changes have occurred, opportunities for female artists to expand their reach via product endorsement and sponsorship deals have expanded, causing artists and their handlers to focus more on their brands and less on their musical offerings.

The industry mandate to make money, particularly by repeating past successes and extending female pop star brands into other related industries, has given rise to what I call the *Lifecycle Model for Female Popular*

Music Stars. Chapter 4 examines this lifecycle, and its component phases, demonstrating that women nearly always adhere to a predictable path in order to succeed at the highest levels of the industry. This model, developed from interviews with industry professionals, offers an insider look at the music industry game as it is commonly played by platinum-selling female artists and their handlers.

4

THE LIFECYCLE FOR FEMALE POPULAR MUSIC STARS

Given my prior experience in the music industry as a journalist and a marketing and business development executive, I had a unique opportunity to interview a variety of music industry professionals about how female artists are branded and managed throughout their career lifecycles (see "Cast of Characters Interviewed for this Book" for short biographies of each named participant).

In researching this book, I conducted initial in-depth interviews of 45 to 120 minutes with 21 respondents in 2006 and 2007, and then conducted numerous follow-up interviews of varying lengths with many of the same respondents and some new ones from 2008 to 2012. I interviewed industry professionals who had worked in the music industry or with music industry companies for 10 to 25 years, and worked in some capacity with gold- and platinum-selling female artists at some point in their careers.

Those interviewed have collectively spent hundreds of years in the music business, and paint an explicit picture of what it takes to succeed as a female popular music star in today's environment. Based on these interviews and my related research, I created the *Lifecycle Model for Female Popular Music Stars*, which shows the predictable path a female star must follow as she navigates the music industry and works to capture the public's attention.

To maintain the integrity of my interviews, I have used the language of the music industry professionals, even when this language is problematic from an academic standpoint. To be sure, "*hot mess*" and "*whore*" are neither kind nor academic terms, but they are common in the music industry and will be used to illustrate two vivid phases of the *Lifecycle Model* because my respondents used the terms when responding to my questions.

It should be noted that more differentiated positioning for female artists occurs at the lower levels of the industry—certainly for artists on independent labels; but these artists fall outside the scope of this book, which concerns itself primarily with the similarities among the top-selling artists in the modern music industry.

The *Lifecycle Model* I built from this interview data does not aspire to provide a roadmap for every female pop star because there are exceptions to every theory and every career path. However, it represents the highly patterned types most aspiring stars must fit into and maintain in order to succeed at the highest levels of the business.

Celebrities are public property—and everyone thinks they own a piece. Those who produce them for public consumption believe they know which norms and stereotypes they must activate to make them resonate with the masses. *Receivers/audiences*, long familiar with post-MTV positioning of female artists, have their own expectations about pop stars' appearance and behavior. These pop stars, *cultural objects* themselves, also measure themselves using societal yardsticks, as they, too, live in the *social world*, where they simultaneously play the roles of *creator/producer*, *receiver/audience/consumer*, and *cultural object/pop star*.

Sex has been a major theme in popular music since rock and roll was named after it, but female popular music stars today feel pressure from all points on the *Cultural Diamond* to overemphasize sexuality in the early stages of their careers. This inevitably shortens their longer-term potential, regardless of their talent for singing, songwriting, and musical performance, which, presumably, should be more important drivers of career longevity.

Several dominant themes recurred throughout the interviews:

- Women have to be exceptionally gorgeous (i.e., they must meet some universal but sometimes ineffable quality of transcendent attractiveness to have a fighting chance of success).

- They must be willing to show and tell all to their demanding audiences.
- They must play a vastly different career game than their male counterparts.
- They must harness the power of personal narrative to construct, maintain, and extend their career lifecycles.
- They must leverage their core product or asset—their bodies and perceived sexual availability—into as many other entertainment arenas (e.g., television, film, fashion, publishing) as possible to maximize short-term success.

These themes will emerge in this and the following chapter, and serve as the basis for my *Lifecycle Model*. It is important to note that some of these major themes transcend particular phases of the *Lifecycle Model* and may, in fact, exist in some form in each of them. Age and appearance, for example, are critical throughout a female popular music star's career. Additionally, many artists only last for one or two phases (*good girl* and *temptress*) before exiting the industry, while other artists are able to occupy multiple phases simultaneously.

There are precious few multi-platinum-selling female recording artists at any given point in time for numerous reasons. Historically, women have not had as many professional opportunities as men; some drop out of the industry to raise children or focus on other things; others find life on the road unsustainable; some make enough money to effectively quit, ego needs met. But most, according to my interviews, are at least partially forced to exit the industry as they age and become less attractive by contemporary music industry standards. Simply put, for all but the exceptional few, the career lifecycle for female artists is much shorter than it is for male artists. Everyone interviewed for this project agreed on this matter. They also agreed that there are common patterns exhibited by the most successful female artists during various phases of their careers.

In an attempt to capture and describe these various career stages, I have explained the characteristics of the various lifecycle phases, illustrating each one with artist examples from my interviews. These anecdotes about artists signal a larger trend within the category and should not be read as isolated examples. In many cases, I have used the most entertaining or the most vivid story provided, although other similar stories certainly exist. I will briefly preview the overall *Lifecycle Model* here, and then describe each stage in detail in this chapter, continuing into the next.

Those interviewed all reported, to varying extents, that the music industry treats women differently than men. Many of these reported differences are captured in the *Lifecycle Model* (see Figure 4.1). High-performing, high-status female artists must cycle in and out of set phases as they advance in their careers. The model provides a roadmap of this game and suggests that in order to become and remain a dominant female popular music star, one must start off as a *good girl*: "cute," "innocent," "stable," and "fun." From there she cycles into a *temptress* phase, where she and her handlers make her sexuality and "hotness" more salient in her public image. For many female artists, the road ends

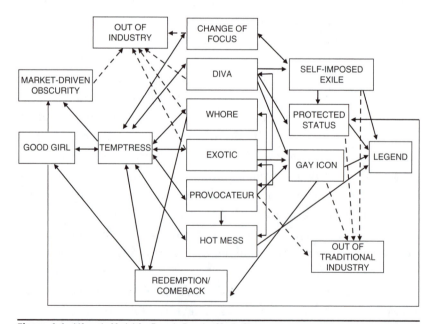

Figure 4.1 *Lifecycle Model for Female Popular Music Stars.*

during her *temptress* phase. For those lucky enough to progress, there are six choices: she can decide she no longer wants to play the game and exit the system (*change of focus*); refine her look and cast herself as best-in-genre musically (*diva*); conclude that her sexual assets are, indeed, her best-selling points and position herself accordingly (*whore*); represent herself as something unusual by virtue of her ethnicity, influences, or behavior (*exotic*); gain notoriety by provoking audiences through counter-normative or offensive behavior (*provocateur*); or engage in public self-destruction (*hot mess*). If an artist opts out of the industry, or chooses the "*whore*" route for too long, she will not remain in the system long enough to pass through another phase of the lifecycle. In contrast, those choosing and succeeding in the "*diva*" and "*exotic*" pathways earn the opportunity to move on to the next gateway: *self-imposed exile*, *protected status*, or *gay icon*. Many *divas* end up in *self-imposed exile*, as they've reached the top of their game and have nobody with whom they can relate, and nowhere to go unless they reinvent themselves or change their genre. A select few achieve *protected status*, most commonly through family connections or marriage to an industry insider, and can more or less do as they please as long as their activity does not compromise or cheapen their established brand. Others, viewed as washed up in the eyes of the public, join the "*gay icon*" aftermarket and live on in an exaggerated or campier version of their former selves. A small number of artists who began their careers well before the MTV era end their careers in the enviable position of "*legend*." These artists built their careers predominantly on musical talent because that was still possible and even expected at that time.

As of 2012, only two artists have gamed the system expertly and lapped the model. Madonna, by virtue of her motherhood, religious affiliations, and age, left the *gay icon* category and re-entered the model as a considerably older *good girl*. She has since re-entered the *temptress* category, where she has improbably remained despite the fact that she is now in her mid-50s. Christina Aguilera was also able to restart as a *good girl*, despite her numerous public blunders, largely because she became a mother. Aguilera's trajectory will be discussed in depth in this chapter and in Chapter 5.

Gender differences

In order to ensure that I was not making an assumption that there were different "come-to-market" strategies for men and women, I asked each of my participants whether there was a difference in the way in which women and men of the popular music star world are presented to the public. One summed up the general consensus in a word: "Absofuckinglutely."

While the focus of this book is on women in the music industry, and it is not structured to include a comparative gender study, I felt that it was necessary and important to gauge whether participants sensed a gender difference up front. My participants unanimously observed a difference in the way in which men and women are constructed for public consumption, though several observed that certain male pop stars, such as Justin Timberlake and Adam Levine (*The Voice* and *Maroon 5*), are also sometimes presented in a hyper-sexualized manner. But as you can see in the links in the notes section, this sexualization is not consistent. For example, they are not nearly as sexualized as the women around them in several of their most popular songs, including "Sexy Back,"[1] "Like I Love You,"[2] and "Moves Like Jagger."[3] In Maroon 5's "Payphone,"[4] Levine is completely invisible, as the video is a cartoon. Others observed that male rap stars tend to be sexualized but differently than women are, as their bodies are displayed in aggressive, powerful stances (rather than the often passive, weak, or reactive representations of female artists). But men are also allowed to present cartoonish characters (Cee-Lo Green) to avoid sexualization.

The differential presentation begins early with adolescent boy and girl bands, which are constructed to play into the fantasies of each gender. Lang calls this a deliberate strategic move made by people who understand teens:

> Boy bands if you look at them—they're very non-threatening, non-sexual. That's done very deliberately because little girls would feel threatened by someone too sexy. I mean, they're not looking at Kid Rock and Tommy Lee, going: "Oh La La!" 'Cause they're very masculine looking. Little girls don't identify with that.

Stephen Thompson, online music producer for NPR, agreed that boys and girls come to market in nearly opposite ways, with girls sexualized and boys neutered. He observed:

> The best way to make a million trillion dollars as a young male pop star is to convey in as many ways as possible that "I will not make any sexual demands on you whatsoever." Justin Bieber is the most non-threatening male artist in the world right now. If you can get the visual and social appeal of being liked by a boy without having to navigate the animal desires of boys, that's enormously appealing. That's the fantasy that gets replayed again and again and again, and will replay itself again and again and again until the end of the culture. It brought us New Kids on The Block, and 98 Degrees, and N*SYNC, and The Backstreet Boys, and Justin Bieber, and the Jonas Brothers. These artists had long stretches in which they were basically sexless boys who sang in perfect harmony about how much they love you and want to hold your hand.

In contrast, young female performers and girl groups are sexualized from the get-go, in order to court little girls, who want to be like them, and little boys, who just want them. Britney Spears's first video, "Hit Me Baby One More Time"[5] serves as an example. Lang elaborated on the strategic intent behind such positioning:

> In the beginning you want to put them out there and they're very pretty, very cute, but you want boys to look at them and go: "Hubba, hubba." Little girls want to be like them, dress like them, do their hair like them, sing like them, dance like them, and the boyfriends have to go: "She's hot."

Sexuality is brought out gradually, over time, to adhere to social norms about young people and to potentially lengthen the artist's lifecycle. Revealing too much too soon can be hard to come back from, and may end a career, particularly if the artist started her career as a children's entertainer.[6] Glickman, who wrote for *Hits* and has also worked as an artist manager and a brand consultant, summarized the problem succinctly: "It's much more difficult to be, like, dry humping your dancers in a video early on and then dial it down later." When and how an artist's sexuality is presented is carefully managed by an artist's stable of handlers, including publicists, artist managers, label managers, stylists, and choreographers.

These gender and sexualization differences continue throughout the respective lifecycles of male and female artists. As male entertainers age, there are numerous positions open to them if they have talent, regardless of their looks. They may use their sex appeal to sell music. But they also may not—male pop stars without much sex appeal, such as Meatloaf, can and do go on to great careers in music, so there are more potential positioning strategies open to them. Doug Melville, broke down the game:

> A woman's come-to-market strategy always includes sex of some sort, in some way, in some form, in some fashion. But guys are looked at as how will they make money? Will they be sex symbols? Where can they go to get their press? It's the opposite funnel in regard to these detailed positions.

The cultural constructions of gender norms that find young boys and girls cast in these nearly opposite roles only intensify as these boys and girls age and develop into men and women. The following *Lifecycle Model* provides a glimpse into how constructed gender norms are amplified as female acts progress through their career lifecycles, demonstrating how little room they and their handlers have to negotiate against social and industrial norms if they are to succeed at the highest level of the industry.

Phase 1: The good girl

Whether a female musician is an adolescent or an adult, she must adhere to set cultural templates of femininity. In all but exceptional cases, which will be covered later in this chapter, aspiring female popular music stars must begin their careers looking, dressing, and acting like "*good girls.*"

Adhering to culturally expected modes of femininity can be a tightrope act throughout a female artist's career. Simply put, she must appear certain ways at certain phases of her career or risk losing relevance, which, in turn, translates into losing financial backing because those footing the bill don't believe she'll draw, sell, or succeed otherwise. Thus, the gatekeepers questioned for this study think long and hard about how artists must be positioned, developed, managed, and leveraged for success.

Those interviewed mentioned Whitney Houston, Britney Spears, Christina Aguilera, Fergie, Miley Cyrus, Taylor Swift, Avril Lavigne, Mariah Carey, and LeAnn Rimes as examples of female pop stars who began in the *good girl*/innocent virgin mold, by virtue of their age at the time they entered the industry or their context (e.g., church, the Mickey Mouse Club) at the time of their market entry. Whitney Houston got her start singing in church; Britney Spears and Christina Aguilera started as Mouseketeers in the Mickey Mouse Club; Stacy Ferguson (Fergie) began her career on television as the voice of Sally Brown in the cartoon *The Charlie Brown and Snoopy Show*; Cyrus was a prominent child star in the family-oriented television series *Hannah Montana*; Swift grew up in the country genre, which is notoriously protective of its young female artists. The general thinking is that handlers do not and should not put such stars into circulation in provocative stances until they approach or reach the age of consent.

Good girls growing up

The process of growing up in public is a tightrope act for young female celebrities, who are often expected to remain exactly as they were when they became famous. But many pressures, from all sides of the *Cultural Diamond*, conspire against that fixed image: Handlers may be eager for their stars to grow up and reach new markets; audiences grow up and want their idols to evolve along with them; or young stars may simply want to grow up and break free from the mold into which they were originally cast.

A November 2010 photo shoot of *Glee* cast members in *GQ* magazine provides a compelling example of one of these progressions. In the spread, *Glee*'s lead female characters, Dianna Agron and Lea Michele, are presented in considerably less wholesome ways than we typically see them in their PG-13 prime-time drama. Michele, in particular, is taken over the top, photographed in panties, stilettos, and a bra. She wears ripped or otherwise revealing partial shirts in every shot she's in. In one shot Michele sits spread-legged, pouting at the camera. Meanwhile, the only male lead involved in the shoot (Cory Monteith) remains fully clothed in all the pictures.[7]

Fine-tuning images of stars as they transition into their adult lives, and adult roles, is tricky, and we often see stars portrayed as too sweet, then too distasteful. The cultural reception of suddenly changed types often creates a critical backlash against the artist and those constructing her. Frank Bruni (2010, p2) of *The New York Times* explained how this phenomenon likely happens despite these reactions: "The process has a physics all its own: G + NC-17 = PG-13." Bruni's equation brings us to the inevitable second step for a popular star: the *temptress* phase. For many stars, their genres provide the code for turning up the heat. For Cyrus, the code was Disney, for Swift it was country, and for Lavigne, it was punk rock. All have begun flirting with the boundaries of their respective norms, which will be discussed later during the *temptress* phase of the *Lifecycle Model*.

Some stars are believed to have jumped too quickly into the *temptress* phase. LeAnn Rimes struggled as she tried to emerge as a young woman in the country music realm. Lang, who was working as Rimes's publicist through this period, explained the trajectory:

> LeAnn wanted to shake that little girl, cute, chubby cheek image—and fair enough, she wasn't a little girl with cute chubby cheeks anymore, she was becoming a young woman.

While Rimes was still a minor, she began dating a considerably older man (Andrew Keegan) and publicly discussing her relationship. Her handlers advised against this because of the larger legal implications for such a relationship, particularly as she began changing her style and wearing more revealing clothing.

In the end, Lang said Rimes "won the battle, but lost the war." This meant selling gold (500,000 units) on her fifth CD release, after selling platinum (1 million units) or multi-platinum (2 million+) on her first four releases. Now in her 30s, Rimes is holding steady in the *temptress* role, scrutinized in the media for her dramatic weight loss and extra-marital romantic exploits. She made the cover of *Shape* magazine, only to see the editor apologize for putting her there due to her extra-marital transgressions. Other stars play musical chairs with romantic partners, but Rimes is called on the carpet for it, perhaps because she framed herself as naughty with her premature move into *temptress* territory. "She's not really a recording artist anymore," Lang said. "In the minds of the general public, she's more of a gossip rag staple."

The backlash was somewhat predictable in that, according to Lang, "the age you are when you become a star is the age you are forever in the mind of the audience." In this case, Rimes was driving the change; but in other genres, artists are pressured to transform for the public eye—ready or not. Being seduced by the trappings or fame and adulthood is common for younger stars as they mature. It's as though the age of innocence is over, and it's time for the age of adulthood, which carries with it images of high fashion and sexuality. Artists entering the music business often do not know, understand, or appreciate the norms of the business. They must learn quickly at the urging of their advisors and handlers, and look to past popular music stars for inspiration and guidance.

In the blues and R&B genres, the *good girl* mold looks slightly different. Often, the girls and women who succeed in these genres "learn how to sing in church," according to Tim Riley, an author and NPR critic who has written several biographies about prominent popular music stars, including John Lennon and Bob Dylan. "Tina Turner and Whitney Houston both learned to sing in church, and that's a big part of their respective stories," he said. Jamie Morris, who worked as a web marketer and database manager for a prominent music retailer (Newbury Comics) and a record label (Atomic Pop) before becoming manager of interactive marketing systems for Paramount Pictures, observed that the difference is more about geography than it is about genre. "The church connection is very important to people from the South, whether it's R&B, or country, or rap—they're all like: 'I'd like to thank God.'" A quick look at past *American Idol* winner Carrie Underwood serves as a perfect illustration. Thompson explained: "[In pop country] there's sort of just one accepted package. It's shaped like Carrie Underwood. She's absolutely the proto-female country singer: Big blonde hair, tight jeans, standing stock still, and sort of wailing about Jesus and boys." In such performances, young *good girls* uphold the cultural norms of their genres: In this case, virginity and religion.

Good girls in a group

Some artists begin their careers—and their *good girl* phase—as part of a larger group, as was the case with Beyoncé Knowles and Destiny's Child. Founded in 1997, this R&B trio from Houston got its start singing in churches and hair salons. Their clean, polished image, pitch-perfect vocals, and catchy songs proved a winning combination, and the trio went on to sell millions of CDs, win three Grammys, and earn frequent comparisons to The Supremes, with Beyoncé cast in the Diana Ross role.

In 2000, Destiny's Child released its breakthrough sophomore album, *The Writing's On the Wall*. It became one of the best-selling CDs of the year, but marked the point at which the band's members elected to pursue solo projects. Beyoncé's debut was delayed repeatedly, but when it ultimately dropped in 2003, it debuted at No. 1 on the *Billboard* 200, ultimately earning her three number 1 hits and five Grammys, which tied the record for most Grammys for a solo female performer in a year.

In terms of imaging, the years 2000 to 2003 saw Beyoncé emerge as a *temptress*, playing Foxxy Cleopatra in *Austin Powers in Goldmember* and performing more adult-themed tracks such as "Baby Boy" and "Crazy in Love." Beyoncé's performance of "Emotion"[8] with Destiny's Child and then "Hey Goldmember"[9] as Foxxy Cleopatra serve as illustrations of the *good girl* and the *temptress*, respectively. Beyoncé also became professionally and romantically involved with Jay-Z after her high school sweetheart dumped her, adding to her new bad girl edge and cachet. Beyoncé will be discussed further in the "*diva*" section of the next chapter.

The *good girl* phase is the necessary starting point for an artist, regardless of her age, if she hopes to stay in the industry long enough to become a *career artist*. The industry is littered with plenty of female artists who emerged as bad girls, scored a major hit album or two, then lost momentum and suffered sales losses on subsequent releases. Recent examples include Amy Winehouse and Lily Allen, who, in Thompson's terms, were "twin towers of self-destruction" who took "short and unpleasant hell rides into oblivion" after bold debuts. Unfortunately, Winehouse subsequently self-destructed and died on July 23, 2011. Medical experts established that she had a blood alcohol level five times the legal driving limit, and her cause of death was ultimately declared "death by misadventure" (Khan, 2011). Allen was virtually invisible by July 2012.

Courtney Love, solo artist and lead singer of the delicately named band Hole, was also cited regularly as a talented artist who refused to play nice and paid for it. Hole's "Miss World"[10] and "Celebrity Skin"[11] exemplify what artists who resist pop star norms look like in comparison. Fiona Apple's name surfaced for similar reasons. Love admitted to using heroin while pregnant in *Vanity Fair* (Hirschberg, 1992), and Apple, who told *Rolling Stone* (Heath, 1998) she had an eating disorder related to her rape at age 12, looked strung out and emaciated, especially in her first video, which depicts her in various stages of party recovery and undress. Apple also looked underage (she was 18 in her first video), which raised concerns from critics due to the sexualized representations of her. Both Love and Apple were considered attractive in alternative music circles, but were too edgy and unconventional looking to be positioned as pop stars without major makeovers. Apple's first video, "Criminal"[12] and her controversial acceptance speech at the 1997 MTV Awards (in which she condemns the power of pop stars and the music industry as cultural influencers)[13] enhanced her contrary image.

Apple was nominated for the Best New Artist Grammy in 1998, but lost to Paula Cole. Still, she won the Grammy for Best Female Rock Performance, and *Tidal* sold multi-platinum and earned extensive critical praise. Apple also won MTV's Best New Artist award. She felt ambivalent about her victory, telling *Rolling Stone* (Heath, 1998, p32): "When I won, I felt like a sellout," she said. "I felt that I deserved recognition but that the recognition I was getting was for the wrong reasons." Apple said she won:

> [...] not because of my talent, but instead because of the fact that somehow, with the help of my record company, and my makeup artist, my stylist and my press, I had successfully created the illusion that I was perfect and pretty and rich [...] I'd betrayed my own kind by becoming a paper doll in order to be accepted.

Then Apple gave into her subversive side again. Her next release, 1999's *When the Pawn Hits the Conflicts He Thinks Like a King What He Knows Throws the Blows When He Goes to the Flight and He'll Win the Whole Thing 'Fore He Enters the Ring There's No Body to Batter When Your Mind Is Your Might So When You Go Solo, You Hold Your Own Hand and Remember that Depth Is the Greatest of Heights and If You Know Where You Stand, then You Know Where to Land and If You Fall It Won't Matter, Cuz You'll Know that You're Right*, was also critically acclaimed, sold platinum, and earned a *Guinness Book of World Records* distinction for longest album title. Those who subvert convention too much in the music business (here by creating an 83-word title that is virtually impossible to market easily or well) regularly find themselves punished. Apple's label refused to release her next effort until her producer, Jon Brion, leaked it to the Internet and fans demanded it (Pareles, 2005; Perez, 2005). After insisting that Apple re-record some of the material with a new producer, the label released the CD as the more conventionally titled *Extraordinary Machine* in 2005. It sold gold. Apple's latest release (in 2012) sees her returning to form and issuing another obvious flip off to her label and its marketing plans. It is fittingly called *The Idler*

Wheel Is Wiser than the Driver of the Screw and Whipping Cords Will Serve You More than Ropes Will Ever Do.

Both Love and Apple were cited as unique talents whose aggressive behavior and positioning compromised the careers they might otherwise have been destined to have. Both remain in the game, so to speak, but both arguably shortened their career lifecycles by skipping the *"good girl"* phase and heading straight for the *"temptress"* and *"hot mess"* categories.

Several of the industry experts I interviewed argued that the problem with starting off so aggressively is that there's nowhere to go in the future. In order to remain viable, such artists can reform and repent or clean up their acts, but these are not necessarily sustainable positions for some artists, who can't "seem to get out of their own way," according to music industry manager and publicist Janet Billig-Rich, who would know, having managed Nirvana and Hole.

Powerful as it is, the fountain of youth and the charm of a *good girl* eventually runs dry, and artists and their handlers are left scrambling for proof—or at least marketable representations—of the artist's continued appeal and relevance. Melville explained the explicit connection between a woman's age and her branding potential: "Once a female singer hits a certain point, they're not marketable."

It is precisely at this point that stars and their handlers pursue other strategies for remaining desirable, popular, and relevant. Increasingly, this takes the form of emphasizing one's physical appearance, sexual availability, and overall accessibility. In terms of the model presented here, this means entering the realm of the *temptress*. However, sometimes these positions ring awkward. "You have to be yourself, and own your shit," Billig-Rich said. "If you're 40, don't act 20."

Several of my respondents noted that representations of purity and virginity create good public images for young teen stars, but as these stars hit their late teens—presumably as they reach the age of consent—they are repositioned as overtly sexual commodities. In this sense, age is clearly one factor driving artists from the *good girl* into the *temptress* phase. Often this process is carefully planned and managed from the beginning. Notorious porn director Gregory Dark directed videos of

Mandy Moore and Britney Spears when they were just teenagers, and *Esquire* author Tom Junod (2001, p132) argued that Dark's job was made easy for him by mainstream America, which fetishizes virginity as regularly as it does sex:

> He was a pornographer, sure, maybe even the worst pornographer [...] but it's not like he sits around plotting to direct Britney Spears, Mandy Moore, and Leslie Carter so that he can corrupt them and the little girls that idolize them. And it's not like he has to worry about making them pornographic, either—about straying over the boundaries of taste, about eroticizing them, about fetishizing them, about doing all the things he used to do as a pornographer. They've already been eroticized by culture itself.

The temptress

As an artist transitions from being presented as a *good girl* to being presented as a *temptress*, several things happen concurrently: She wears more provocative, form-fitting clothing; she begins an active seduction of her audience; and she becomes more publicly accessible—that is, we begin to learn everything about her—through tabloids, print and broadcast interviews, web sites, friends, and family.

"The *American Idol effect*," as defined by media including *USA Today*, *People*, and CNBC.com, has seen numerous American Idols lose a substantial amount of weight once they are launched from the realm of the *good girl* next door into the *temptress*-laden music industry. Carrie Underwood and Kelly Clarkson represent the most prominent early examples of this trend, while Jennifer Hudson and Jordin Sparks serve as more recent examples.

Interestingly, these musicians are dissected not for their lack of musical ability, but for their lack of model-esque looks! This is a strong indication of what the majority of those interviewed report—that looks are actually the most important aspect of a female pop star's portfolio. If you can't pose near naked on the cover of a magazine and be well received, that's a career roadblock.

Industry executives and audiences notice the obvious change in the star's appearance in the transition between phases. One former personal assistant who worked for a multi-platinum-selling artist and preferred not to be named, observed a radical image change that occurred between Carrie Underwood's second and third videos:

> They came out with her third video, and I did not believe it was her. She was so thin. And she was fine before. I just think it's amazing that we cultivate this culture of anorexia and then turn around and criticize people's appearances.

Underwood's 2012 release, *Blown Away*, finds her squarely in the *temptress* category.[14]

So what's considered attractive or "hot" in contemporary music industry terms, at least for women, is less about charisma, musicianship, and the sexiness associated with someone performing at the top of their professional game, and more about how a star looks naked and how close she'll come to showing her audience her naked body in promoting her musical wares. Imagine for a moment that the same standards were applied to male popular music stars. Save for Justin Timberlake, Adam Levine from Maroon 5, a handful of rap and R&B artists, and perhaps Justin Bieber, in time, few would pass the test. Yet, for decades, Steven Tyler (lead singer of Aerosmith)[15] and Mick Jagger[16] (lead singer of the Rolling Stones) have been viewed as sexy—arguably more for their stage charisma and talent than for their looks.

Whether you're a pop star reaching the age of consent, or a more mature musician moving into a sophomore or junior effort, chances are your image will become more sexualized and more scrutinized—and this will continue until you are considered too mature to sexualize or too old to be worthy of consideration. Again, it's a fine line. This is the phase in which artists test the limits.

Even artists who are not perceived as sex-first artists use considerable skin to market themselves and their music in this phase and beyond. According to Thompson, the path to stardom is paved with bare midriffs, and that seems to be fine even with more conservative music audiences:

> Midriffs seem to be really big. If you are a female pop singer, I've probably seen your navel. And I can't think of any exceptions besides Norah Jones. Gwen Stefani is not a "come hither" sex kitten, but Lord knows I've seen what her belly looks like. It goes right down the line.

These kinds of recurring representations are par for the course in our contemporary musical culture. In the *temptress* phase, artist handlers try to make her as ubiquitous as possible before her stardom expires. The pop star's personal assistant articulated what she perceived to be the formula and thought process:

> When you hit on something, and you see that it's going to be financially profitable, you will just permeate the market. And I don't think longevity is an issue. I get the idea that it is like we have to make as much money as we possibly can right now. Because (a) who knows how long it's going to last, and (b) when it's a person, they are going to get wrinkles, 35 is old, and you have a limited amount of time.

Thus, the desire to "cash in" on good looks before one "expires" is not only tempting, but also appears to be a marketplace imperative. It is therefore unsurprising that we see these methods employed so regularly. Lang noted that Avril Lavigne's desire to "grow up too fast" caused her to lose resonance quickly. The beginning of her downfall was in June 2007, when Lavigne appeared on the cover of *Blender*, a well-known youth-targeted music publication, topless, save for a banner across her chest, reading: "Hell Yeah, I'm Hot."[17] In this image, her pants are so low-riding that one wonders if she is looking at the sort of magazine that comes in a brown paper wrapper. However, there is a strategically placed belt buckle and mailing label to obscure her nether regions just enough to make the photo passable. Contrast this image with her first

CD cover, in which she's covered from neck to toe.[18] In a grand stroke of irony, I was unable to secure photo clearances for the magazine and CD covers referenced throughout this chapter because all of the rights holders wanted to see how they would be used in context. Ultimately, they did not care for the way I was presenting their stars and publications, and they rejected my requests. Still, one can find all of the images mentioned in this chapter on the web, and I have provided links to some of the more stunning visuals. Glimpsing these stars' visual trajectories provides a frighteningly coherent visual narrative about "maturing" in the music industry.

In 2007, Lavigne also released the video "Girlfriend," in which she conveniently plays two roles—the *good girl* and the *temptress*, both vying for the same boy. In the end, the *temptress* gets the guy and the *good girl* ends up face down in a porta-potty—a fittingly symbolic ending for a music industry tale.[19]

In this case, the artist is believed to be behind her image change. My participants indicated that Lavigne earned the right to influence her own projected style by selling millions on early efforts. But the question of agency is tricky. Would Lavigne have had this "say so" if she wanted to change her image in a manner that was not consistent with music industry norms? I would argue no—that Lavigne's agency is bounded by the norms of the music industry, which, in turn, is bounded by the norms of society. If she can make only one choice and remain relevant, does it really matter whether the choice was hers or someone else's? It sometimes seems the contemporary music industry offers no choice at all. So, in this case, we see a *good girl*—in Lavigne's case a non-sexual skater chick—turn into a *temptress* hottie after several short years in the industry. Lavigne's transformation was likely premature because so much of her identity was wrapped up in being different from the other pop stars. Glickman observed:

When Avril Lavigne first came out in 2002 or 2003, we were coming off of Britney's latest album. With Avril, they were tapping into the market of the girl who wasn't *that*. She was never glammed up. She was like, into like, Skater Boys or whatever the hell it was.

Her current sexy packaging is not consistent with her old punk rock position, and she has not been able to integrate them effectively. But still, Lavigne, now in her late 20s, keeps trying, as is evident in the November 2010 issue of *Maxim*, where the focus is clearly on her body, not her music.[20]

So, what is going on with Lavigne's music? Billig-Rich was the only respondent who had an immediate answer: "She's popular with kids, like 11-year-olds." This makes her current positioning even more bizarre, given the gap between the age of the target market and the "maturity" of her positioning.

Nearly every female pop star enters the *temptress* stage eventually, as appearance requirements for women have become more limited over time. Sexuality, once suggested, is now explicit. Peter Adams, a professional musician who has toured with a wide range of artists and bands, explained how styles or poses have changed over the past 25 years, starting with Madonna:

> In the '80s, there was Madonna, and she was kinda slutty for the time, but it was more about what she was wearing. Now it's not about what they're wearing, it's the fact that they're actually on the cover of *Playboy*. That's the style.

Indeed! Mariah Carey appeared on the cover of *Playboy*,[21] one month after Beyoncé appeared as *Sports Illustrated*'s *Swimsuit Issue* cover model in 2007.[22] Anthony Colombo, a former *Billboard* chart manager who tracked popular music for nearly 20 years in this capacity, suggests this is part of a wider cultural phenomenon: "The images that we see on TV have become more and more mature, whether it's just the regular television show, or whether it's commercials. So I think seeing Beyoncé in a bathing suit is a natural extension of that."

As usual, there's a catch. If a pop star is deemed sexy enough for such activity, she had better not take it too far. Female popular music stars must observe well the fine line by appearing appealingly sexy and sexually available, but not too much so. Those who push it too far enter the "*whore*" category, which will be discussed in the next chapter. Those who do not have the physical assets to make it as a hottie/*temptress* likely dead-end in the first phase of their career, whether as a good girl with a bright future, or as a rebel without one.

There is one other option for those who are not attractive enough to play the *good girl* and *temptress* roles effectively. Many of those women wind up selling their songs to someone who is hot enough to give them a fighting chance. Several of my participants named Linda Perry as an example of someone who probably could not be a pop star for long based on her looks, even though she was successful as the front woman for 4 Non-Blondes.[23] Now she's known as a background player, writing major hits for other artists, such as "Beautiful," which was performed and popularized by Christina Aguilera. Arguably, "Beautiful"[24] is a song about empowerment and self-acceptance that shouldn't have been sold to a sexier singer, but there are those who write the songs in the background and those who perform them publicly. Sometimes the singer and the songwriter are one and the same, but oftentimes they're not—and not by the writer's choice. Billig-Rich observed:

> I think they all want to be stars—Linda Perry [...] Kara DioGuardi [...] they'd all love to have the careers that they're the hit makers for. It's interesting, if you sit down and talk with any of those people, their aspirations were always to be front and center on stage, having the hits. Being a hit maker for a 22-year-old is kind of depressing.

Ironically, DioGuardi, a former *American Idol* judge, was deemed hot enough to participate in a *Maxim* profile in 2010.[25] She was also judged attractive enough to meet the strenuous appearance requirements of prime-time television. But still she may not have the right look to be a pop star, despite her obvious talent.

In other industries, continuously objectifying women in these ways is arguably illegal; but in the music industry, such treatment of women is so commonplace that it is hardly noticed—people are so used to it, they aren't seeing it. In Raymond Gregory's book *Unwelcome and Unlawful: Sexual Harassment in the American Workplace*, he cites an appellate court decision that stated: "Title VII prohibits sex discrimination. Although 'sex' has several common meanings, in Title VII it describes a personal characteristic, like race or religion" (Gregory, 2004, p85). The decision continued: "Likewise, hostile or paternalistic acts based on perceptions about womanhood or manhood are sex-based or 'gender-based.'" (Gregory, 2004, p.86). Gregory sums up these types of sex and gender discrimination as power acts to "keep women in their place." He argued: "Harassment devalues a women's role in the workplace by directing attention, not only to her sexuality, but also to her gender" (Gregory, 2004, p86).

There is literally nowhere for a singer to go if she wants to sell big numbers but is not believed to be hot enough to invest in. Melville observed: "There are no female character singers in the contemporary music industry. That unattractive or average-looking person would never even make it that far. As depressing and disgusting and horrifying as it is, that's the reality."

Three of today's most popular contemporary *temptresses* are Taylor Swift, Miley Cyrus, and Katy Perry. Swift's music has been praised by some, but dismissed by others as being too sophomoric. As music critic Bob Lefsetz put it in his October 25, 2010 email to his subscribers: "*Speak Now* does not augur well for longevity. It's both too cutesy and too dramatic, just like an adolescent girl. The question is whether Taylor Swift can grow." Since then, Swift's portrayals have been more gamorous and more inclined to feature full-body shots as she has aged. On the eve of her 22nd birthday, Swift did a cover for Vogue.[26] Swift then released *Red*[27] in October 2012, which by November 2012 had sold platinum, and arguably positions her on the borderline of *good girl* (songs) and temptress (appearance) as she approaches her 23rd birthday.

Farther along the *temptress* cycle is Miley Cyrus, whose Hannah Montana character has sold more than 13 million CDs to date. Trying desperately to break free of her Disney origins, Cyrus, now in her 20s, finds herself lambasted in the media for her notorious pole-dancing performance at the 2009 Teen Choice Awards, her portrayal of a wild-but-caged sex-starved-bird-creature in her "Can't Be Tamed,"[28] a home video of her smoking pot in 2011, and photos of her preparing to chomp on a penis cake intended for her boyfriend in 2012.[29] Ordinarily, this might not be a deal-breaker for American audiences, but given Cyrus's age and core audience, people react with either disgust or comedic interpretations. When Cyrus took a bite out of the aforementioned penis cake, Bill Mahr and Jay Leno incorporated it into their late night talk show routines. "She just jumped the shark," Hungs said. "She's shown us what she really wants to be, which is apparently a sex object," laughed veteran publicist Lang. To see her shocking visual progression, look at a photo of Cyrus as *good girl* Hannah Montana,[30] and then in her *temptress* mode a few years later.[31]

Even further along the *temptress* continuum is Katy Perry, a former Christian artist. She's playing the tease ("I Kissed a Girl and I Liked It"), chronically appearing near-naked in her photos and videos, and playing on cheesy double entendres in her songs. Some suggest recent antics find her dancing on the borderline of the *temptress* and the *whore* categories. Hung questioned: "How many lollipops can you hold over your hooch before that act gets tired?"

Thompson described Perry's schtick as "plastic invulnerability" that is symbolic of contemporary popular culture, but not at all interesting. "Katy Perry's whole persona is an airbrushing of a wax doll of a real doll," he said.

Likewise, the critic who reviewed *Teenage Dream* for iTunes called Perry a "hybrid of Alanis Morissette's caterwauling and the cold calculation of Britney Spears in her prime" who is "singing with the desperation of a fading burlesque star twice her age" (Erlewine, 2008, p1). Perhaps that is because the clock is ticking, and she knows time is the fuse of her career.

Riley indicated that most discussions of objectification of women in the music and film industries result in endless loops of people trying to establish whether Britney Spears is a legitimate artist, or whether Madonna was all good or all bad for women in music. These "critical distinctions" are, in his view, "beside the point." He explained:

> The takeaway should be different than what the takeaway normally is. The takeaway should be "this problem reflects serious dysfunction within culture, and a serious double standard and dynamic way that we think of the sexes very differently." The prejudice is very alive, and it really acts itself out in the cultural heroes we choose. It's all a reflection of who we are and what we're thinking about. In this culture we sort of have this dominant adolescent

mode. It's alive and powerful, and it expresses itself continuously, day in and day out.

"There are so many channels, but only one message," Lang said. "You can give her a candy stripe and call her Katy Perry, or wigs and call her Rihanna, or a bob haircut and call her Jesse J, but it's all the same person. It's Britney Spears. It's the princess model. And it works."

Summary

From the time a young pop star arrives on the market, there are significant gender differences in the way that sexuality figures in artist positioning. Interviews with music industry professionals, supplemented with supporting examples, demonstrate that female performers must implicitly (when young) or explicitly (when at the age of consent or older) use sex to position themselves, while men have sex and sexuality available to choose as just one option from a range of other positioning strategies (such as the poet, the working-class hero, the storyteller, and others, as described in Chapter 1). This differentiation begins at a young age; as noted in this chapter, girl and boy bands are positioned differently from the very beginning. Little boys are portrayed as "sexless" and "neutered" and little girls are packaged to be aspirational for little girls and attractive to little boys.

Most solo female pop stars begin their careers playing the role of the *good girl*. This phase takes different forms for different artists, and these differences typically stem from age and genre. As the female pop star's career progresses, she typically transitions into playing the role of the *temptress*, wearing more revealing clothing, appearing in more provocative poses in media appearances and promotional materials, and generally putting her looks and appearance at the center of her brand.

The *good girl* and the *temptress* are important roles to consider, as virtually all female pop stars must embody these roles if they wish to have prominent careers in the industry. These two initial phases of the *Lifecycle Model for Female Popular Music Stars* create a rigid dichotomy that perpetuates feminine stereotypes and, almost without exception, set the stage for a female pop star's options later in her career. The next chapter looks at the limited range of role choices available to pop stars once they move beyond their *temptress* roles.

5

THE LIFECYCLE MODEL CONTINUED

The *temptress* phase is thrilling, indeed, but no woman in history has been able to remain a *temptress* forever. Age drives many female pop stars to the end of their temptress phase, but others may cycle out of it due to commercial pressure, cultural shifts, or personal decision-making. After all, our pop stars are part of the *social world* and must constantly respond to it. It's important to note that for many female pop stars, the *temptress* phase is simply the end of the road. Those who move on generally fit into one (or more) of six stages. These six stages are *change of focus*; *diva*; *exotic*; *provocateur*; *whore*; or *hot mess*.

A change of focus

After playing the game as a *good girl* and a *temptress*, some artists elect to play a different game, redirecting their focus. My informants mentioned such artists as Sarah McLachlan, Sheryl Crow, Melissa Etheridge, and Queen Latifah as examples of artists who are no longer primarily musicians. McLachlan is best known for starting Lilith Fair, a tour featuring only female singers or female-fronted bands during the 1990s, and for raising more than $10 million for women's charities. Crow is best known for her breast-cancer advocacy work on behalf of Susan G. Komen for the Cure. Etheridge receives most of her current attention for being openly gay, a breast cancer survivor, and a general-purpose left-wing activist, and Queen Latifah maintains her visibility through film appearances and celebrity endorsement deals. My informants indicated that these artists manifested *temptress* differently than did younger pop stars, arguably due to their genres, target markets, age, and looks. McLachlan was a buttoned-up *temptress*, while Crow was already over 30 when her first album debuted, and then aged out of her *temptress* mode quickly. Etheridge came to market more aggressively posed and in more comfortable-looking clothes than most female popular music stars of the time. Latifah came to market in a different way, too; she was a rough-but-feminine rap artist, not hard enough to be one of the boys, but not seductive or submissive enough to be one of the girls. These women were all *temptresses* to a degree, but a critical difference between them and, say, Britney Spears, is that they were positioned to distinct but predominantly female audiences. When the target market is not men, several respondents speculated, norms around female attractiveness and how to represent it may be more open and accommodating.

On and off the stage, McLachlan, Crow, Etheridge and Latifah all appear wise, powerful, smart, and sophisticated—which arguably stands at odds with the other *temptress* poses evaluated. But these very qualities enabled them to move seamlessly into a more comfortable realm, where they may find greater career longevity.

My informants' experience with top-selling artists led them to speculate that these artists achieved what they wanted to in music and began using their money and stature to do what they really wanted: Effect positive social change in the greater *social world*. Sometimes artists leverage their known brands to promote causes or products, particularly to fans who have aged along with them. A *change in focus* can signal an artist's evolution or maturity, whether a step toward their eventual exit from the industry or simply buying an artist time to regroup or pursue a new passion. Hung speculated:

> People come to you and they need money, and they need your name to try to raise money for a cause, and what are you gonna do?

Say no to these causes? If you're a good person, you've evolved after hitting the pinnacle, you'd do anything to help these organizations that are advocating for children, or curing cancer, or helping after natural disasters.

If you're like Sheryl Crow, or Queen Latifah, or Sarah McLachlan, you're like 0.00001 percent of musicians. You're so successful you're like a unicorn—you're not supposed to exist. You got good from the universe, how are you gonna give it back?

The diva

The music industry's best-in-class "songstresses" (a term Glickman offered) may develop into *divas*, with big budgets, big demands, and big performances. This is the classiest, most elegant stage in a female pop star's lifecycle—should she have the chops and the desire to visit it. Most do not. Past and present exemplars of this category include Barbra Streisand, Madonna, Mariah Carey, Whitney Houston, and Celine Dion. Beyoncé and Adele were cited as artists who appear on their way to one day becoming *divas*.

Being a *diva* is one of the most enviable positions for women in the music industry in that one's voice and musical talent is foregrounded, and everything else is backgrounded. When an artist reaches this place in the industry, she can begin to call some of her own shots, as her talents have generated considerable revenue and are expected to do so over a comparatively long career. Being a *diva* is about what an artist can do vocally and what she can command as a result of this prowess.

One of the only drawbacks to being considered a *diva* is that many women's voices change as they age, thus threatening their longevity in this capacity. Whitney Houston provides a recent example. After falling from grace through public drug and marriage problems, Houston, with the help of Clive Davis and her label, attempted to wage a major comeback. However, it didn't work because her voice had changed and was not as strong as it once was, presumably due to age and substance abuse. Hung recalled: "People were like, 'What happened to her voice? She really can't sing anymore.'" Without an exceptional voice, a performer simply can't be a *diva*. And thus ended Whitney Houston's run as a *diva*. Sadly, about a year later, Houston died at the age of 48 after drowning in a bathtub due to a drug overdose.

The exotic

Pop stars who fall outside the traditional pop star mold for some reason, including race or ethnicity, can sometimes trade on their image as *exotic* creatures. For the purposes of this model, *exotic* has been operationalized to mean a little different, hard to classify, and somewhat unusual or mysterious. It is a potentially problematic term, but one that came directly out of discussions with industry experts. The term was retained with the intention of it being viewed as an ironic category title, which explains very little about these stars beyond the fact that they are typically not white. Stars currently residing in this category include Norah Jones, Beyoncé, Shakira, and Adele. For these artists, their *exoticism* adds to their sex appeal and protects them from direct comparisons to more mainstream competitors. But because it's harder for audiences to stereotype less common or *exotic* types, they often lump all *exotic* performers together to make sense of them. In feminist scholar Jean Kilbourne's (Kilbourne and Jhally, 2010) view, these images are confusing to those consuming them as truth. She observed:

> So the image isn't real. It's artificial. It's constructed. But real women and girls measure ourselves against this image every single day. It's an impossible ideal for just about everyone, but it's absolutely impossible for women who aren't white. Women of color are generally considered beautiful only if they approximate the white ideal—if they are light-skinned, have straight hair, Caucasian features.

Norah Jones, born Geethali Norah Jones Shankar, emerged from relative obscurity to become one of the most successful *exotic* female pop stars of the last decade. Jones's success bubbled up from her listeners, so she didn't have to posture like a star—she was one, authentically. This star power came from her blood (her father is a legendary sitar player), her ethnicity (her parents are Indian and Anglo-American, though

Jones could pass for any number of ethnic types), and the fact that her music is genuinely different than most of what's available in the marketplace. Glickman recalled:

> Radio only played her when they had no choice, when people were calling up and saying, "Play Norah Jones! Play Norah Jones! Play Norah Jones!" And they would look stupid, but they really resisted it. This is somebody who was a cash machine for the music industry, in spite of itself. Basically she defied all of the prescriptions and suggestions and was hugely successful [...]. Her label made buttloads of money by just letting her do her thing.

My respondents reported that although Jones's early positioning was wholesome, there was something a little bit different about it. "She has this kind of smoky allure about her where you don't entirely know what she looks like," observed Thompson. He believes that Jones was "packaged to obscure traits as well as to enhance them," "photographed very carefully," and that "there was probably a discussion about maybe less is more where skin is concerned."

Notably, Jones's first CD cover (*Come Away with Me*)[1] features a headshot, which is uncommon for female pop artists. Several of those interviewed said it made them give her more consideration as a serious artist, not less.

Adams, observed a marked difference in the way that Jones was presented to the public during the run of her first two albums (*Come Away with Me* and *Feels Like Home*), and how she was being presented in March 2007 in support of her third album, *Not Too Late:*[2]

> I have noticed in the latest Norah Jones promotional stuff, they've definitely got her looking a little hotter. Like they're showing her a little bit more. I bet she feels pressure now, too.. So to stay popular and stay in the spotlight, you gotta show a little sexiness. I think that's ridiculous, but it seems to be the way it is.

So, in this case, Jones's *exoticism*, familial relationships, and early radio support may have spared her the worst of the *good girl* to *temptress* progression, but not all of it.

Adele is also *"exotic"* in her look, her sound, and her ability to cross formats with ease. Her first two albums, *19* and *21*,[3] both went platinum, and her singles were and are played across radio formats, which is uncommon. Adele won the Best Song ("Rolling in the Deep") and Best Record (*21*) categories at the 54th Annual Grammy Awards in February 2012 (Ehrlich and Horvitz, 2012). Still, reviewers and critics try to fit her into cookie-cutter modes of understanding female musicians. "The way people come at her about her looks—it's like the first thing in every review," Billig-Rich said. "They say she doesn't look like a pop star, she doesn't look like a soul singer. That's intense."

But according to Billig-Rich, Adele's handlers are nailing her positioning and overall strategic management:

> I think they've done everything right. She's being herself, and she's got it going on. Her songs were like 80 percent there and they brought in people to tune her up and make her a little more mature, or a little more soulful, and whatever else they did to tidy it up— it's still really who she is. They didn't buy into the stylists, and the get-skinny mentality, and the show your midriff thing. She's not wearing *these* clothes to *that* event. But she's a pop star. A multi-format pop star—it's amazing!

The efforts of Adele's team also won praise from a respondent who is the director of entertainment marketing for one of the top professional sports leagues. This respondent, who spoke to me under the condition of anonymity, said he would be delighted to book Adele as a live performer at one of his events, given her nearly universal appeal. "Adele very much reminds me of a Josh Groban or a Michael Bublé, or a Harry Connick, Jr.," he said. "You can't identify their songs, but you know the artist's name," he said.

Melville agrees that Adele is distinctive and says she will likely remain so for the next few years. He also dubbed her "the new Norah Jones—a wholesome, normal human being"—and quickly added how unlikely this is in female pop star circles.

Melville suggested that there's only room for one of these "types" at a time in the "character-driven" music industry, which operates "like a play. You need a character for each revenue element of the show," he explained. "You're building an ecosystem of characters to make a play work."

One of the newer *"exotic"* artists on the block is Nicki Minaj, a rap dynamo who has collaborated with everyone from Drake, to Rihanna, to Taylor Swift, to Usher. She relies on numerous distinct and deliberate personalities to get into character and tell her stories. At the core of many of these stories is sexuality—though she communicates it differently than many of her peers. For example, Minaj says she has a rebellious, gay alter ego, Roman, living inside her, which explains some of her elaborate costuming and stage antics. But she also says Roman's mother is living inside of her, thus making for a presumably tumultuous inner-life.

Minaj's flamboyant designer costumes and crossover musical stylings make her appear *exotic*, but her use of hip-hop swagger in her lyrics, interviews, and marketing makes her represent as a *temptress* as well. She toys with the media, particularly with respect to her sexuality. In *Details* (Weiner, 2010), Minaj was openly bisexual, but the same year she told *Vibe* that she does not "date or have sex with women" (O'Connor, 2010). When questioned about this by *Out* magazine, she explained inconclusively: "I don't date men either" (Ganz, 2010). Minaj remains mysterious and *exotic* by obscuring the truth, using sexual innuendo targeting both men and women in her songs, and generally keeping people guessing about her.

Chapter 6 will provide a more elaborate discussion of female pop stars' representations of their sexuality to mainstream audiences, and consider the ways in which such personal disclosures may enhance their positioning as *temptresses*, *exotics*, and *provocateurs*. Minaj appears to be straddling the line between *exotic* and *provocateur*, as her 2012 Grammy's performance[4] was a bizarre Gaga-inspired spectacle in which she tried to exorcise the aforementioned Roman (Ehrlich and

Horvitz, 2012). She was also photographed on the red carpet with a man dressed as the Pope.

The provocateur

If the music industry is, indeed, like a play, as Melville suggested when talking about Adele's enviable role, enter the *provocateur*, whose role is to toy with social and cultural norms and delight in the reactions she gets from her button-pushing antics. Lady Gaga is the lone exemplar of this category because most artists who are this provocative are not also as commercially viable as Gaga has been.

Ironically, before Lady Gaga was "Lady Gaga" she was Stefani Germanotta,[5] a plain-looking girl with long brown hair playing a brand of piano rock closer to Norah Jones or Fiona Apple than her current club music. But after being dropped from her first major label, Island/ Def Jam, after only three months, she re-emerged as Lady Gaga and to better commercial effect. In Paul Lester's (2010) biography of Gaga, she recounted some of the turning points along the way. The most telling, perhaps, was that one night, when nobody was paying attention to her set, she stood up, took off her pants, and held the audience's attention for the rest of the night. Arguably, moves such as this might place her in the *temptress* or *whore* categories, but this exhibitionism has remained present in everything she has done since—her bizarre wardrobe choices and general aesthetic are clearly designed to provoke discussion and reactions. Gaga is also a figurative exhibitionist, and the confessional approach she takes to her audience and the marketplace clearly reflects the exhibitionist tendencies of the modern *social world*, with its obsession with expression, self-help, and what's ultimately authentic or real.

Critics and observers do not know how to classify Gaga, so they offer characterizations that never quite fit, comparing her to performance artists, drag queens, Madonna, Alice Cooper, Marilyn Manson, and so on. In essence, she's all of these things at once, applying plays from each respective playbook simultaneously in a completely non-linear fashion. Most artists move slowly through the lifecycle; Gaga seems determined to occupy every position a female artist has ever held in four years flat.

But sometimes provocative positioning successfully differentiates an artist who might otherwise fade into the background, guaranteeing her at least 15 minutes of fame. M.I.A., who scored a hit in 2007 with "Paper Planes,"[6] had become all but invisible since. But when she took the stage of the 2012 Super Bowl halftime show with Madonna and Nicki Minaj, she inherited an associative bump in popularity and one of the world's largest televised platforms. She used the moment to build her brand—arguably at the expense of the others—by swearing and flipping the bird.[7] Her juvenile antics worked and she emerged from that performance as the most talked-about brand of the spectacle. These actions may compromise her brand in the long-term, but as a self-proclaimed "*bona fide* hustler making her name,"[8] she struck while the iron was hot.

The whore

Another term that recurred throughout my interviews with music industry professionals was "*whore*," which, while problematic on numerous levels, was retained because it was the natural language of my industry participants.

Although other stages offer elements of the *whore* category (overt sexualization; sexualized images, songs, and videos; unsavory personal stories; a willingness to do anything for money), this stage collects these scattered elements and brings several of them together at once. It's also a matter of degree. *Temptress* activities, turned up several notches, may resonate as *whore*. If an artist is parked in the *whore* stage, she becomes a sex-first commodity, through and through. In this stage, an artist's dress, behavior, videos, songs, and public behavior all make explicit her sexuality, sexual availability, and sexual prowess.

Christina Aguilera was mentioned as an artist who has crossed into and out of the *whore* category several times already. Those interviewed predicted that most other pop stars could not straddle the line so expertly or get away with what Aguilera does. It is not an industry of generous second chances.

Britney Spears provides an illustrative and regularly cited example of a nice girl passing through the *temptress* stage and into *whore* territory.

All of my informants mentioned different elements of how Spears's image and brand were compromised during 2006 to 2007. Spears's problem was that she was representing as a "*whore*" at the same time she was becoming a mother, which is a clear violation of one of the most sacred rules of the *social world*. Participants said that the "teenage kitten" act that had worked so well for her was no longer fitting, and the incongruity between private Britney and public Britney was too jarring for many to handle.

Several of my participants cited the rise and ubiquity of the Pussycat Dolls as a more extreme three-dimensional example of this trend of sex-first positioning for female artists. The Pussycat Dolls appear to be what the Spice Girls might have become if they had focused more on stripping and less on being cute. In other words, the Pussycat Dolls bypassed the *good girl* and *temptress* phases and headed straight for *whore*. This was a short-term strategy, but one that paid great dividends (via albums, tours, television shows, etc.) while the window of success was still open.

Both acts are obvious marketing constructions, built with sexual fantasies (and fantasy types) in mind to sell to wide audiences. But such positions leave little to the imagination and consequently limit their potential longevity. Such acts may be fun for audiences for a short time, but not interesting, unique, or entertaining enough to survive the long haul. Thompson explained:

> There must be an artist development playbook somewhere that says don't give it up right away. Don't come out like the Pussycat Dolls. They're anonymous automatons, interchangeable fuckbots. Where do you go from there?

Nowhere, as is evidenced by Dolls' singer Nicole Scherzinger's 2011 solo single "Right There."[9] In the song, she offers an explicit play-by-play account of what she likes in bed to 50 Cent and anyone else who wants to listen.

Again, the key is being sexy enough to be consumable, but not so sexy you're deemed over the top and disposable. Glickman illustrated this point by way of example: "If a female artist does push that envelope to the extent where her sexuality is foregrounded, it starts to become a distraction from everything else." Thompson observed that Britney Spears, Christina Aguilera, and Janet Jackson all went from hot to not through physical and musical overexposure. Spears and Aguilera managed to regroup and wage successful comeback efforts, which will be discussed later in this chapter, but Jackson's image remains compromised. "Openly, all of her songs became about sex, bumping and grinding, heavy breathing, basically porn soundtracks," Thompson noted. "This is a far cry from the mewing pussycat tracks on *Control*. There's no established path for a forty-something sex kitten who has been making the same boring R&B album for ten years. Like everybody else, I tuned her out." Many tuned back in again, if only for a minute, to view her 2004 Super Bowl "wardrobe malfunction,"[10] which only further reinforced Thompson's stated ideas about what she's known for now.

Christina Aguilera also learned this lesson the hard way when she stepped out of the temptress mode in 2003 and planted both feet squarely in a realm my respondents call *whoredom*. Many of my participants mentioned her "Dirrty"[11] video by name in discussing stars who had ventured too far away from the mainstream positioning in the pursuit of short-term commercial success. Interestingly, participants often responded from a position of personal offense. Hanley described her own reaction to the video: "The video was gross, she looked like a whore. It was filthy. The song was just so over the top." Still, Hanley understood why Aguilera made her bold move into whorishness. "This was at a time when everybody was putting her and Britney and Mandy Moore and all these other lame pop divas on the same page. There was no way that she was ever going to escape from those comparisons, yet she did." So, in some sense, the error in judgment actually gave her the opportunity to redeem herself for it. She used the recovery process to rebrand and differentiate herself. (This will be a critical point to which I return when I address artist comeback strategies later in this chapter.)

It can be difficult to gauge what is enough and what is too much for audiences in the contemporary *social world*. Aguilera revisited old territory in *Maxim* in March 2007 in her photo spread called "Christina

Aguilera & the Art of Seduction." Aguilera's 2007 and 2003 covers are *Maxim*'s two best-selling issues of all time.[12]

On the 2007 *Maxim* cover, she kneels on a bed in shiny black pumps, covering herself with a pillow and wearing nothing but lace panties. This, presumably, is what Caputi (2003) means by "everyday pornography" — the pornographic images that are so pervasive in contemporary advertising culture that we hardly even notice them. Veteran music publicist and maketing executive Elizabeth Lang attributes such moves to the "show us your vagina" mentality that our culture encourages through voracious consumption of such photos, explicit videos, and revealing stories in celebrity gossip magazines.

The *whore* stage can end a career, particularly if the artist came to market in that pose, as was the case with the Pussycat Dolls and Nicole Scherzinger. For others, if managed successfully, a stint in the *whore* phase can reinvigorate their career. But no one can remain in this stage for too long because, as my informants stated earlier, there is nowhere for a bad girl to go strategically, except for good again—if the marketplace will allow it. Ultimately, Aguilera was one of the lucky ones who earned a chance at redemption and rebirth as a "*good girl*" through motherhood. Her tale will continue in the discussion of the redemption/comeback loop stage toward the end of this chapter.

The hot mess

Those relegated to the mercilessly named "*hot mess*" category have typically succumbed in some way to the relentless demands of fame and the music industry so that the public's focus is directed to their behavior, not their talent.

Often there is an element of self-destruction, on top of drug abuse or appalling behavior. These performers are dubbed "*hot messes*" when their acts become unappealing and unsustainable. Ke$ha, Amy Winehouse, Britney Spears, and Courtney Love surfaced regularly as exemplars of this category.

Ke$ha is known for her drunken party lyrics and bizarre public storytelling. She sings about brushing her teeth with Jack Daniels and carrying whiskey in her purse, and reported that she peed on the floor of Paris Hilton's closet while attending her party (*US Weekly*, 2010).

"She's a cartoon character—drunken, dirty, no style, no taste, no class, not too bright, not fascinating, can't sing, can't perform, really just a disaster," Lang explained. "She's just capitalizing on the sound of the moment. It's going to be gone in a year, and so will she."

Others speculated that Ke$ha, who writes her own songs, will become a background player when her pop star run is over, and that her "*hot mess*" persona is intended to be an entertaining placeholder until then.

Amy Winehouse was once a cartoon character, too, but her story took a tragic turn when she died in July 2011. Media outlets focused on the fact that in her untimely death, Winehouse joined the circle of 27-year-old rock legends before her who died from health issues related to drug and alcohol abuse or suicide (Morrison, Hendrix, Joplin, Cobain). Lang offered this perspective on that news angle:

> Everyone keeps talking about the mystery of this 27 club. I just want to say, perhaps 27 years old is the life expectancy of a hard-core drug addict. Maybe we should start thinking in those terms, not thinking of it as a mythical club that the super-talented elite end up in. Twenty-seven is how long your heart and body can take it. Everyone wants to think they're Keith Richards, but the harsh reality is that most musicians aren't.

Lang indicated there was "a lot of enabling going on" with Winehouse. In 2008, the Grammys allowed her to perform via satellite from London because her travel privileges had been suspended due to drug charges. Until her death, her handlers insisted she was getting better when she clearly was not. "The public doesn't like to be lied to," Lang said. "We have eyes, we have ears. It reinforces the fact that this is all a joke."

Several of those interviewed indicated that drug and alcohol abuse is so prevalent it is practically expected of contemporary musicians— it's what fans have come to expect from experience, so they're almost OK with it. Lang echoed the sentiment: "It's shocking, but we laugh—there's not a lot of empathy," she said. "These pop stars are out there for our judgment and commentary. So when they act like clowns, we laugh."

But often the "*hot mess*" behavior is not funny at all—suggesting deep psychological problems or addictions that are difficult, if not impossible, for some to manage. So what may look like "funny" violations of social norms and harmless partying may be much more sinister, as was the case with Winehouse. Combine personal difficulties with the industry's ferocious bottom-line demands and you have a recipe for disaster. Lang explained:

> There's only one purpose for the music industry—only one—it's not entertainment—it's to sell records. Everybody wants to forget that, but it's true. There's not a long shelf life on any artist. So it's like if this record is selling—if her *hot mess* is selling—well, if it ain't broke, don't fix it. Just keep her moving, keep her out of jail, keep her alive, and keep her moving.

Lang noted that while she does not blame the recording industry for Winehouse's death or think that they had an obligation to "clean her up," she does think there were moments—such as at the 2008 Grammys—when the industry enabled her rather than asking her to face the real consequences of her actions.

"Amy Winehouse obviously sang the song 'Rehab'," Lang said. "Who wanted her to go to rehab? Her manager. The label took a song about it and made a ton of money. Oh, the irony."

Unfortunately, Winehouse did not live long enough to feel genuine empathy from her fans—she died as a uniquely talented and highly differentiated performer who had the goods and the resonance to become a *career artist*, but instead became a short-term caricature. But other performers are lucky enough to go through hell, emerge on the other side, and find compassion and empathy.

Britney Spears engaged in a series of bizarre public behaviors (including shaving her own head and hitting paparazzi photographers with an umbrella) before it was clear that she was becoming unhinged.

And, as Lang observed above, the audience laughed until it realized it was probably more appropriate to cry. Britney hit rock bottom— losing custody of her children and being committed to a psychiatric hospital against her will—before her audience grasped her humanity and vulnerability. "It went from kooky to heartbreaking," Lang said. "She wasn't a drug addict—to my knowledge—she was mentally ill. She needed help."

In July 2011, Spears was in the midst of a semi-effective comeback, but my respondents reported that it was time to take a more radical change of direction for the sake of her longer-term career. Hung observed: "Maybe it's time for her to change it up a little bit, leave some clothes on. She's 30 now, not 21. There's a new Britney now." Hung suggested that Spears needs to "evolve more than she's evolving" and strategically execute a legitimate and comprehensive comeback, involving a new look, a new kind of tour, and a different style of music.

Courtney Love had a different ride, as explained by Billig-Rich, her former manager. "She came in as the bad girl, she cleaned herself up, she became hot in the mainstream, then she screwed it up," she said. "I love her—no one thinks more of her than I do. But as a manager and a facilitator of artists, you can't want it more than your client." Ironically, Love, who is no stranger to drug abuse and the hazards of addiction (having lost her husband Kurt Cobain to drugs and eventually suicide), tried to help Winehouse sober up. In a quote that has now traveled all over the country in various forums, Love said: "I'm f***ing gutted. I tried with her, I tried twice"[13] (Jill, 2011).

A common thread between Spears and Love is that they both violated a sacred societal norm and did one of the worst things you can do as a woman in modern United States society: They challenged our notions and expectations of the sanctity of motherhood. Spears did this by driving with her child on her lap and Love did it by telling *Vanity Fair* (Hirschberg, 1992, p8) that she used heroin "for a couple months," including during her pregnancy. This made recovery difficult, but not impossible. As of February 2012, Spears is enjoying a comeback of sorts as a judge on *X Factor*, while Love remains somewhat invisible.

The *hot mess* category and all that it entails runs the gamut from hilarious to tragic. This is not a category you want to inhabit for long if you're a pop star; but for some, unfortunately, this phase marks the end of their careers.

The Lifecycle Model phase 3: In exile, protected, or iconic

The next round of stages includes three categories: *self-imposed exile*, *protected status*, and *gay icon*. Most artists never travel through the necessary channels to make it into these stages.

Self-imposed exile

In this stage, an artist decides to take herself out of the traditional music industry game for a year or more. According to my informants, this often happens after an artist has been a *diva* for a long time and is no longer surrounded by people who will tell her the truth. Some in this category feel it is easier to disappear on your own accord than to slowly lose relevance and fade away.

Participants mentioned Celine Dion as an example of someone who accrued enough power to play her own game on her own terms. For her, this meant having a venue (the Colosseum) built for herself in Caesar's Palace in Las Vegas and then performing in residence there, to sell-out audiences, for five consecutive years. Dion then did a year-long tour during 2008 to 2009, took time off to be with her family, and returned to performing at Caesar's in 2011 ("Return to Las Vegas", 2012).[14] For others, like Mariah Carey, self-imposed exile reads more like a time-out taken for personal reasons. In Carey's case, one of these *self-imposed exile* periods followed hospitalization for "extreme exhaustion," on the heels of her *Glitter* release, and a semi-public meltdown on her web site. *Self-imposed exile* may also follow periods of recovery in rehab.

Protected status

Those who have achieved *protected* status have men who have saved them, fairy-tale style, at different points in their careers. Exemplars include such stars as Celine Dion, Mariah Carey, and the late Whitney Houston, all of whom experienced the protection of powerful men in the industry. *Protected status* can occur within any stage, or it can be a consequence of a successful run as a *diva*. When an artist has *protected status*, it means that someone important is watching out for her. Often this is a family member or an influential friend who has great influence in the music industry. Protectors can help with career by creating opportunities or family needs by enabling time off to have a child or address health issues. Examples include Celine Dion and current husband René Angelil and Mariah Carey and former husband Tommy Mottola (Clarke and Chin, 2012; Mock and Wang, 2012).

Dion made her first record, and met her future manager and husband, René Angelil, at age 12 (Angelil was 38 at the time). Dion's voice was undeniable, but she was awkward, as many adolescents are. Angelil mortgaged his house to release Dion's first CD and become her manager. This affiliation, along with Dion's obvious talent, was enough to warrant investment in her career development. Dion and Angelil married in 1994, and their relationship has enabled Dion to make some unorthodox career moves (e.g., taking time off to be with their child and setting up a one-woman show in Las Vegas).

Mariah Carey and her handlers knew that she was attractive from the get-go and wanted to capitalize on this asset, but they wagered that her best asset was her remarkable voice. Not wanting to erode her brand prematurely by sexualizing her too much in the early stages, they chose more elegant headshots and somewhat conservative body shots to indicate her stature. This subtle presentation of her beauty, not her sexuality, slowed down her path through the lifecycle, thereby extending her career long enough to have subsequent releases. Several of my interviewees reported that this protective attitude toward Carey's positioning came from Carey's romantic involvement and subsequent marriage to label president Tommy Mottola. Such relationships give the artist *protected status* as long as they last. Carey and Mottola divorced in 1998 (Weagle, 2002), leaving Carey free to dabble in other phases of the lifecycle.

Before her death in 2012, Whitney Houston spent many years under the protection of Arista label president Clive Davis, who launched her career in the 1980s. Over the years as Houston descended into drug abuse, Davis gave her chance upon chance when others may have deemed her a liability and dropped her. Even in the week of her death, Davis was holding out the possibility that she would perform at the Grammys. It's unlikely that any star without the protection of a mogul such as Davis would have received so many chances to revive a damaged career.

The gay icon

This phase of the *Lifecycle Model* is said to be "the last vestige," and for most who visit it, it functions as a final stopping point. What are the characteristics of a *gay icon*? For starters, they are often vocal in support of gay rights issues, and they court gay audiences through theatricality and dramatic storytelling. This is not to say that fans of *gay icons* are necessarily gay, just that they enjoy similar spectacles. Thompson offered more specific criteria:

> You have to have suffered [...] struggled with your weight or substance abuse. You can choose from the menu. You may also have an outsized personality, be candid, and be relatable to gay men and have a sort of dishy quality. Or you can just be a run-of-the-mill fat girl, perceived to have struggled given your appearance.

Madonna, Cher, and Barbra Streisand were cited regularly as artists who occupy this space in the female popular music star landscape. David Thomson (2004, p865) succinctly summarized the plight of Streisand, one of the best-selling artists of all time:

> She is, or was, a great singer. She was never a beautiful woman, and so the drama of her singing sometimes seemed a battle with her looks. After all, opera singers are not required to be gorgeous—but those who sing love ballads have to face the test of sexiness.

Of course, Streisand[15] sold many of her CDs decades ago, and does not compete head to head with many of the women mentioned in this study.

Thompson picked up this thread in his own narrative about gay icons, citing Christina Aguilera as a "perfect *gay icon*" who writes songs about recovering from being ugly and misunderstood. "They're self-pitying songs of self-empowerment," he said. "Now I'm a beautiful butterfly, so FUCK YOU. Her songs are about survival and comeback. No wonder she was able to survive and come back—not a bad strategy."

Lady Gaga appears to be the prototypical *gay icon*, appealing to this market with campy songs and videos, costumes so over the top they make her look more like a female impersonator than a female musician, and lyrical double entendres à la "Poker Face." Her notorious meat dress, Gaga said, was meant to show her support of abolishing Don't Ask Don't Tell.

In 2012, Gaga is less than four full years into her career, and yet she arguably inhabits five phases at once: *temptress, exotic, provocateur, whore,* and *gay icon.* According to my *Lifecycle Model,* this suggests she may be somewhere between the middle and the end of her musical career.

The Lifecycle Model phase 4: Legends and comeback queens
The legend

Some female artists achieve the rare air of "*legendary*" status, generally after building their public profiles in the "*diva*" and "*gay icon*" categories. Exemplars of this category include Barbara Streisand, Cher, Madonna, Tina Turner, Aretha Franklin, and Liza Minnelli. It's important to note that only Madonna got her start in the MTV era. The others began their careers during the 1960s and 1970s, before modern-day appearance requirements took effect, and, arguably, when looks were secondary to talent. This begs the question of whether there will even be future *legends* as appearance standards intensify, news cycles shorten, and distribution and circulation methods change and allow people immediate access to what's hot right now. As Lang observed: "I don't think Aretha could become Aretha today, unless she looked like Taylor Swift."

Tina Turner is perhaps the least likely but longest enduring *legend* of all, given her complicated backstory and her 50 years as a performer. Turner (then Anna Mae Bullock) was given her first break by Ike

Turner, who invited her to sing with his Kings of Rhythm in the late 1950s, before forming The Ike and Tina Turner Review together in 1960. The duo married in 1962, and Ike was notoriously physically abusive (Winfrey and Turner, 2005; Boucher, 2007). Ironically, Tina had achieved *protected status*, but was suffering abuse at the hands of this protective other. From an attractiveness standpoint, she did not need the protection—people still talk about her great looks and chiseled body. But from a personal standpoint, she needed to go solo. That's where her next protector, Mick Jagger of the Rolling Stones, stepped up to the plate. Riley explained: "Mick Jagger's a very important figure in her career. He has her open for the Stones. People on the inside knew she was one of the greats, and they wanted to figure out how to keep her working." Once Turner's protectors got her in front of audiences, she became known as one of the great live performers in the industry. Her attitude and appearance made her an early MTV smash, and this, in turn, led *Private Dancer* to sell more than 5 million copies (RIAA, 2012).

Premature death can also lead an artist to enter the legend category, as long as she had a significant run as a *diva* or an *exotic*. Whitney Houston was poised to become a *legend* based on her vocal ability, but arrived in this category prematurely at age 48 due to her untimely death.

The comeback/redemption

Over the past couple of decades, the *comeback* has become a vital stage in an artist's career. This comeback can take several forms—an artist who was considered "over" can launch a successful new tour or album; a woman who has publicly fallen on her face can get up, shake off the failure, and start again; a woman who has gone dangerously astray from industry norms can simply have a child, reform in the eyes of the public, and be forgiven. My informants focused primarily on three artists in discussing this stage: Mariah Carey, Madonna, and Christina Aguilera.

Mariah Carey started out as the ultimate *good girl* who married an industry insider, became a *diva*, and seemed to have it all. But in 1998 she got divorced and saw a decline in popularity. At the same time, according to my informants, she began taking the *temptress* stage too far. According to Glickman:

> Mariah Carey wore the little black dress and was mega successful for years and years in the little black dress. She was sexy but elegant. She really had a certain kind of cachet as an artist, but really what she wanted to do was put on short shorts and hang out with Jay-Z.

Glickman argued that elegance and class were Carey's strong suit, and the short-short phase compromised these associations. Her style of dress wasn't the only way in which Carey compromised herself and her brand. She started sounding sexually aggressive in songs, too, as is evidenced by "Sweetheart," her duet with superstar producer Jermaine Dupri. In the song, she phones Dupri to dirty-talk him, eventually cutting to the chase to indelicately tell him: "We fuckin' tonight."

EMI/Virgin signed her and then dropped her after only one CD, *Glitter*, and a public breakdown due to "fatigue" in 2001. The company even paid Carey $28 million in 2002 to buy her out of her contract. Four months later, she was re-signed by Island/Def Jam, part of the Universal Music Group. Her subsequent release, *The Emancipation of Mimi*, was the best-selling album of 2005 and won three Grammys in 2006. This was victory for Island/Def Jam and vindication for Carey. Glickman shared his thoughts about these events:

> I thought the Virgin decision was [...] influenced by poor executives looking purely at the spreadsheets as opposed to saying, "All right, what's common sense here?" Mariah Carey can still sing. Yeah, she screwed up, she fell on her face. America loves comebacks. Get her with the right producer and look what's going to happen.

Most recently, Carey became a mother, thus enabling the possibility of her rebirth as a *good girl*. But some of my participants think she's blowing her opportunity by overexposing herself. Carey courts the tabloids relentlessly, but Hung pointed out that much of the attention Carey receives is negative:

> Her life has become such a train wreck that people are more interested in her personal life than her creative life. When you're in the tabloids, people just want to see what you're wearing because they want to know if you're fat. They're watching the sideshow, and Mariah's the sideshow freak. If you have a child and you name him Moroccan, people just think you're bat-shit crazy.

Some artists seem to thrive on the comeback. My informants mentioned Madonna (in nearly every interview), Christina Aguilera (in nearly every interview), and Tina Turner (twice) as female artists with unusually long careers. Thompson commented:

> Artists have a finite number of news cycles. The fact that someone like Madonna got as many as she did is remarkable. And I'm sure she still has a comeback or two left.

Glickman speculated that Madonna's success comes from her understanding and manipulation of her audience's needs as well as her keen comprehension of the dynamics at play in the greater *social world*:

> She reinvents her persona from the audience's point of view [...] it's the installation she's doing now, and it's really light years beyond where most pop artists are able to think. She can go from being Marilyn Monroe to being like a bedroom dominatrix character [...]. She's saying that all these people are part of who I am. So there's a part of me who's a hippie girl who likes the Kabbalah, there's a part of me that's like a German transsexual who's into S&M.

Other participants took a more macro-level view of Madonna's contributions to popular music, and held her up as a women's crusader and business mogul. Music biographer and industry historian Riley observed that by writing and producing her own songs and heading her own corporation (Maverick Records), Madonna paved the way for those wanting to be entertainers and CEOs:

> It's a huge symbolic boundary she has crossed that makes someone like Jennifer Lopez just unimaginable without Madonna. You're a movie star, you have a breakout movie, and then all of a sudden, you're an industry.

Christina Aguilera is clearly one of the beneficiaries of Madonna's groundbreaking work. Now in the midst of her third comeback, Aguilera (who in 2012 is only 31 years old) is making music, starring in films, and judging and coaching on *The Voice*, the top-rated new show in the spring 2011 season, and the third-ranked overall show in spring 2012 (behind NBC's *Sunday Night Football* and only 0.04 ratings points behind Fox's *American Idol*) (Gorman, 2012a, 2012b).

These new roles cast Aguilera in the position of expert judge and singing coach, and critics following the show are surprised by what it is doing for her popularity. In Season 1, Aguilera proved to be a champion of women who do not look like typical pop stars (e.g., Beverly McClellan and Frenchie Davis, both heavy-set women with shaved heads[16]) and she gained considerable goodwill by showing that she could be kind, nurturing, and intelligent.

Rob Sheffield (2011, p38) of *Rolling Stone* magazine wrote:

> The real shocker here is Christina Aguilera—who has never been the most likable star on the block, which is why pop fans take sadistic pleasure in watching her crash and burn, whether she's stripping with Cher in *Burlesque* or disemboweling the National Anthem at the Super Bowl. She's even pouncing on the opportunity to remodel herself as a full-fledged human being, the way J. Lo did on *Idol*.

Sheffield is humorously pointing out the downside of being perceived as too much of a *diva*. Aguilera did not have a sense of humor about forgetting the words to the National Anthem, and if she had, the story may have died down quicker, as people empathized with the person behind the public error.

"It's weird how [her handlers] ignored it—like nobody was gonna call her on it," Billig-Rich said. "Just own your shit. People want to forgive you. You just have to say the words."

Billig-Rich's assessment is in line with media studies literature, which suggests that the most effective celebrities are both aspirational—they can do or be things that most of us can't—and real—they are human beings with limitations and flaws (Ellis, 2007). In any case, she's come back yet again, and only time will tell how many lives she'll have before she's done with the music industry.

Billig-Rich speculated Aguilera's talent is enough to carry her through the tough times. "She had such giant hiccups—a divorce, and getting arrested, and singing the wrong words, and then, all of a sudden, she's beloved again because of *The Voice*," she said. "But she can sing and she can write. It's a rarity, and she's incredible."

Summary

This chapter has described the phases of my *Lifecycle Model* that lie beyond the *temptress*—for those artists lucky enough to survive beyond that point. It explored the worlds of the *diva*, the *exotic*, the *provocateur*, the *whore*, and the *hot mess*—the phases that artists inhabit in the middle to late stages of their careers. For those artists lucky enough to survive beyond the second set of stages, we also explored the phases of *self-imposed exile*, *protected status*, and *gay icon*, where many of the most successful female artists will likely end their careers. Finally, this chapter discussed those rare artists who succeed in reviving a declining career in order to play the enviable role of the *comeback queen*, and the lucky few who end their careers as superstars and live on as *legends*.

The lifecycle is admittedly reductive—no young woman starting out in the music industry foresees herself following this regimented path. But it is a clear reflection of nearly every pop star's career during the past three decades. This is a phenomenon worthy of consideration by both the producers and the receivers of popular culture. As audiences have come to expect a beautiful face, body, and voice to travel together in one person as a perfect packaged good, the societal impact of female popular music stars has intensified, making them good fodder for academic consideration. The next chapter examines research from related disciplines (sociology/women's studies/pop culture studies, mass communication/media studies, marketing/branding) that helps to provide better context for the themes and stages arising from my *Lifecycle Model*.

6

THEORETICAL FOUNDATIONS
FOR THE LIFECYCLE

The *Lifecycle Model* arose from industry sources' pointed commentary about the way in which pop stars are marketed, but it speaks to broader principles of cultural production and contemporary social issues, particularly the growing power of celebrity.

Celebrities are *cultural objects* who attract audiences by simultaneously being ordinary and extraordinary, public and intimate, present and absent (Ellis, 2007). Some celebrities earn their status through achievement, while others rise because "the publicity machine focuses on the worthy and unworthy alike, churning out many admired commodities, called celebrities, famous because they have been made to be" (Gamson, 1994, pp15–16). As powerful, persuasive, and sought-after celebrities whose images and public behavior are shaped by a multitude of forces, female popular music stars exemplify the aforementioned dualities. Despite the intimacy that audiences feel they have with a celebrity, and the star's power in helping audiences shape and refine their hopes and identities, the audience would be wise to remember that these stars are "artificially manufactured" investments who "often require a good deal of processing before they are marketable" (Kendall, 1962, pSM19). Thus their handlers, who assist them with everything from makeup application to wardrobe decisions to interview coaching, play a vital role in constructing stars to be simultaneously accessible and inaccessible.

Female popular music stars invariably embody these required dualities, and layer on top of them complicated gender performances (Butler, 1990) that will be addressed later in the chapter. But how did our female pop stars come to look and behave as they do? And how do they become so popular as to be ubiquitous, if only for a short time? Many studies indicate that a woman's attractiveness and self-presentation can affect the way in which she is evaluated, treated, and processed in society (Kilbourne, 1999; Wolf, 2002; Andsager, 2005). Chapters 4 and 5 gave us an inside look at how music industry professionals shape and evaluate pop stars; but as the *Cultural Diamond* suggests, the music industry itself exists within the greater context of the *social world*, so its contributions must also be addressed. It is also important to evaluate the roles of the pop stars themselves (as *cultural objects*) and of audiences in producing pop star types. At the end of the chapter, after tracing the collaborative forces that have helped to shape the modern pop star, we will consider the effects of her current likeness on the audiences who consume her, and how this feeds back into the mutually reinforcing system of the *Cultural Diamond*.

Popularity

For all the defiant spirit contained within rock and roll, rap, country, and other forms of contemporary popular music, the manner by which such music becomes popular is highly systematic. The recipe for popularity appears to call for enough mainstream appeal to attract many, but enough deviation to attract people at the margins. But what are the elements of popularity?

Theodor Adorno (1990, p302) posits that commercial pressure forces songwriters to produce "standardized" patterns and replicate age-old themes because they are easier for audiences to recognize and for industry professionals to popularize and distribute. In simpler terms, Adorno recognizes that it is easier to sell something that has already been successfully sold than it is to determine how best to sell something new. By setting the production context with revenue demands, and requiring the same of products that do not fit the template as those that do, the music industry commodifies music (Adorno, 1990). In so doing, it erases meaningful differences between songs and emphasizes similarities. The popular music hit effectively "hears for the listener" and becomes "a multiple choice questionnaire" (Adorno, 1990, pp306, 309) due to its strict adherence to genre—and song—conventions. Arguably, this explains why most contemporary popular music is made by already-established musicians. Such music is more likely to be a "hit" with the audience because the same system has already made the artist popular. In Adorno's (1990, p306) terms, such music has already been "predigested" for public consumption.

Since the mid twentieth century, various communications media (e.g., network and cable television and the World Wide Web) have amplified the impact of the popular song by carrying its messages to ever-more viewers and listeners in their preferred formats. According to Harvard Business School Professor Anita Elberse (2008, p7), the impact of these technological changes has reinforced the blockbuster model, not broken it: "A few winners will still go a long way—probably even futher before." Thus, the tenets of popularity described above remain firmly intact.

Hinojosa argues that the music industry makes and markets similar products repeatedly. When a breakout hit happens, Hinojosa says, it is in spite of the rigid, conservative industrial norms, not because of them. "The music companies have a template they use over and over again," he said. "It's like McDonald's."

As *cultural objects*, each female pop star must integrate the realities and expectations of the *social world*, the music industry (*creator/ producer*), and the *receiver/audience* (*consumer*) as she makes herself available for public consumption. Cultural anthropologist-turned management scholar Grant McCracken (1986, 1989) explains that modern celebrities are powerful and popular because of their ability to embody the lifestyle aspirations of their audiences, while still conveying similarity or relevance to such audiences in terms of gender, class, and status. This relevance can be real or constructed. Hall and Whannel (1964, p35, citing Edgar Morin) suggest that it is the "need for her which creates the star." In other words, the audience is desperate for stars on which they can pin their hopes, desires, and dreams. By consuming different dimensions of their favorite celebrities, audiences get a bit closer to meeting their own identity needs, which might involve fitting in, being "hot," or transitioning from who they are to who they want to become.

In this capacity, female pop stars *"do gender,"* or *"perform gender norms,"* mainly for the *"male gaze,"* in the *"gendered spaces"* of the music industry. The resulting product often constitutes *"everyday pornography,"* which is consumed and internalized to different extents by men, women, boys and girls. This process raises the issues put forth in Frederickson and Roberts's (1997) "Objectification Theory." This chapter will explore each of these ideas in the context of the music industry, showing their specific application to female popular music stars.

Doing gender and gender performance

In "Doing Gender," West and Zimmerman (1987) argue that gender is a routine, and that women *"do gender"* in their everyday lives as they interact with others in ways that adhere to culturally established norms of femininity. Those who don't "do" gender properly risk opening themselves up to critical gender assessment (West and Zimmerman, 1987, p136). Judith Butler extends this idea, offering the notion of a *"gender performance."* Despite the concept's name, a *gender performance* is not typically a grand action performed in a theatrical setting (Butler, 1990). Butler asserts that gender is unstable, arguing that it is discursively produced and has no essential core. Thus, gender performances are often simple acts, learned through exposure, and normalized and perfected through repetition. When a woman performs her gender, she indicates to others, often through minute actions, that she has encoded the norms around the societal expectations of her gender. Think about a woman crossing her legs as she sits, or a man sitting with his legs spread apart. We see both of these things occur daily and we think nothing of them. But if a man sat with one leg crossed tightly over his knee or if a woman sat with her legs spread apart, we would notice them because they would be performing gender acts contrary to their given gender. Society teaches us that there are consequences for such transgressions, so many of us unconsciously exhibit the behavior that gains us rewards, while studiously avoiding other behaviors that might cause us embarrassment or punishment (Butler, 1990). As West and Zimmerman (1987, p147) note: "Gender is a powerful ideological device, which produces, reproduces, and legitimates the choices and limits that are predicated on sex category."

As usual, the stakes are higher for female pop stars, who arguably set a standard of femininity for the rest of us by amplifying and celebrating pre-existing societal gender norms through highly feminized performances of gender. Given the artificiality of such roles, performing gender on the world's stage can be tricky business for artists. *Gender performances* as interpreted by pop stars may look a bit more like grand actions performed in theatrical settings—virtually any of Lady Gaga's public personas serve as illustrations of this, as did Janet Jackson's "wardrobe malfunction" at the 2004 Super Bowl. But, as *gender performances* go, those enacted by pop stars are critically important and highly influential because regular people, particularly young people developing their identities, look to aspirational pop stars to figure out how to act, dress, and behave, not only from a gender standpoint, as Butler suggests, but from a more general social standpoint, as Albert Bandura (1976) explains in his book *Social Learning Theory.*

As stated at the beginning of this chapter, female pop stars are carefully constructed representations of women, so this becomes complicated for all involved. Girls engaging in social comparison essentially end up mimicking women who are in some sense *acting* like women, rather than just *being* women. So they learn to be a *representation* of a woman, arguably a female impersonator, rather than a three-dimensional woman. This becomes confusing in a hurry.

So, where do pop stars look to decide how they should represent their gender? To other pop stars, of course, and to those behind the camera, who construct such stars for the public eye.

Entertainment industries that pursue blockbuster business models (e.g., music, film, television) look to what's been popular before to predict what will become popular in the future. Pop stars, too, look in the rearview mirror to determine how to position themselves. Gaga became one of the most ubiquitous artists of the last decade by updating Madonna's playbook, adapting its strategies for contemporary culture and its audiences. But if Gaga is the new Madonna, what on Earth will the new Gaga look like?

As queer theorist Judith (Jack) Halberstam (2010) observes on her blog: "You cannot Gaga Gaga, honey, so don't even try! She is camping camp, she is dragging drag, she is ironing irony (ok [...] ok), she has done it, been it, worn it."

However comprehensive it may be, Gaga's ironic use of gender doesn't enable her to escape its trappings. Thus, whoever accepts the Gaga mantle of the future will likely struggle with the same issues, *performing gender* to societal specification, while simultaneously attempting to redefine it.

The male gaze

Butler (1990) argues that all gender is socially constructed, and that we learn to be men and women by watching repeated impressions of femininity and masculinity in our everyday lives and through media representations. Thus, those creating media images for public consumption wield a great deal of power in shaping our views of gender. During the 1970s, scholars such as John Berger and Laura Mulvey began to analyze why, in society and film, men were always looking, while women were always looked at. Berger (1972, p47) observed: "Men look at women. Women watch themselves being looked at."

Mulvey (1975, p837) explains how the *male gaze*, constructed by men and internalized by women, works in film:

> In a world ordered by sexual imbalance, pleasure in looking has been split between active/male and passive/female. The determining male gaze projects its Fantasy on to the female figure, which is styled accordingly. In their traditional exhibitionist role women are simultaneously looked at and displayed, with their appearance coded for strong visual and erotic impact so that they can be said to connote to-be-looked-at-ness. Women displayed as sexual object is the leitmotif of erotic spectacle: from pin-ups to strip-tease, from Zigfield to Busby Berkeley, she holds the look, plays to and signifies male desire.

Those behind the camera have the power to look, while those in front of it can only be looked at. Men represent both locations, as filmmakers and actors, while women have historically inhabited only the latter space. Mulvey sees this as gender inequity playing itself out on the big screen, as a woman serves both filmmakers and audiences as they gaze upon her. Mulvey (1975, p843) calls this reality a part of the "cinematic code," and argues that it cannot be revised until it breaks free of the "external structures" enabling it. These external structures include film industry norms, social constructions of gender, and audience expectations. According to esteemed actress Meryl Streep, these structures are holding strong today. Streep, who has been nominated for Oscars 16 times and won twice, told *60 Minutes* (Safer, 2011) that she probably had a longer shelf life than most actresses because women have directed the last four films she's appeared in. Another likely factor in Streep's success is that she has rarely, if ever, been portrayed in a purely sexual light. She also offered that she gets annoyed when people observe that she plays strong-minded women. "No one has ever asked an actor, 'You're playing a strong-minded man.' We assume that men are strong-minded, or have opinions. But a strong-minded woman is a different animal" (Safer, 2011).

Streep is one of the few who operate against the grain of gender norms. But most female performers find it easier to go with the flow, playing to gender norms and the eager eye of the *male gaze*. Perhaps this explains why, in the video for her No. 1 hit "London Bridge," Fergie grinds against a policeman, writhes on a pool table, and performs a boardroom table striptease. It might also account for why in her follow-up video, "Fergalicious,"[1] she entertains her audience as a Girl Scout, a fitness fanatic, and, ultimately, a stripper, who emerges from a cake, smears it all over herself, and proceeds to initiate some cake-wrestling fun with several other women. If this video is not a male fantasy constructed for a *male gaze*, I'm not sure what is.[2]

Psychology scholars have found support for a similar phenomenon when studying media portrayals of men and women. Social psychologists have defined *face-ism* or *facial prominence* as the relative prominence of the face in relation to the body in photographs. Archer et al

(1983, p726) hypothesized that because the head and face are viewed as centers of mental life, more prominent faces would convey stronger messages about a person's "intellect, personality, identity and character." In contrast, the media focus on women's bodies activates thoughts about sex and sexuality rather than intellect and character. A visual survey of the Top 10 CDs of 2011 illustrates the point. At number 1, Adele's *21*[3] features a rare headshot of a female artist, in which she looks down, not at the camera. She is avoiding the *male gaze*; she has not been deemed worthy of it because she is overweight and was thus not constructed for its inevitable evaluation. In the No. 2 position, Lady Gaga's *Born This Way*[4] offers a more predictable objectification shot, with an open-mouthed head on a motorcycle body. Rounding out the Top 10 are Nicki Minaj's *Pink Friday*[5] (No. 9) in which she is represented as a Barbie doll, and Katy Perry's *Teenage Dream*[6] (No. 10), which features her naked but strategically robed in clouds. The other covers featured male artists and were not overtly sexual. However, it is worth noting that Chris Brown's *F.A.M.E.*[7] (No. 7) finds him glaring at the camera in seeming defiance of it. This is an interesting choice, given his history of domestic violence against ex-girlfriend Rihanna.

Thus, the objectification of women for the benefit of the *male gaze* has effects that last beyond the end of the cinematic experience. As Kilbourne and Jhally (2010) explain: "When men are objectified they generally are bigger, stronger, more powerful. When women are objectified we're more fragile, more vulnerable, less powerful." As female pop stars increasingly cross over into film, they must adhere to the norms of the music industry (as described in previous chapters) *and* the film industry, leaving little room for realistic portrayals of mature adult women.

This cinematic code, as enforced by external structures, keeps women in passive cinematic roles, while stifling the imagination of female viewers gazing upon them for inspiration. Young girls looking for new female types to transition into are invariably looking at women who have been constructed by men, and who anticipate their gaze, for ideas about who they might one day become. In essence, little girls learn how they should look when they are being looked at, not how to actually develop into something other than the object of a *male gaze*. These days, they also learn to internalize a mainly white ideal of beauty, and a highly sexualized one at that, regardless of their own race and ethnicity, as noted in "the *exotic*" section of Chapter 5.

As Kilbourne and Jhally (2010) point out, we have numerous public health problems in the United States related to body image disturbances. These are perhaps caused and definitely exacerbated by unrealistic notions of what men and women should look like. By teaching students how to be critical of media as part of their formal education, they have a better chance of interrupting the punishing and overwhelming messages sent to them through various media systems. When students realize that these messages are often sent by commercial organizations with financial interests in preserving the manufactured status quo, they are more likely to take exception to them and resist them as falsely normative. Media literacy efforts in high schools and junior high schools are particularly critical in preparing students to question media messages.

Hegemony, ISAs and the male gaze

The formation of cultural objects is also greatly affected by cultural *hegemony*, which Marxist philosopher Antonio Gramsci (1971) characterizes as a process in which subordinate classes consent to the dominant class system, even though it promises to continue their subordination, because they perceive enough benefit in the system to not rebel against it. In music industry terms, this means that the system of releasing a CD through a major label system might be prohibitively costly and onerous, but artists still pursue this path because they do not see a better or less threatening alternative. Similarly, a female popular music star may not wish to be sexualized in her promotional materials, but because this method has been known to work for other artists she feels more at risk by not doing so. Thus, there is constant tension or contradiction between the ideology of the dominant class and the social experience of the subordinate class. In order to ease this tension, the dominant class relies on what Marxist philosopher Louis Althusser (1977) calls *ideological state apparatuses* (ISAs)—social institutions (schools, media outlets, religious institutions) that encourage people to behave in socially acceptable ways benefiting the interests of those in power. Althusser indicates that each institution is distinct from the others, but acknowledges that they all share common goals (or ideological similarities) at a high level. For example, all of them may espouse the merits, or perhaps the requirement, of women conforming to societally sanctioned gender roles (focusing on family, not career, or appearance, not personal development). These norms may be interpreted by some as natural, but they are artificially constructed by those making the rules within a social or political system, and thus the tension in observing them. In the United States, the powerful people who make the rules are still disproportionately white, male, straight, and middle to upper class, and thus may have a different sense of justice and equity from those in different social locations.

Althusser (1977) considered the network of ideological interrelationships between ISAs and determined that their "independence" gives them their credibility, but their congruence is what gives them their power. In other words, when a person hears the same story told everywhere, such as how important it is to be attractive, she might be more inclined to believe it. In Althusser's model, an individual becomes a subject as soon as she is born into society, molded by the ISAs around her. In other words, she becomes a product of her environment or her culture. She will be "hailed" or addressed in specific ways by others based on her particular social location, or her place in the world with respect to race, class, gender, age, and myriad other personal factors (Althusser, 1977). She will be spoken to in ways the dominant culture finds befitting of her position in society (e.g., ISAs might address older women differently than younger women, and lower-class people differently than higher-class people). It can also be argued that people will be trained to listen for things that resonate with them given their understanding of their social position or location. Furthermore, through "interpellation," ideology dictates the language, along with the terms of conversation, for both parties in a social exchange (e.g., a critic might call a female pop star a "whore" in an article, and she might be offended and call him a "hack") (Althusser, 1977).

But, as Stuart Hall (1980, p136) observes, "decodings do not follow inevitably from encodings," so however one is addressed or constructed, she ultimately decides how to interpret the meaning for herself. She may accept what is served to her at face value, negotiate the meaning of it, or reject it. In the scenario offered above, the artist may want to be decoded in sexual terms, and she may even embrace the critic's name-calling, owning it as part of her current positioning and future performances. So while Althusser believes in a more passive, more malleable audience, scholars such as Hall (1980) and Fiske (1993) believe in a more active audience who uses popular culture to make their own meanings from it.

Pop stars and sexuality

Audiences looking to pop stars for cues about sexuality also find a narrow range of types available for consideration. Even when stars are attempting to be subversive in this respect, they often provide relentlessly heterosexist ideas and imagery, in part to satisfy the demands of the *male gaze*. Sometimes these efforts ring false, and rather than extending ideas about sexuality, they serve to further constrict them, framing them through the lens of *heteronormativity* (Diamond, 2005).

Former Christian artist Katy Perry's song, "I Kissed a Girl,"[8] provides an example of such *heteronormativity*, with its base promiscuity masquerading as sexual exploration and discovery. While it poses as a gay-friendly anthem about the joys of same-sex kissing, it actually presents bisexuality and lesbianism as fleeting, meaningless, and trashy fun, thus confirming stereotypes about bisexuals being promiscuous and lesbianism being a phase. Perry declares she doesn't want to know the name of the girl she kisses because it "doesn't matter." Further, her kiss is an "experimental game," which "don't mean I'm in love tonight." Perry's pursuit of the *male gaze*, and the duplicitousness involved in getting its undivided attention, is alarming, even for the world of popular music. While posing as a girl-kisser, Perry comments that she "hopes [her] boyfriend don't mind it," engaging the fantasy precisely for the performative nature of it and its likely reception.

Others might read the song as a simple representation of "*bicuriosity*" or "*heteroflexibility*" (Diamond, 2005). *Bicurious* or *heteroflexible* people are predominantly straight, but experiment with same-sex partners occasionally, in some cases to confirm their own heterosexuality (Diamond, 2005). Perry could argue this type of representation was her intent, but if that's the case, her exploitation of this kind of experimentation comes across as self-serving and immature rather than open-minded or progressive. To begin with, Perry is singing about "kissing a girl," even though she is a grown woman and would presumably kiss another grown woman. The video is set up as an adult slumber party, which focuses on images of Perry lying in bed stroking her cat, her companion stuffed bunny, and ultimately primping, prancing "girls" rather than the substance of the reported encounter, which is discarded as a dream by the video's end. Sociologist Dawne Moon observes this type of exploitation is happening repeatedly at the hands of a new wave of "party lesbians" who participate in a "*Maxim* culture where it's all a performance. It's like, 'I'm being transgressive because I want men to want me more'" (Jessica G., 2008). As near-nakedness has become the norm among pop stars, some, like Perry, have escalated their sexual propositions and widened their perceived sexual availability by pretending to be open to things they are not. Such moves don't aid the progressive social agenda, but rather pander to the pornographic culture, which keeps pop stars locked in pornified, objectified positions.

Nicki Minaj employs similar attention-getting tactics and has been confronted by various media outlets for her inconsistencies. Writing for AfterEllen.com, Trish Bendix (2010) laments Minaj's potential "*fauxmosexuality*":

> Assuming that Nicki is telling the truth, that she's not really bisexual, this is certainly a huge issue. A large part of her appeal and her career has been her innuendos […]. If we take Nicki's statement that she doesn't date or sleep with women as a truth, then I think it is fair to be disappointed if not upset about how she portrays

herself as an artist. She spits lines like "I only stops for pedestrians, or real real bad lesbians," signs her female fans' boobs and makes reference to bedding other women.

Bisexuality

In contrast, in 1995, openly bisexual singer Jill Sobule also released a song called "I Kissed a Girl." Sobule was more sincere in her approach to and treatment of the subject, framing her same-sex kiss in a narrative structure that made it important but not voyeuristic. She concludes, "I kissed a girl. And I might do it again." This led to different meaning-making opportunities for her audience. In a *Billboard* interview with Eric Boehlert (1995, p97), Sobule observed:

> I played a show in Phoenix [in 1995] and there were a bunch of young girls with braces on their teeth, and they were yelling for the song. And I thought, this is so great, because I remember having braces on my teeth and having a crush on my best friend, and feeling so friggin' ashamed of it. If I would have heard a song like that, that would have made me feel much better.

Sobule, while playful, is conveying genuinely progressive sex and gender ideas through her music, whereas Perry poses as bi-curious in order to play to the times, the camera, and those intrigued by seeing her in this different role. Perhaps it's ironic that the more progressive song was written nearly two decades ago, or perhaps it's just an indication of the limitations of superstardom. Sobule was never a superstar. With a low profile and modest sales, she was able to make nuanced, authentic music that served to suggest an alternative sexuality to the dominant culture. Today, as a blockbuster hit-maker still capable of selling millions of CDs in the contemporary marketplace, Perry can sing provocative lyrics in revealing outfits, but her every move supports *cultural hegemony*—namely, *performing her gender* in a highly sexualized fashion.

Representations of people who are not completely homosexual or heterosexual are becoming more common for a variety of reasons. Arguably, we live in a more open culture than ever before in the United

States, so people feel more comfortable sharing who they are in this respect. In cases such as Sobule's, such disclosures and related celebrations of them through music contribute to general cultural awareness and the healthy discussion of sexuality in society. Representations like those presented by Perry, however, might stimulate cultural conversation by helping to keep public biases locked in place through reinforcement of stereotypic content.

The post-modern gaze?

While the *male gaze* is alive and well, some scholars have questioned whether women have developed a comparable "*female gaze*" as they have stepped behind the camera. E. Ann Kaplan (1987) applied the idea of the *male gaze* to music videos, specifically those on MTV. She observed that the medium was not gender specific and that men as well as women are the subjects of a new kind of gaze. In this new gaze, everyone looks at everyone for a complicated set of sexual and non-sexual reasons.

Kaplan (1987) attributes this new gaze to the breakdown of sexual stereotypes and the emergence and recognition of new sexual categories. She acknowledges that some age-old psychological ways of looking are still intact—she cites close-ups as an example of a pre-Oedipal, child-mother look—but also points to new gazes taken in relation to female popular music stars. Kaplan notices that the gaze employed in these videos is *post-modern* in nature. In other words, we don't really know whether some of the things we see are sexist, or are instead commenting on sexism. (Think back to my previous example of Fergie—is she playing with sexual stereotypes as she tears through them? It scarcely matters—she's repeating and reinforcing them, whether joking or not.) This is what Kaplan means when she says the audience no longer knows whose gaze to adopt. In her view the medium has stopped seeing *for* us.

Feminine types in music videos

However, more recent studies serve to uphold and extend Mulvey's work, effectively arguing by exemplification that the cinematic code may be locked in place for some time. Julie Andsager (2005) offers the most specific take on women in video, establishing a typology of feminine portrayals on MTV. She calls them "metamorphosis" (as exemplified by Christina Aguilera's "Dirrty"); "fantasy fulfillment" (as exemplified by Faith Hill's "The Way You Love Me," in which she poses as a nurse, a waitress, and a stripper); and "power" (as exemplified by Madonna in "Express Yourself"). Andsager is careful to say that she does not expect these three types to apply to most female pop videos. Rather, she asks that readers regard them as the beginning of a framework explaining types of female gender constructions in music videos. Andsager mixes critical theory with quantitative analysis in order to effectively and efficiently summarize the existing body of work in this area and establish a working model of "types" for examination and consideration. She draws on content analyses that indicate that as far back as 1990, 89 percent of videos featured sexual content, which was then defined by lip-licking, crotch-grabbing, gyrating, and other similar actions. Andsager reports that sexual portrayals have become even more graphic, "nearly naked" in her terms, but are now a requirement for commercial success.

The "metamorphosis" type described by Andsager is particularly common with young stars transitioning into adulthood. According to Tom Junod (2001, p128) in *Esquire*, when female artists are in their early teens, they are presented as "aggressively wholesome, given over to a wholesomeness that [is] unreal and fetishized." Gregory Dark, a pornographer "famous for making the worst pornography, a pornography of transgression and violation, a pornography that seemed intended less to glorify sex than to advertise the death of the soul" actually *directed* early Britney Spears and Mandy Moore videos (Junod, 2001, p128). Christina Aguilera and Britney Spears serve as exemplars of innocent teens who "metamorphize" by adding sexually explicit edges to their existing images of purity (Andsager, 2005). In one *Brandweek* writer's estimation, Aguilera's image changed from "teen temptress to street whore" (Van Munching, 2002, p30). Aguilera's "Dirrty" (2002) and Spears's "I'm a Slave 4 U" (2001) are reflective of this idea even at the level of song title, but the videos deepen the impression. The set for "Dirrty" looks like a dog-fighting-ring-turned-dance-club, and the viewer is taken on a tour of raunchy images from dirty bike gears, to mud wrestling, to dog fighting, to the inevitable lesbian shower orgy.[9] "I'm a Slave 4 U"[10] is comparatively tame, though Spears's lyrics articulate the story of her metamorphosis from little girl to sexual beast. The video concludes with her sandwiched in a three-way between two men.

The fantasy fulfillment type is also real and prevalent. These types appear to hold regardless of genres, as long as an artist is big enough to have crossed over into the "popular" music realm. Lady Gaga's "Bad Romance"[11] and Fergie's "Fergalicious"[12] videos find the artists cycling through various feminine types at warp speed.

The post-modern era also allows for a "powerful" type, which French (1985) constructs in two ways: "power to" and "power over." "Power to" manifests as controlling one's situation, while "power over" represents as controlling another's choices. Madonna exemplifies both types of power in various videos. In "Express Yourself" (1989),[13] she is an executive who grabs her crotch, Michael Jackson-style, as evidence of her power to do as she pleases, however unconventional or masculine. She uses her sexual power over men in myriad ways in her "Material Girl"[14] (1984) video—for example, to collect cash, jewelry, and adoration—while offering nothing real in return.

Everyday pornography

There are many reasons we only see certain types of women depicted in the media, and, increasingly, they relate to the concept of *everyday pornography* (Caputi, 2003). This theory maintains that pornography has become so mainstream that people do not recognize it for what it is— material that sexualizes, degrades, and objectifies women—and what it does: "eroticizes domination, subordination, violence and objectification" (Caputi, 2003, p434) and cultivates a manner of thinking in which violence toward women is normalized. Caputi (2003, p435) writes: "It is not always easy to recognize the oppressive character of pornography and its popular culture manifestations precisely because it is so normal." It may also explain why nobody flinched when Beyoncé became *Sports Illustrated*'s *Swimsuit Issue* cover model in February 2007.[15] Or when Mariah Carey became a *Playboy* cover girl in March 2007,[16] or when

Christina Aguilera posed near-naked on a centerfold for a particularly porn-leaning issue of *Maxim* in the same month.[17] As Kilbourne and Jhally (2010) note: "The problem isn't sex, it's the culture's pornographic attitude toward sex. It's the trivialization of sex." Kilbourne goes on to say that representations of women in advertising are "more extreme and graphic and pornographic than ever before." Caputi and Kilbourne both observe that this is particularly troublesome when little girls are sexualized and grown women are infantilized to look as though they are little girls being sexualized.

Pop stars' related imaging is symptomatic of the music industry's desire to comply with, or perhaps even amplify, societal standards of feminine beauty. It is no secret—academic or otherwise—that women are treated differently by virtue of their physical attractiveness (Kilbourne, 1999; Wolf, 2002; Andsager, 2005). Increasingly, attractiveness has taken the form of sexualization, which is said to occur when, according the American Psychological Association (APA, 2007, p1):

> A person's value comes from only his or her sex appeal or behavior, to the exclusion of other characteristics; a person is held to a standard that equates physical attractiveness (narrowly defined) with being sexy; a person is sexually objectified—that is, made into a thing for others' sexual use, rather than seen as a person with the capacity for independent action and decision making; and/or sexuality is inappropriately imposed upon a person.

All of these elements need not be present for sexualization to occur, but as evidenced by the aforementioned "Fergalicious" video, they often occur in clusters.

In *Killing Us Softly 4*, Kilbourne and Jhally (2010) argue that the overall message such images send to women is: "You have the right to remain sexy." Female popular music stars integrate this message, upstaging their own music by literally trying on different sexualized, idealized portrayals of women for the pleasure and approval of those watching. Andsager (2005, p42) articulates the business formula behind these representations of women perfectly: "If you don't care for me *that* way, try this." It's as though these women are being constructed to appeal to myriad fantasies, presumably so they take longer to lose their resonance. They can't stay the same—even for the duration of a single live performance! In a telling moment in Katy Perry's 2012 biopic, *Part of Me*, her dancers, who shield her with a cylindrical changing station each time she switches costumes, begin to stalk her, signaling time for another wardrobe change. She exclaims: "What? Me? Change? OK!"

Some might say these costume changes and revealing print appearances are all in good fun, and if the artists are OK with such representations, we should be too. But there are consequences arising from the increasingly normative objectification of women.

Kilbourne and Jhally (2010) observe:

> As girls learn from a very early age that their sexualized behavior and appearance are often rewarded by society, they learn to sexualize themselves—to see themselves as objects. They're encouraged to see this as their own choice, as a declaration of empowerment, to reframe presenting oneself in the most clichéd and stereotypical way possible as a kind of liberation.

This is called *self-objectification*, and it and other effects of consuming objectified images of women are neatly and efficiently organized in Frederickson and Roberts's (1997) influential article "Objectification Theory," and supported by numerous follow-up studies by these and other authors and media critics. For example, Kilbourne and Jhally (2010) report that between 1997 and 2007 procedures ranging from Botox and laser surgery to liposuction and breast implants rose 457 percent to approximately 12 million procedures per year. Women constituted 91 percent of the market for such procedures.

Objectification theory

Objectification theory argues that "girls and women are typically acculturated to internalize an observer's perspective as a primary view of their physical selves," (Frederickson and Roberts, 1997, p173). The implications and consequences of looking upon one's own body through the lens of an outsider range from "habitual body monitoring" to increased "shame and anxiety," to decreased "opportunities for peak motivational states," to "diminished awareness of internal bodily states" (Frederickson and Roberts, 1997, p173). Frederickson and Roberts also specify that as these negative experiences and effects accumulate, they have the potential to deepen into unipolar depression, sexual dysfunction, and eating disorders—afflictions more common in women than men.

Many of these ideas have been tested and confirmed by follow-up studies. Frederickson et al (1998) demonstrated through experiments that when women are in a state of self-objectification (e.g., they have just tried on bathing suits), their distraction causes cognitive abilities to be compromised. Similarly, Quinn et al (2006) also found that participants in a state of self-objectification performed worse on tasks than when they weren't self-objectifying. Szymanski and Henning (2007) found that habitual body monitoring interrupted work performance, induced greater body shame, and led to greater appearance anxiety. These conditions, in turn, led to depression and have also been linked to eating disorders.

It's no secret that even the stars aren't immune to these effects. At her peak, Fiona Apple famously told *Rolling Stone*: "Of course I have an eating disorder. Every girl in fucking America has an eating disorder" (Heath, 1998, p36). Juliana Hatfield, quoted earlier in this book, entered rehab for an eating disorder in 2008 and even blogged about it to share her experience with fans and others who were similarly afflicted (Lapatine, 2008). In 2010, Demi Lovato canceled her tour to enter eating disorder rehab (MSN, 2010). Kelly Clarkson, the most successful *American Idol* veteran, told the show *Access Hollywood* in 2012 that the scrutiny of her weight makes her want "to punch people sometimes" (Martin, undated).

Objectification can be blatant, but it can also be insidious. When objectification is communicated through non-verbal cues via mass media channels and carriers, it is arguably more powerful because it is less noticeable and, thus, presumably more likely to be accepted or internalized by gatekeepers and audiences without negotiation. (It is difficult to reject or perceive something as false if you have never registered it consciously in the first place.) The stakes are higher than ever before, as audiences have near-constant access to pop stars via thousands of magazines and blogs and hundreds of cable stations circulating their stories and images. If we see the same pictures and hear the same stories repeated ad infinitum, they reset our cultural norms to the extent that we can't be surprised by them or even notice them, really. If we don't notice them, we can't question why there are few genuinely new images or stories, despite the fact that there must be individual differences among stars.

Apple's criticisms of the music industry made her an outlier—and a target for other celebrities who believed she was hypocritically railing against the music business while perpetuating its stereotypes, particularly its fetishistic obsession with thinness. When questioned about that in a *Rolling Stone* interview, Apple cried, explaining:

> Every girl has an eating disorder because of videos like that ("Criminal"). Exactly. Yes. But that's exactly what the video is about. When I say, "I've been a bad, bad girl, I've been careless with a delicate man"—well, in a way I've been careless with a delicate audience, and I've gotten success that way, and I've lived in my ego that way, and I feel bad about it. And that's what the song's about, and therefore, that's what the video looks like.
>
> (Heath, 1998, p36)

In the same interview, Apple said she sought to control her body type for highly personal reasons: She had been raped as an adolescent and didn't want to develop body parts that might make her a target for unwanted advances. "For me, it wasn't about getting thin," she said. "It was about getting rid of the *bait* that was attached to my body" (Heath, 1998, p35).

Such personal narratives peel away the veneer of the molded, coached pop star to reveal an actual person whose real-life experiences shaped her music, her looks, her public representation of herself, and the way in which she connects with her audience. These stories also let audiences know that pop stars, however aspirational, are not above the cultural factors that plague "every girl in fucking America" (Heath, 1998, p36).

Production of popular culture

Fiske and Adorno disagree somewhat about who holds the power in cultural production. Adorno thinks it's the *creator/producer*, while Fiske believes it's the *creator/producer* and the *receiver/consumer*. In Fiske's (1997, p1) terms, popular culture "is made by various formations of subordinated or disempowered people out of the resources, both discursive and material, that are provided by the social system that disempowers them."

The Super Bowl is arguably the most hegemonic and anticipated entertainment event in American culture each year. It is created by the dominant culture (the NFL, the television network, and its advertisers, among others) to sell things to the masses while simultaneously entertaining them. But within this hegemonic display, the athletes and entertainers create their own spectacles for consumption by the audience, which interprets their behaviors to produce popular culture.

M.I.A.'s swearing and bird-flipping at the 2012 Super Bowl offers a case in point. M.I.A., who had been figuratively and ironically missing in action since her 2007 hit "Paper Planes," got the opportunity of a lifetime when she was invited to perform with Madonna and Nicki Minaj at the 2012 Super Bowl. This "hustler"[18] used her provided platform to upstage the spectacle in which she had been invited to play a small role. Media outlets and the Super Bowl audience paid more attention to M.I.A.'s momentary, immature transgression than to the extraordinary performer who was defying age expectations by rocking the halftime show as a female solo artist more than 30 years into her career.[19] Ensuing news coverage of the Super Bowl rarely discussed Madonna,[20] the intended centerpiece of the halftime show, instead focusing squarely on M.I.A.'s deliberate transgressions. Producers of the halftime show, and certainly Madonna herself, probably wanted the audience to receive the cultural message that female pop stars can still "have it" 30+ years into their careers. Instead, the audience resisted that message, choosing to focus on one rude gesture. Is our cultural attention span becoming too short to pay attention to talent devoid of shock tactics? Do we simply value the shocking over the talented?

Fiske (1997, p5) asserts that the mass public ultimately decides which "commodities they will use in their culture." Similarly, those making cultural products, such as artists and musicians, can also resist the dominant culture of the time in favor of putting forth their own ideas. "It's boring to make the same thing over and over," Hinojosa said. "You have to do something unexpected to get the extraordinary." But those who break with tradition too much don't stand a chance of success. They must work within existing structures to begin to subvert them.

The 2011 season of *The Voice* provided an interesting illustration, with Christina Aguilera selecting artists with amazing voices who did not fit the cookie-cutter appearance templates of herself or her peers. In shows such as *The Voice* and *American Idol*, the audience ultimately selects its cultural winners. But the coaches and judges, who must accept the public's verdict, do their best to influence popular opinion along the way by praising contestants they deem worthy and dismissing those they deem amateurish or deficient. In the music industry, there is a professional class of *cultural intermediaries* who work with musicians to popularize their work to the masses, and the coaches on *The Voice* and the judges on *American Idol* serve as a contemporary example of this, bringing contestants into millions of homes via popular television shows and telling people how to think about them.

Cultural consumption involves a person taking the culture and pop culture served to her and making her own meaning from it, depending upon her own personal history, disposition, experiences, and beliefs. The act of consuming culture, whether it's a book, or a movie, a CD, or a television show, is also a political act in that a person's choice of what to consume, and what sense to make of what she's consuming, tells us numerous things about her. We know from mass communication literature that people like to see reflections of themselves in what they consume. For this reason, historically, gays and people of color have had slim pickings with respect to seeing themselves on television (Greenberg et al, 2002). Television scholar George Gerbner established through his cultivation theory (Gerbner, 1998; Gerbner et al, 2002) that heavy users of television are more likely to experience greater effects than light users. Gerbner joined forces with Larry Gross, Michael Morgan, and Nancy Signorelli during the 1970s and 1980s to run a cultural indicators study, which "used the concept of cultivation to describe the resulting influence of television in viewers' conceptions of social reality" (Gross, 2001, p6). They observed a pattern called *mainstreaming*, which indicated that heavy television users tended to agree with the "viewpoints proffered by television" (Gross, 2001, p7). According to Gross (2001, p6) "Heavy television use is thus associated with a convergence of outlooks, a mainstreaming of opinion." In this way, television has the power to introduce viewers to their first known black person, gay person, Mormon person, or polyamorous person, thus paving the way for the viewer to be more accepting of such people in real life.

As music competition shows began to play larger roles in creating American pop stars, *American Idol* received criticism for having no openly gay contestants (though Clay Aiken and Adam Lambert came out after their seasons ended). Thus, one noteworthy change in this venue occurred in the debut season of *The Voice*. Three semi-finalist contestants, Beverly McClellan, Vicci Martinez, and Nakia, were all openly gay, with families, friends, and partners featured in the audience and in the singers' back stories. These relatively new television images went a long way in showing fans that when judging someone's vocal ability, looks and sexuality do not determine outcomes. Such images were also validating for gay audiences, who do not often see themselves reflected in network television shows.

Such representational changes have the capacity to excite audiences craving something new and to convince other producers to consider whether innovation, not copycat antics, might be the best roadmap to a future hit. These changes also promise to transform power dynamics through culture. While changing power dynamics on one contest show might not seem like a big deal, the possible ripple effects are worth noting. Media scholar John Fiske (1997, p1) observes that:

> *Culture* is the constant process of producing meanings of and from our social experience, and such meanings necessarily produce a

social identity for the people involved [...]. [Culture] is a constant succession of social practices; it is therefore inherently political, it is centrally involved in the distribution and possible redistribution of various forms of social power.

Similarly, cultural studies scholar David Hesmondhalgh (2002, p40) observes:

Cultural studies explores the complex ways in which systems of aesthetic value feed into cultural power. Whose voices are heard within a culture and whose voices are marginalized? Which (and whose) forms of pleasure are sanctioned and which/whose are felt to be fickle, banal, or even dangerous?

In such a framework, the opportunities enabled by representational changes on a show such as *The Voice* are enormous, as they can enable people without pop-star looks to be heard without distraction and people who have been underrepresented on television to be seen and heard based on their voices.

But such representation will not change society overnight, so while *The Voice* is encouraging in some ways, it's treading water in others. Christina Aguilera's breasts remain on regular display on the show, and Blake Shelton tells young female contestants how beautiful they are and then infantilizes them by positioning himself as their most able protector. Shelton seems to come from a well-meaning but paternalistic place, while Aguilera's blonde, buxom appearance reinforces what women should look like if they want to make it in the music business. Thus, the coaches and the show send mixed signals. The audience is left to make its own sense of what has happened, whether celebrating the progressive victories, or being comforted by the familiar show structure and conversation. During a March 2012 episode, Shelton and Aguilera both reacted strongly to Erin, a former model wearing a revealing dress. Shelton told her: "Erin, I'm so glad you wore that. I'm married now and seeing women wear outfits like that is all I have left." Then Aguilera said "Hi, hot momma, gorgeous person in front of me," before telling her that the song she performed was not a good choice for her. The implicit message was that her poor song choice was ultimately OK because people were focusing on her appearance, anyway.

Production of culture literature is useful in explaining the way in which the various pieces of a cultural system (e.g., values, norms, institutions) work together to produce popular artifacts, or those things that resonate widely throughout a given culture. These artifacts might take the form of a CD cover, a public performance, a marketing campaign, or an article about a given artist. This literature also gives us a glimpse inside the forces at work within cultural industries. Such literature also demonstrates how production and consumption are not separate entities but, rather, "different moments in a single process" (Hesmondhalgh, 2002, p34).

A careful reading of the *The Voice* as a cultural artifact seems an apt way to showcase the concepts of *culture*, *meaning-making*, and *multivocality*. The brand-within-a-brand structure (with the show, the coaches, the teams, and the contestants all serving as brands) enables the show's *multivocality*, and it effectively speaks with many different voices, some traditional and some progressive, simultaneously.

The show, based on the conceit of choosing contestants based on their voices only, appeals to those who believe that musicians should be evaluated and given professional opportunities based primarily on their talent, not their looks or showmanship. Yet the show's structure rings traditional and familiar—we are accustomed to the setup of this contest show, thanks to its most direct predecessor, *American Idol*. We expect contestants to get comments about their appearance from our past experience in culture, generally, and from watching *American Idol*, specifically, and they do. But they typically only hear praise for looking hot or sexy—rather than browbeating for not being as hot as their competitors, as was the case on *Idol*—and both male and female contestants are objectified. While the judges on *Idol* mocked weaker contestants for sport, *The Voice* takes a more compassionate approach, as judges tell the passed-over contestants that they too have faced such rejection, and that they should power on in their careers until they succeed. The brand of *The Voice* is pro-talent and pro-people, whereas the brand of *American*

Idol focused more on contention and humiliation. It does not hurt that *Voice* judge Christina Aguilera is on her third or arguably fourth life as a female pop star, making her the perfect embodiment of the show's brand in terms of cultural resonance, meaning-making, and the representation of those we don't expect to see on TV—like the unicorn of the female pop star on her third or fourth life! It is critical to remember that Aguilera likely earned her multiple lives because of her legendarily powerful voice—and the fact that she has maintained her pop star looks throughout her trials.

Feminist geography and gendered space

Feminist geographers understand space as a feature of social relations because "space is not merely an arena *in which* social life unfolds, but *through which* social life is produced and reproduced" (Rose, 1993, p19). Thus, in their view, there are actual spaces in which and through which popular culture, for example, is produced and consumed. Certain spaces are considered more *gendered* than others because the nature of those spaces encourages the construction and performance of gender—a key ingredient in people's social identity (Rose, 1993; Longhurst, 2000). Such spaces also facilitate the consumption of such produced and reproduced gender performances by audiences and thus perpetuate gender inequalities (Spain, 1992; Fortuijn et al, 2004). Music videos and magazine covers are arguably two of the most gendered spaces in the music industry.

The videos described earlier in this chapter (e.g., Katy Perry's "I Kissed A Girl," Britney Spears's "I'm a Slave 4 U," and Christina Aguilera's "Dirrty"), as well as the aforementioned magazine covers (e.g., Carey on the cover of *Playboy*, Beyoncé on the cover of *Sports Illustrated*'s *Swimsuit Issue*, and Aguilera, Fergie, Avril Lavigne, and countless others on the cover of *Maxim*), are apt depictions of the power and consistency of the types of *gendered spaces* produced by the music industry and its associated media partners.

Women have slowly but surely advanced into positions of power within the music industry, so this dynamic is arguably changing, but men continue to hold the lion's share of power across industry verticals;

thus, old patterns, such as representations of female artists and characters, remain firmly intact. The cultural artifacts that the modern music industry nurtures and distributes, and the ideas it espouses through its performers and their performances, lock in place the types of careers possible for female artists. By solidifying the appearance requirements that female artists must meet if they wish to be invested in for any length of time, the industry guarantees a steady supply of looks-first artists.

The consequences of evaluating female musicians based on their looks over their talent/professional capabilities are potentially more extreme than they might appear at first. Not only do they harm the lifecycles of the pop stars in question, they harm the *receivers* of these bodies-first messages.

For adolescent girls looking to pop stars as attractive, aspirational figures to represent, admire, or emulate, the limited range of choices available to them via mass media channels proves troublesome. Consider the constrained celebrity types available for young women to compare themselves to as they try to determine who they want to "be" and "look like." For example, not all girls are born of the *"good girl"* template—many explore different modes of being until social norms coach them into compliance. Later, naturally occurring or socially constructed *"good girls"* don't automatically transition into *"temptresses"* due to some biological imperative. They begin dressing differently in their teenage years in large part because of what's made available to them in retail venues and because of how they see celebrity versions of themselves looking, dressing, and acting.

The artificially small range of types available for social learning and role experimentation means that young girls essentially have to choose from various sexualized and/or dysfunctional types, which likely confuses them and compromises their creativity in regard to who they can become as they transition into adolescence and, ultimately, adulthood. As Kilbourne and Jhally (2010) observe in the documentary *Killing Us Softly 4*: "When the culture offers girls and women only one way to be sexy it can hardly be considered an authentic choice to choose it." The solution? Broaden our cultural definitions of beautiful, sexy, and healthy.

Historically, women have been underrepresented in the music industry (e.g., in 2012, there are still shockingly few female producers) and in society (e.g., women only got the right to vote in 1920—less than 100 years ago). This makes the few representations of women that we see all the more important from a social influence standpoint. As previously noted, subconscious messages produce potentially dangerous effects, as audiences don't notice them consciously enough to consider or resist them. Rance Crain (1997, p25), former editor-in-chief of *Advertising Age*, wrote: "Only 8% of an ad's message is received by the conscious mind. The rest is worked and reworked deep within the recesses of the brain." Kilbourne and Jhally (2010) argue that it is critical to notice the patterned nature of gender portrayals in advertising because:

> Ads sell more than products, they sell values, they sell images, they sell concepts of love and sexuality, of success and perhaps most important, of normalcy. To a great extent, they tell us who we are and who we should be.

They conclude that ads tell women "what's most important is how we look." Clearly, anyone critically examining this assertion rejects it as false, but still the statement bears interrogation, particularly as it is reinforced again and again by the *social world* and the *creator/producer* points on the *Cultural Diamond*.

Summary

If media organizations and music companies set the agenda for what people see, and how they think about what they see (McCombs and Shaw, 1972), their message about female celebrities is clear: They are valued predominantly for their use to or consumption by others (Frederickson and Roberts, 1997), and their bodies are their most marketable asset (Lieb, 2007). If such stars, their handlers, or their audiences internalize such ideas, they may find themselves focusing on the "wrong" things, as least as far as music is concerned.

This poses numerous problems, which I have identified and addressed using theory from sociology/women's studies/pop culture studies, mass communication/media studies, marketing/branding and related disciplines. These problems include hyper-sexualization and objectification, body image dissatisfaction and eating disorders, depression, violence against women, and a lack of strong, positive female figures for young women to aspire to be.

In recognition of these problems, theories related to patterns of representation (e.g., the *male gaze* and *everyday pornography*) were used to better contextualize and understand the patterns that emerged in previous chapters. Such theories were also used to convey the importance of defining the social problems underlying such representations so that those involved in various ways (e.g., *receivers/consumers, creators/ producers*) can begin to more immediately recognize and fix them.

Book summary

The music industry is in a state of constant flux, but for female pop stars, some things never change. For more than three decades there has been an imperative to look beautiful and be willing to emphasize sexuality in order to sell their music. Today, with technology speeding the pace of the industry and ever-younger starlets popping up, the impulse to sell sex above music is stronger than ever. This book has highlighted the social forces underlying the patterned and problematic representations of female artists, and explained how they become so culturally embedded using frameworks, theories, and ideas from multiple disciplines, including communication/media studies, sociology/ gender studies/pop culture studies, and marketing/branding. It also sought to convince students how the process of building and popularizing pop stars influences both the stars who are marketed and packaged to the hilt and their various audiences.

My research isolated two critical-but-understudied concepts—the short-term brand and the person brand, and merged them to birth the new concept of the short-term person brand. My research for this book also yielded my data-driven Lifecycle Model, which can be used as a framework with which students and academics can view short-term person brands and analyze pop star careers. The intent was to provide a motivation for all who read it to think more critically about who becomes a celebrity and how this process happens, and what their chosen field has to say about it. Finally, this book was written as a reminder that if students aren't finding deeply resonant musical artists or reflections of themselves in such artists, there are definite reasons for that, but there are now ways to access artists they identify with, whether through social media, cable, or specialized labels and magazines.

Many of the lessons shared throughout this book are disheartening, while others are completely heartbreaking. My hope is that the themes of this book will leave an impression, and make students more critical of the messages they receive about women though pop star images in the future. My intention is that by pointing out the wide-ranging social implications and effects associated with pop star representations, my readers will credit courageous artists such as Adele and Fiona Apple, and their correspondingly brave handlers, with being genuinely distinctive (and supremely talented) in an industry that continuously looks for this year's version of last year's girl.

The representation of women in popular culture is a growing field of academic study. Those who study systems of representation have the potential to contribute positively to the media literacy of future generations and to help reshape cultural notions of attractiveness in the United States. Given the types of courses this book is being used in, some readers might actually end up *working with* pop stars in the future (whether in a music, television, film, marketing, PR, advertising, journalism, or social media capacity), and I hope reading this book will convince them to be mindful of the importance of their influential positions and the power of the ideas and images they present to *audiences* and our greater *social world*.

People to watch

As I finished this book, there were exciting developments on the horizon. Given the upsetting patterns regarding representations of female performers chronicled throughout the book, I wanted to shed light on several rays of hope that emerged from various corners of the music/ entertainment industry.

Ashley Judd

After reading wildly speculative accounts of why her face looked "puffy," actor Ashley Judd wrote a scathing article for *The Daily Beast* in April 2012, which sparked a "viral media frenzy" about media representations of women and girls (Judd, 2012). In it, Judd (2012, p1) observed:

> The Conversation about women's bodies exists largely outside of us, while it is also directed at (and marketed to) us, and used to define and control us. The Conversation about women happens everywhere, publicly and privately. We are described and detailed, our faces and bodies analyzed and picked apart, our worth ascertained and ascribed based on the reduction of personhood to simple physical objectification. Our voices, our personhood, our potential, and our accomplishments are regularly minimized and muted.

Judd (2012, p2) said she generally ignored her own press, but chose to respond this time because:

> The conversation was pointedly nasty, gendered, and misogynistic, and embodies what all girls and women in our culture, to a greater or lesser extent, endure every day, in ways both outrageous and subtle. The assault on body image, the hypersexualization of girls and women and subsequent degradation of our sexuality as we walk through the decades, and the general incessant objectification is what this conversation allegedly about my face is really about.

Judd understands well, from living under the microscope of celebrity scrutiny, the intricacies of what the theorists presented in this chapter have painstakingly analyzed and brought to life. Sometimes a celebrity is what a cause or a movement needs to gain traction, and Judd may be in the best position to make a case against the hyper-sexualization, objectification, and dismissal of women as equal beings in contemporary American society. Her efforts, if resonant, could serve to ameliorate conditions for her peers in popular music.

Adele

After making her looks an issue in a fair number of early-stage magazine articles, journalists and critics have finally stopped talking about Adele's anti-pop star looks and started focusing instead on her exceptionally catchy but elegant songwriting and phenomenal voice which was recently saved by vocal surgery (Gottlieb, 2011) so she may be expected to sing for a long time to come. There may not be room for many like her at this point in time, as one respondent noted, but one artist like her having the best-selling CD of 2011, ahead of household names such as Lady Gaga, Justin Bieber, and Katy Perry, is a good start toward building a stronger model for female performers seeking to be career artists.

Kelly Clarkson

The original *American Idol* winner also gives us reason for hope. Her weight has gone up and down, but her sales have been strong for a decade—a rare feat for female pop stars. Clarkson is adamant about claiming her position as an artist, telling media outlets that it's her choice if she wants to eat more or less, or change her hair color. Her music-first posture is refreshing, and it's just what the career doctor ordered for promising acts coming up behind her. In 2012, Clarkson became a participant/judge/activist in *Duets*, where she coaches young artists. She gives great advice, telling one to look away from her male partners and at her *real* audience, and demanding that another watch herself perform to grasp how talented she is. She is joined by participant/judge/activist Jennifer Nettles (lead singer of Sugarland), who told another contestant (who performed barefoot one week, and in 4-inch heels the next) that she looked uncomfortable, probably due to her shoes, and that she should simply refuse to wear them. To this, Clarkson responded: "I do."

Alabama Shakes

Alabama Shakes[21] features formidable lead vocalist Brittany Howard, whom critics have compared to Aretha Franklin and Janis Joplin. Charmingly, Howard deflected such comparisons in a 2012 NPR interview with Terry Gross, comparing herself instead to the late Bon Scott, the original and notorious lead singer of AC/DC, whose masculinity, authenticity, and impassioned performances survive him (NPR, 2012). Howard often performs in comfortable-looking casual clothes, focusing exclusively on her vocal and musical performance. Imagine that!

Madonna

Madonna wrote the playbook for building a career, an empire, and a legacy as a contemporary female pop star. As she approaches the 30th anniversary of her debut release in 1983, she has much to celebrate. In 2012, she set a new record for most No. 1 albums by a solo singer with the release of *MDNA* (Glennie, 2012). She rocked the Super Bowl as its marquee halftime-show performer, and continued to garner favorable comparisons to Lady Gaga—all at age 53.

My analysis of the lifecycle of a female pop star makes clear that a young singer with a burgeoning career will be quickly painted into one of two corners—the *good girl* or the *temptress*—as she launches her career. Those early portrayals will set the stage for the rest of her career, as the economic mandate to create a strong brand duels with social concepts of gender, beauty, sex, and power.

Watching Madonna on stage at the Super Bowl, and considering the length and magnitude of her career, it's hard to believe that she ever could have been painted into the reductive, restrictive corners of the *temptress*, or the *gay icon*, or the *whore*. Over the course of 30 years, she has embodied nearly everything her audience might wish to see, yet she appears to have called nearly all her own shots. She continues to use beauty and sexuality, but they have never been her sole focus. When we watch Madonna, we see power, and creativity, and constant innovation. Artists coming up behind her would be wise to learn from her history, so they can apply it in pursuit of protecting and owning their personal and professional futures. Those of us studying Madonna from a critical perspective should take note of what female pop star careers can and should look like if the artists possess genuine talent, take a proactive approach to career planning, and select professional managers who are more interested in focusing on their artists' compelling points of difference rather than their reductive points of parity.

NOTES

Preface

1 In *I Want My MTV* (Marks and Tannenbaum, 2011), Ann Wilson reported that her sister Nancy was objectified relentlessly, while she herself was dismissed and downplayed visually because she "didn't look like a porn star" (p302).

2 Literal video parody of Bonnie Tyler's smash hit/MTV video: "Total Eclipse of the Heart", http://www.funnyordie.com/videos/f03d464867/total-eclipse-of-the-heart-literal-video-version-original.

3 Rod Stewart's "Hot Legs" video, http://www.youtube.com/watch?v=AHcjjxYbgNM.

4 Pat Benatar's "You Better Run," the second video ever aired on MTV: http://www.youtube.com/watch?v=IvSbQB6-UdY/.

5 Fergie's "Fergalicious" video, http://www.youtube.com/watch?v=5T0utQ-XWGY.

6 Some interview data is also used in Chapter 2, but it does not provide the backbone of the chapter.

7 This is a particularly interesting case because Melissa Etheridge's market skews more female than male.

Chapter 1

1 On November 26, 2012, Gaga was the most followed person on Twitter with 31,529,953 followers. As of the same date, she also boasted 53,845,549 likes on Facebook. These are staggering figures for each venue.

2 Gaga's ten favorite outfits: http://www.youtube.com/watch?src_vid=eK_KTG2tEIs&v=GpU_K-eKHaY&annotation_id=annotation_549740&feature=iv.

3 Lady Gaga's "Bad Romance" video: http://www.youtube.com/watch?v=qrO4YZeyl0I.

4 One could counter-argue that there are two allegories at play in the video: first, Gaga has to embrace the industry's hegemonic codes of feminine conduct; and, second, despite this, Gaga is using the industry to gratify herself, as is evidenced by her killing her lover after receiving sexual gratification from him in the video.

5 Mead is best known for framing the mind and the self as social processes, distinguishing the "I" (self as subject/one's impulses) from the "me" (self as object/how one believes she is perceived by others). The mind, he argues, is the interaction between the "I" and the "me."

6 Traditionally, women have not been rewarded for provocative behavior. Part of the shock and appeal of Gaga is that her provocative stunts defy conventional gender expectations, pleasing some and horrifying others.

7 The story of Gaga's meat dress: http://www.youtube.com/watch?v=ms8j5g6OKZU.

8 The idea that reality is "socially constructed" means that although we take many ideas or processes for granted as objective or universal truths in our social world, they are not—they are actually subjective, and constructed by various social structures and through social interaction. Through repetition, these ideas and processes become norms, which we interpret to be objective. Social constructionism bred the idea of post-modernism, which, in turn, influenced the development of cultural studies.

9 It is important to note that while this book focuses on pop stars' roles in the United States, many pop stars are global sensations. Popular culture is a dominant export of the United States, and thus these pop star representations often travel to many parts of the world without modification.

10 Lady Gaga performs as Jo Calderone: http://www.youtube.com/watch?v=Fem7eZlBR4U.

11 Based on articles by *Entertainment Weekly*, MTV, and *E*, and readers' related feedback to them.

12 Media literacy efforts aim to teach people how to critically read, watch, and listen to the messages they receive on an ongoing basis. For example, one might learn how to analyze an advertisement based on the perceived financial interest of the advertising company. In short, such efforts help people know what to watch for as they process messages, particularly commercial messages.

13 Madonna's "Like a Virgin" video: http://www.youtube.com/watch?v=s__rX_WL100.

14 Madonna's "Papa Don't Preach" video: http://www.youtube.com/watch?v=RkxqxWgEEz4.

15 Madonna's "Material Girl" video: http://www.youtube.com/watch?v=_gWqc7pTNn0.

16 Madonna's "Justify My Love" video: http://www.youtube.com/watch?v=Np_Y740aReI.

17 Madonna's "Music" video: http://www.youtube.com/watch?v=Sdz2oW0NMFk.

18 Madonna's "Hang Up" video: http://www.youtube.com/watch?v=EDwb9jOVRtU.

19 Madonna Kisses Britney Spears and Christina Aguilera at the 2003 VMA: http://www.youtube.com/watch?v=T_SI_EoBTx8.

20 U2 Vertigo IPod: http://www.youtube.com/watch?v=nljs4kzpebU.

21 *A Very Gaga Thanksgiving*—Gaga performs "Edge of Glory," reflects on grandparents: http://www.youtube.com/watch?v=jQ7BQuoRmbs.

22 Christina Aguilera's botched National Anthem: http://www.youtube.com/watch?v=hj5NPNe3jNU.

Chapter 2

1 For bands in the 1990s, many of which espoused a do-it-yourself ethic, selling out by becoming too business minded or bottom-line focused was the kiss of death. See Kay Hanley's quotes as examples.

2 But as this book went to press in 2012, Gaga released "Fame," her new fragrance, which she said she designed to smell like semen and blood, so apparently she's still trying to shock audiences.

3 Beyoncé and Shakira's "Beautiful Liar" video: http://www.youtube.com/watch?v=EIhbfu_R-R4.

4 Shakira's "Waka Waka" video: http://www.youtube.com/watch?v=pRpeEdMmmQ0.

5 Sasha Fierce: http://www.youtube.com/watch?v=nX1WSsfe2Qs.

Chapter 3

1 I know this from personal experience. I ran Newbury Comics Interactive, the company's mail order division, from 1996 to 1998.

Chapter 4

1 Justin Timberlake's "Sexy Back": http://www.youtube.com/watch?v=Fz1BXF7bVpM.
2 Justin Timberlake's "Like I Love You": http://www.youtube.com/watch?v=FQ3slUz7Jo8.
3 Maroon 5's "Moves Like Jagger": http://www.youtube.com/watch?v=tyL9H5n_sxQ.
4 Maroon 5's "Payphone": http://www.youtube.com/watch?v=5FlQSQuv_mg.
5 Britney Spears "Hit Me Baby One More Time" video: http://www.youtube.com/watch?v=C-u5WLJ9Yk4.
6 Britney Spears and Justin Timberlake on MMC: http://www.youtube.com/watch?v=76pYZjhVylw&feature=related.
7 Cast of *Glee* at *GQ* photo shoot: http://www.youtube.com/watch?v=eHAzv46DYmk.
8 Destiny's Child's "Emotion" video: http://www.youtube.com/watch?v=xWKdMmH0B-E.
9 Beyoncé as Foxxy Cleopatra performing "Hey Goldmember": http://www.youtube.com/watch?v=39tDBqTQL80.
10 Hole's "Miss World": http://www.youtube.com/watch?v=mS1Ckczz0LQ.
11 Hole's "Celebrity Skin": http://www.youtube.com/watch?v=O3dWBLoU--E.
12 Fiona Apple's "Criminal": http://www.youtube.com/watch?v=FFOzayDpWoI.
13 Fiona Apple's world is bullshit: http://www.youtube.com/watch?v=GSLwYrPbuts.
14 Carrie Underwood's "Blown Away" video: http://www.youtube.com/watch?v=gDooiYMagTs/
15 Aerosmith lead singer Steven Tyler as *American Idol* judge in 2012: http://www.youtube.com/watch?v=TAVIgq2Bbgw.
16 Mick Jagger "Top Ten" video: http://www.youtube.com/watch?v=joi6G1wTyEk.
17 Avril Lavigne's "Blender Cover (Hell Yeah, I'm Hot)": http://www.alavigne.org/Avril-Lavigne-Blender-Pictures/.
18 Avril Lavigne Let Go album cover: http://www.amazon.com/Let-Go-Avril-Lavigne/dp/B000066NW0/ref=sr_1_1?ie=UTF8&qid=1355466856&sr=8-1&keywords=avril+lavigne+let+go+cd.
19 Avril Lavigne's "Girlfriend" video: http://www.youtube.com/watch?v=Bg59q4puhmg.
20 Avril Lavigne's November 2010 *Maxim* cover shoot: http://www.google.com/search?q=November+2010+issue+of+Maxim+avril+lavigne&hl=en&prmd=imvnso&tbm=isch&tbo=u&source=univ&sa=X&ei=WvnoT8_tNorZ0QHrisiwDQ&ved=0CFgQsAQ&biw=1512&bih=895.
21 Mariah Carey's *Playboy* cover in 2007: http://www.youtube.com/watch?v=Z2ma_r7Bm7o.
22 Beyoncé's *Sports Illustrated Swimsuit Issue* photo shoot: http://www.youtube.com/watch?v=Kd9oB3Ywer0.
23 Linda Perry performs as lead singer of 4 Non Blondes: http://www.youtube.com/watch?v=HXW8tjpL_MM&feature=related.
24 Christina Aguilera's "Beautiful" video (written by Linda Perry): http://www.youtube.com/watch?v=eAfyFTzZDMM.
25 Kara DioGuardi, a songwriter and former *American Idol* judge, in a video about her *Maxim* profile in 2010: http://www.youtube.com/watch?v=LhymFXGw5Y4.
26 Taylor Swift's *Vogue* cover shoot on the eve of her 22nd birthday: http://www.youtube.com/watch?v=qog5hr-yidw.

27 Taylor Swift's "Red" album: http://www.amazon.com/Red-Taylor-Swift/dp/B008XNZMOU/ref=sr_1_1?ie=UTF8&qid=1353954012&sr=8-1&keywords=taylor+swift+red

28 Miley Cyrus's "Can't Be Tamed" video: http://www.youtube.com/watch?v=sjSG6z_13-Q.

29 Miley Cyrus bites into her boyfriend's "penis cake": http://www.youtube.com/watch?v=XOae6EnjZGw.

30 Hannah Montana: http://www.amazon.com/Hannah-Montana-Complete-First-Season/dp/B001EOQWNK/ref=sr_1_3?s=movies-tv&ie=UTF8&qid=1342392046&sr=1-3&keywords=hannah+montana.

31 Miley Cyrus: "Can't Be Tamed": http://www.amazon.com/Cant-Be-Tamed-Miley-Cyrus/dp/B003K025V4/ref=sr_1_1?s=music&ie=UTF8&qid=1342392100&sr=1-1&keywords=miley+cyrus.

Chapter 5

1 Norah Jones's *Come Away with Me* cover: http://www.amazon.com/Come-Away-With-Norah-Jones/dp/B00005YW4H.

2 Norah Jones's *Not Too Late* cover: http://www.amazon.com/Not-Too-Late-Norah-Jones/dp/B000KCHZK6/ref=sr_1_1?s=music&ie=UTF8&qid=1340669268&sr=1-1&keywords=not+too+late+norah+jones.

3 Adele's *21* cover: http://www.amazon.com/21-Adele/dp/B004EBT5CU/ref=sr_1_1?s=music&ie=UTF8&qid=1340669508&sr=1-1&keywords=adele+21.

4 Nicki Minaj performs at the 2012 Grammys: http://www.youtube.com/watch?v=8qT3PGToUzU.

5 Stefani Germanotta performs at NYU before becoming Lady Gaga: http://www.youtube.com/watch?v=NM51qOpwcIM.

6 M.I.A.'s "Paper Planes" video: http://www.youtube.com/watch?v=7sei-eEjy4g.

7 M.I.A. offends at the 2012 Super Bowl: http://www.youtube.com/watch?v=GzOEijWdr6o.

8 Direct quote from M.I.A.'s "Paper Planes."

9 Nicole Scherzinger's 2011 solo single "Right There": http://www.youtube.com/watch?v=t-vTaktsUSw.

10 Janet Jackson's 2004 Super Bowl wardrobe malfunction: http://www.youtube.com/watch?v=TPtbHc02mYk.

11 Christina Aguilera's "Dirty" video: http://www.youtube.com/watch?v=lN3qvrZVzIo.

12 Christina Aguilera's *Maxim* photo shoots: http://www.google.com/search?q=Maxim+Christina+Aguilera+Covers&hl=en&prmd=imvnso&tbm=isch&tbo=u&source=univ&sa=X&ei=4K7oT4X3BYqt0AGQpPz3CQ&ved=0CFIQsAQ&biw=1024&bih=895.

13 Courtney Love talks about Amy Winehouse: http://www.examiner.com/article/courtney-love-talks-helping-amy-winehouse-i-tried-twice.

14 Ad for Celine Dion at Caesar's Palace: http://www.youtube.com/watch?v=pZJFNpq8ToE.

15 Gay icon Barbra Streisand: http://www.amazon.com/The-Essential-Barbra-Streisand/dp/B00005V3WH/ref=sr_1_3?ie=UTF8&qid=1340655917&sr=8-3&keywords=barbra+streisand.

16 *The Voice*'s Beverly McClellan and Frenchie Davis: http://www.youtube.com/watch?v=vMdwza78IHo.

Chapter 6

1 Fergie's "Fergalicious" video: http://www.youtube.com/watch?v=5T0utQ-XWGY.
2 Think back to Rod Stewart's "Hot Legs" video from the Preface for another example of the male gaze.
3 Adele's *21* cover: http://www.amazon.com/21-Adele/dp/B004EBT5CU/ref=sr_1_1?s=music&ie=UTF8&qid=1340669508&sr=1-1&keywords=adele+21.
4 Lady Gaga's *Born This Way* cover: http://www.amazon.com/Born-This-Way-Lady-Gaga/dp/B004K4AVAG/ref=sr_1_1?s=music&ie=UTF8&qid=1340671750&sr=1-1&keywords=lady+gaga+born+this+way.
5 Nicki Minaj's *Pink Friday* cover: http://www.amazon.com/Pink-Friday-Nicki-Minaj/dp/B0042RUMEQ/ref=sr_1_1?s=music&ie=UTF8&qid=1340671845&sr=1-1&keywords=nicki+minaj+pink+friday.
6 Katy Perry's *Teenage Dream* cover: http://www.amazon.com/Teenage-Dream-Katy-Perry/dp/B003L77TZI/ref=sr_1_1?s=music&ie=UTF8&qid=1340671907&sr=1-1&keywords=katy+perry+teenage+dream+album.
7 Chris Brown's *F.A.M.E.* cover: http://www.amazon.com/F-A-M-E-Deluxe-Edition-Chris-Brown/dp/B004LFO0EW/ref=sr_1_1?s=music&ie=UTF8&qid=1340671963&sr=1-1&keywords=chris+brown+f.a.m.e.
8 Katy Perry's "I Kissed a Girl" video: http://www.youtube.com/watch?v=tAp9BKosZXs.
9 Christina Aguilera's "Dirrty" video: http://www.youtube.com/watch?v=_b0okuftqng.
10 Britney Spears's "I'm a Slave 4 U" video: http://www.youtube.com/watch?v=Mzybwwf2HoQ.
11 Lady Gaga's "Bad Romance" video: http://www.youtube.com/watch?v=qrO4YZeyl0I.
12 Fergie's "Fergalicious" video: http://www.youtube.com/watch?v=5T0utQ-XWGY.
13 Madonna's "Express Yourself" video: http://www.youtube.com/watch?v=GsVcUzP_O_8.
14 Madonna's "Material Girl" video: http://www.youtube.com/watch?v=_gWqc7pTNn0.
15 Beyoncé's Sports Illustrated Swimsuit Issue photo shoot: http://www.youtube.com/watch?v=Kd9oB3Ywer0.
16 Mariah Carey's Playboy cover in 2007: http://www.youtube.com/watch?v=Z2ma_r7Bm7o.
17 Christina Aguilera's Maxim photo shoots: http://www.google.com/search?q=Maxim+Christina+Aguilera+Covers&hl=en&prmd=imvnso&tbm=isch&tbo=u&source=univ&sa=X&ei=4K7oT4X3BYqt0AGQpPz3CQ&ved=0CFIQsAQ&biw=1024&bih=895.
18 Lyrics from M.I.A.'s "Paper Planes."
19 M.I.A. offends at the 2012 Super Bowl: http://www.youtube.com/watch?v=GzOEijWdr6o.
20 Madonna performs at the 2012 Super Bowl aged 53: http://www.youtube.com/watch?v=X3ik_8QjM3U.
21 Alabama Shakes, "Hold On," on David Letterman: http://www.youtube.com/watch?v=sWG-n0CXnrg.

REFERENCES

Preface

Ahlkvist, J. A. and Faulkner, R. (2002) "'Will this Record Work for Us?': Managing Music Formats in Commercial Radio," *Qualitative Sociology*, 25(2), pp189–215.

Coates, N. (1997) "(R)evolution Now? Rock and the Political Potential of Gender," in S. Whiteley (ed) *Sexing the Groove: Popular Music and Gender* (pp50–64), London: Routledge.

Dickerson, J. (1998) *Women on Top: The Quiet Revolution that's Rocking the American Music Industry*, New York, NY: Billboard Books.

Gamson, J. (1994) *Claims to Fame: Celebrity in Contemporary America*, Berkeley, CA: University of California Press.

Marks, C. and Tannenbaum, R. (2011) *I Want My MTV: The Uncensored Story of the Music Television Revolution*, New York, NY: Dutton (Penguin).

McClary, S. (2000) "Women and Music on the Verge of a New Millennium," *Signs*, 25(4), pp1283–1286.

RIAA (Recording Industry Association of America) (2012) http:// www.riaa.com, accessed May 1, 2012.

Chapter 1

Aaker, D. (1991) *Managing Brand Equity*, New York, NY: The Free Press.

Aaker, D. (1995) *Building Strong Brands*, New York, NY: The Free Press.

Baran, S. J. and Davis, D. K. (2003) *Mass Communication Theory*, Belmont, CA: Thomson/ Wadsworth.

Belk, R. W. (1988) "Possessions and the Extended Self," *Journal of Consumer Research*, 15(2), pp139–168.

Berger, P. L. and Luckmann, T. (1966) *The Social Construction of Reality: A Treatise in the Sociology of Knowledge*, Garden City, NY: Doubleday.

Berlo, D. K. (1960) *The Process of Communication*, New York, NY: Hold, Rinehart and Winston.

Blumer, H. (1986) *Symbolic Interactionism: Perspective and Method*, Berkeley, CA: University of California Press.

Blumler, J. G. (1979) *Communication Research*, 6(1), pp9–36.

Connell, R.W. (1987) *Gender and Power: Society, the Person, and Sexual Politics*, Stanford, CA: Stanford University Press.

Cooley, C. H. (1902) *Human Nature and the Social Order*, New York, NY: Charles Scribner's Sons.

Cravens, K. S. and Guilding, C. (1999) "Strategic Brand Valuation: A Cross-Functional Perspective," *Business Horizons*, July/August, pp53–62.

Entman, R. (1993) "Framing: Toward Clarification of a Fractured Paradigm," *Journal of Communication*, pp51–58.

Ferris, K. O. (2007) "The Sociology of Celebrity," *Sociology Compass*, 1(1), September, pp371–384.

Fiske, J. (1992) "British Cultural Studies and Television," in R. C. Allen (ed) *Channels of Discourse, Reassembled* (2nd ed.) (pp284–326), Chapel Hill, NC: University of North Carolina Press.

Fiske, J. (1994) *Understanding Popular Culture*, London: Routledge.

Fiske, J. (1997) *Reading the Popular*, London: Routledge.

Fournier, S. (1998) "Consumers and their Brands: Developing Relationship Theory in Consumer Research," *Journal of Consumer Research*, 24(4), pp343–373.

Fournier, S. and Herman, K. (2004) *Taking Stock in Martha Stewart: Insights into Person-Brand Building and the Cultural Management of Brands*, Unpublished manuscript, Hanover, NH: Tuck School of Business, Dartmouth College.

Fournier, S. and Herman, K. (2006) *Taking Stock in Martha Stewart: Insights into Person-Brand Building and the Cultural Management of Brands*, Unpublished manuscript, Boston, MA: Boston University.

Fournier, S., Solomon, M. R., and Englis, B. G. (2008) "When Brands Resonate," in B. H. Schmidt and D. L. Rogers (eds) *Handbook on Brand and Experience Management* (pp33–57), Northampton, MA: Edward Elgar.

Goffman, E. (1959) *The Presentation of Self in Everyday Life*, New York, NY: Anchor Books.

Goffman, E. (1967) "Gender Display," *Studies in the Anthropology of Visual Communication*, 3, pp69–77.

Grant, J. (2001) *The New Marketing Manifesto*, New York, NY: Texere Publishing, Ltd.

Grazian, D. (2010) *Mix It Up: Popular Culture, Mass Media, and Society*, New York, NY: W. W. Norton and Company.

Hall, S. (1980) "Encoding and Decoding in the Television Discourse," in S. Hall (ed) *Culture, Media, Language*, London, Hutchinson.

Hall, S. (1993) "Encoding and Decoding," in S. During (ed) *The Cultural Studies Reader* (pp90–103), London: Routledge.

Holt, D. B. (2003) "What Becomes an Icon Most?," *Harvard Business Review*, 81(3), pp43–49.

Holt, D. B. (2004) *How Brands Become Icons*, Boston, MA: Harvard Business School Press.

Katz, E. and Lazarsfeld, P. (1955) *Personal Influence: The Part Played by People in the Flow of Mass Communications*, New York, NY: Free Press.

Kotarba, J. and Vannini, P. (2009) *Understanding Society through Popular Music*, New York, NY: Routledge.

McCracken, G. (1986) "Culture and Consumption: A Theoretical Account of the Structure and Movement of the Cultural Meaning of Consumer Goods," *Journal of Consumer Research*, 13(1), pp71–84.

McCracken, G. (1989) "Who Is the Celebrity Endorser? Cultural Foundations of the Endorsement process," *Journal of Consumer Research*, 16(3), pp310–321.

Mead, G. H. (1934) *Mind, Self and Society*, Chicago, IL: University of Chicago Press.

Mead, G. H. (1982) *The Individual and the Social Self: Unpublished Essays by G. H. Mead*, ed. by D. L. Miller, Chicago, IL: University of Chicago Press.

Petty, R. E. and Cacioppo, J. T. (1986) *Communication and Persuasion: Central and Peripheral Routes to Attitude Change*, New York, NY: Springer-Verlag.

Petty, R. E. and Wegener, D. T. (1999) "The Elaboration Likelihood Model: Current Status and Controversies," in S. Chaiken and Y. Trope (eds) *Dual Process Theories in Social Psychology* (pp41–72), New York, NY: Guilford Press.

Rein, I. J., Kotler, P., and Stoller, M. R. (1987) *High Visibility*, New York, NY: Dodd, Mead, and Co.

Rindova, V. P., Pollock, T. G., and Hayward, M. L. (2006) "Celebrity Firms: The Social Construction of Popularity," *Academy of Management Review*, 31(1), pp50–71.

Ruggiero, T. E. (2000) Uses and gratifications theory in the 21st century. *Mass Communication and Society*, 3(1), pp3–37.

Schramm, W. (ed) (1954) *The Process and Effects of Mass Communication*, Urbana, IL: University of Illinois Press.

Schroeder, J. E. (2005) "The Artist and the Brand," *European Journal of Marketing*, 39(11), pp1291–1305.

Shannon, C. E. and Weaver, W. (1949) *The Mathematical Theory of Communication*, Urbana, IL: University of Illinois Press.

Silverman, S. M. (2006) "Fergie: Crystal Meth 'Hardest Boyfriend'," *People Magazine*, 11 September, http://www.people.com/people/article/0,,1533526,00.html.

Solomon, M. R. (1983) "The Role of Products as Social Stimuli: A Symbolic Interactionism Perspective," *Journal of Consumer Research*, 10(3), pp319–329.

Sullivan, A. (1989) "Buying and Nothingness," *The New Republic*, May 8, pp37–41.

Van Munching, P. (2002) "The Devil's Adman," *Brandweek*, November 11, 43(41), p30.

Watson, J. B. (1913) "Psychology as the Behaviorist Views It," *Psychology Review*, 20(2), pp158–177.

West, C. and Zimmerman, D. H. (1987) "Doing Gender," *Gender and Society*, 1(2), pp125–151.

Wipperfurth, A. (2005) *Brand Hijack: Marketing without Marketing*, New York, NY: Penguin.

Chapter 2

Best, J. (2006) *Flavor of the Month: Why Smart People Fall for Fads*, Berkeley, CA: University of California Press.

Christensen, C. (1997) *The Innovator's Dilemma: The Revolutionary Book that Will Change the Way You Do Business*, Boston, MA: Harvard Business Review Press.

Fiske, J. (1992) "British Cultural Studies and Television," in R. C. Allen (ed) *Channels of Discourse, Reassembled* (2nd ed.) (pp284–326), London: Routledge.

Fiske, J. (1997) *Reading the Popular*, London: Routledge.

Fournier, S. and Herman, K. (2004) *Taking Stock in Martha Stewart: Insights into Person-Brand Building and the Cultural Management of Brands*, Unpublished manuscript, Hanover, NH: Tuck School of Business, Dartmouth College.

Fournier, S. and Herman, K. (2006) *Taking Stock in Martha Stewart: Insights into Person-Brand Building and the Cultural Management of Brands*, Unpublished manuscript, Boston, MA: Boston University.

Gladwell, M. (2000) *The Tipping Point: How Little Things Can Make a Big Difference*, New York, NY: Little Brown and Company.

Gottlieb, J. (2011) "Singer Adele's Vocal Cord Surgery in Boston Called a 'Success'," *Boston Herald*, November 7, http://bostonherald.com/entertainment/music/general/view/2011_1107singer_adeles_vocal_cord_surgery_in_boston_called_a_success.

Hall, S. (1980) "Encoding and Decoding in the Television Discourse," in S. Hall (ed) *Culture, Media, Language*, London: Hutchinson.

Herman, D. (2002) *Think Short: Short-Term Brands Revolutionize Branding*, November, http://www.allaboutbranding.com/downloads/a283/Think_Short.pdf, accessed December 1, 2011.

Holt, D. B. (2003) "What Becomes an Icon Most?," *Harvard Business Review*, 81(3), pp43–49.

Holt, D. B. (2004) *How Brands Become Icons*, Boston, MA: Harvard Business School Press.

Keinan, A. and Avery, J. (2008) *Understanding Brands: Case Study*, Boston, MA: Harvard Business Publishing.

Kotler, P. and Armstrong, G. (2011) *Principles of Marketing* (14th ed.), Boston, MA: Prentice Hall.

Lane, V. (1998) "Brand Leverage Power: The Critical Role of Brand Balance," *Business Horizons*, 41(1), pp75–84.

Negus, K. (1999) *Music Genres and Corporate Cultures*, London: Routledge.

RIAA (Recording Industry Association of America) (2012) http://www.riaa.com, accessed May 1, 2012.

Rindova, V. P., Pollock, T. G., and Hayward, M. L. (2006) "Celebrity Firms: The Social Construction of Popularity," *Academy of Management Review*, 31(1), pp50–71.

Chapter 3

Ahlkvist, J. A. and Faulkner, R. (2002) "Will this Record Work for Us? Managing Music Formats in Commercial Radio," *Qualitative Sociology*, 25(2), pp189–215.

Business Wire (2011) "Digital Music Industry Revenues Plummet as Consumers Demand Music Everywhere," *Business Wire*, May 26, http://www.businesswire.com/news/home/20110526006070/en/Digital-Music-Industry-Revenues-Plummet-Consumers-Demand.

Christman, E. (2008) "Dollars & Cents: iTunes Store Has Sold 4 Billion Tracks – But Is It Profitable?," *Billboard*, March 15, http://www.billboard.biz/bbbiz/content_display/industry/news/e3i174d24f4a4bd6a9273308815a9663bfc.

Christman, E. (2010) "Slipped Disc," *Billboard*, 122, October 16, p5.

Christman, E. (2011a) "Mixed Tidings U.S. Album Sales Fall 12.8% in 2010, Digital Tracks Eke Out 1% Gain," *Billboard*, January 8, http://www.billboard.com/news/u-s-album-sales-fall-12-8-in-2010-digital-1004137859.story#/news/u-s-album-sales-fall-12-8-in-2010-digital-1004137859.story.

Christman, E. (2011b) "Rap, Non-traditional Retail Are Bright Spots in Glum 2010 Year-End Numbers," *Billboard*, January 6, http://www.billboard.biz/bbbiz/industry/retail/rap-non-traditional-retail-are-bright-spots-1004138189.story.

Christman, E. (2012) "Universal Music Group Tops Sony to Lead 2012 Mid-Year Market Share," *Billboard*, July 5, http://www.billboard.biz/bbbiz/industry/record-labels/universal-music-group-squeaks-past-sony-1007508952.story.

Edgecliff-Johnson, A. and Nuttall, C. (2011) "Amazon's new front in the digital media war," *Financial Times*, March 30, 2011.

Elberse, A. (2008) "Should You Invest in the Long Tail?," *Harvard Business Review*, July/August, pp1–9.

Fried, I. (2003) "Will iTunes Make Apple Shine?," *CNET*, October 16, http://news.cnet.com/2100-1041-5092559.html.

Jobs, S. (2007) *Thoughts on Music*, http://www.apple.com/hotnews/thoughtsonmusic/, accessed February 6, 2007.

Kirk, M. (director) (2004) "The Way the Music Died," Television series episode, May 27, in M. Kirk (producer) *Frontline*, New York, NY: Public Broadcasting System.

Lewin, K. (1947) "Frontiers in Group Dynamics," *Human Relations*, 1(2), p145.

McCracken, G. (1986) "Culture and Consumption: A Theoretical Account of the Structure and Movement of the Cultural Meaning of Consumer Goods," *Journal of Consumer Research*, 13(1), pp71–84.

McCracken, G. (1989) "Who Is the Celebrity Endorser? Cultural Foundations of the Endorsement Process," *Journal of Consumer Research*, 16(3), pp310–321.

McNeill, B. (2011) "Apple's Steve Jobs Unveils iCloud," *SNL Kagan Media and Communications Report*, June 7, ABI/INFORM Trade and Industry, Document ID: 2371501961, accessed April 17, 2012.

Miller, R. K. (2008) *The 2009 Entertainment, Media and Advertising Market Research Handbook*, Loganville, GA: Richard K. Miller and Associates.

Negus, K. (1999) *Music Genres and Corporate Cultures*, London: Routledge.

Radio Dimensions (2010) New York, NY: Media Dynamics.

RIAA (Recording Industry Association of America) (2006) http://www.riaa.com, accessed May 1, 2006.

RIAA (2008) *2008 Consumer Profile*, http://web.archive.org/web/20100820202007/http://76.74.24.142/8EF388DA-8FD3-7A4E-C208-CDF1ADE8B179.pdf.

RIAA (2012) http://www.riaa.com, accessed May 1, 2012.

Segal, D. (2004) "Requiem for the Record Store: Downloaders and Discounters Are Driving Out Music Retailers," *Washington Post*, February 7, pA01.

Semuels, A. (2006) "Tower Records to Sell Off Inventory: Liquidation Specialist Great American Group, which Bought the Bankrupt Music Retailer for $134.3 Million, Plans To Close All 89 Stores," *Los Angeles Times*, October 7, pC2.

Shoemaker, P. J. (1991) *Gatekeeping*, Newbury Park, CA: Sage.

Smith, E. (2007) "Sales of Music, Long in Decline, Plunge Sharply," *Wall Street Journal*, March 21, http://online.wsj.com/article/SB117444575607043728.html.

Specter, M. and Trachtenberg, J. (2011) "Borders Forced to Liquidate, Close All Stores,"
    Wall Street Journal, July 19, http://online.wsj.com/article/SB10001424052702303661904576454353768550280.html.

Telecommunications Weekly (2011) "Strategy Analytics: U.S. Digital Music Sales Will
    Overtake CDs in 2012," *Telecommunications Weekly*, April 13, p1105.

Van Buskirk, E. (2012) "iTunes App Store: 30 Billion Downloads. $7.14 Billion in
    Revenue," *Billboard*, 11 June, http://www.billboard.biz/bbbiz/industry/digital-and-
    mobile/itunes-app-store-30-billion-downloads-7-1007294562.story.

Wills, R. (2011) "CDs Going the Way of Records, 8-Tracks, Cassette Tape," *Tribune
    Business News (McClatchy)*, May 26.

Chapter 4

Bruni, F. (2010) "Good Girls Gone Wild," *New York Times*, October 29, http://www.
    nytimes.com/2010/10/31/fashion/31Starlet.html?_r=1andpagewanted=print.

Erlewine, S. T. (2008) "Review: Katy Perry's 'One of the Boys'," *Allmusic*, http://www.
    allmusic.com/album/r1388803, accessed 11 March 2012.

Gregory, R. (2004) *Unwelcome and Unlawful: Sexual Harassment in the American Workplace*,
    Ithaca, NY: Cornell University Press.

Heath, C. (1998) "Fiona Apple: The Caged Bird Sings," *Rolling Stone*, 778, January,
    pp30–36, 68.

Hirschberg, L. (1992) "Strange Love," *Vanity Fair*, September, pp230–233.

Junod, T. (2001) "The Devil in Greg Dark," *Esquire*, 135, February 1, pp128–135.

Khan, A. (2011) "'Death by Misadventure': Amy Winehouse and Alcohol Poisoning,'
    Los Angeles Times, October 27, http://articles.latimes.com/2011/oct/27/news/
    la-heb-amy-winehouse-blood-alcohol-20111027.

Pareles, J. (2005) "The Lost Apple," *The New York Times*, April 3, http://www.nytimes.
    com/2005/04/03/arts/music/03pareles.html.

Perez, R. (2005) "Whatever Happened to Fiona Apple? Online Campaign Tries to Find
    Out," *MTV News*, January 26, http://www.mtv.com/news/articles/1496301/whatever-
    happened-fiona-apple.jhtml.

Chapter 5

Ask.com (2012) "Whitney Houston obituary," Aks.com. (2012). Retrieved June 28, 2012,
    from http://www.ask.com/web?q=whitney%20houston%20obituary&askid=7fc2fb83-
    76a3-4a19-bf66-fb43f7ce68d2-0-us_gsb&kv=sdb&dqi=whitney%20houston%20
    cause%20of%20death%20tmz&qsrc=999&o=102246&l=dir

Boucher, G. (2007) "Rock pioneer was known for abusing wife Tina Turner," *L.A. Times*,
    December 13, http://articles.latimes.com/2007/dec/13/local/me-turner13.

Caputi, J. (2003) "Everyday Pornography," in G. Dines and J. M. Humez (eds)
    Gender, Race, and Class in Media (2nd ed.) (pp434–450), Thousand Oaks, CA:
    Sage.

Clarke, E. and Chin, S. (2012) "We Now Pronounce: The Most Extravagant Celebrity
    Weddings (Celine Dion and Rene Angelil)," *iVillage*, June 11, http://www.i
    village.com/celine-dion-rene-angelil-wedding/1-b-123448, accessed
    June 28, 2012.

Ehrlich, K. (producer) and Horvitz, L. J. (director) (2012) *54th Annual Grammy Awards*, Television broadcast, February 12, New York, NY: CBS.

Ellis, J. (2007) "Stars as Cinematic Phenomenon," in S. Redmond and S. Holmes (eds) *Stardom and Celebrity: A Reader* (pp90–97), Thousand Oaks, CA: Sage.

Ganz, C. (2010) "The Curious Case of Nicki Minaj," http://www.out.com/entertainment/music/2010/09/12/curious-case-nicki-minaj?page=0,1, September 12.

Gorman, B. (2012a) "Complete List of 2011–12 Season TV Show Ratings: *Sunday Night Football* Tops, Followed by *American Idol, The Voice and Modern Family*," *TV by the Numbers*, 24 May, http://tvbythenumbers.zap2it.com/2012/05/24/final-list-of-2011-12-season-tv-show-ratings-sunday-night-football-tops-followed-by-american-idol-the-voice-modern-family/135747/, accessed June 28, 2012.

Gorman, B. (2012b) "Complete List of 2011–12 Season TV Show Viewership: *Sunday Night Football* Tops, Followed by *American Idol, NCIS* and *Dancing with the Stars*," *TV by the Numbers*, 24 May, http://tvbythenumbers.zap2it.com/2012/05/24/complete-list-of-2011-12-season-tv-show-viewership-sunday-night-football-tops-followed-by-american-idol-ncis-dancing-with-the-stars/135785/, accessed June 28, 2012.

Hirschberg, L. (1992) "Strange Love," *Vanity Fair*, September, pp230–233.

Jill, J. (2011) "Courtney Love Talks Helping Amy Winehouse: 'I Tried Twice'," *Examiner*, July 24, http://www.examiner.com/article/courtney-love-talks-helping-amy-winehouse-i-tried-twice.

Kilbourne, J. and Jhally, S. (directors) (2010) *Killing Us Softly 4*, DVD, Northampton, MA: Media Education Foundation.

Lester, P. (2010) *Lady Gaga: Looking for Fame – the Life of a Pop Princess*, New York, NY: Omnibus Press.

Mock, J. and Wang, J. (2012) "Mariah Carey," *People Magazine*, http://www.people.com/people/mariah_carey/0,,,00.html.

O'Connor, S. (2010) "Character Study: Just How Real Is Nicki Minaj?," *Vibe*, June 23, http://www.vibe.com/article/character-study-just-how-real-nicki-minaj-pg-2.

"Return to Las Vegas" (2012) *Celine Dion website*, http://www.celinedion.com/return-las-vegas, accessed June 28, 2012.

RIAA (Recording Industry Association of America) (2012) http://www.riaa.com, accessed May 1, 2012.

Sheffield, R. (2011) "*The Voice*: Idol's Wild Child," *Rolling Stone*, 1132, June 9, p38.

Thomson, D. (2004) *The New Bibliographic Dictionary of Film*, New York, NY: Alfred A. Knopf.

TMZ Staff. (2012a). "Whitney Houston: Family told she died from Rx NOT drowning." TMZ.com. Retrieved June 28, 2012, from http://www.tmz.com/2012/02/13/whitney-houston-cause-of-death-prescription-drugs-drowning-atlanta/

TMZ Staff. (2012b). "Whitney Houston: Cocaine in system at time of death." TMZ.com. Retrieved June 28, 2012, from http://www.tmz.com/2012/03/22/whitney-houston-cause-of-death-drowning-cocaine/

TMZ Staff. (2012c). "L.A. coroner's Whitney report: Drug spoon & coke found, possible overdose." TMZ.com. Retrieved June 28, 2012, from http://www.tmz.com/2012/04/04/whitney-houston-autopsy-cocaine-residue/

US Weekly (2010) "Ke$ha Talks about Puking in Paris Hilton's Closet, Breaking into Prince's House," *US Weekly*, January 20, http://www.usmagazine.com/entertainment/

news/keha-talks-about-puking-in-paris-hiltons-closet-breaking-into-princes-house-2010201.

Weagle, S. (2002) "Mottola, Tommy," in *Encyclopedia.com*, http://www.encyclopedia.com/topic/Tommy_Mottola.aspx.

Weiner, J. (2010) "Nicki Minaj: Hip-Hop's Hottest Sidekick Goes Solo," http://www.details.com/celebrities-entertainment/music-and-books/201005/hip-hop-artist-nicki-minaj, May.

Winfrey, O. and Turner, T. (2005) "Oprah Talks to Tina Turner," *O, the Oprah Magazine*, May, http://www.oprah.com/omagazine/Oprahs-Interview-with-Tina-Turner/.

Chapter 6

Adorno, T. W. (1990 [1941]) "On Popular Music," in S. Frith and D. Goodwin (eds) *On the Record: Rock, Pop, and the Written Word* (pp301–314), New York, NY: Routledge.

Althusser, L. (1977) *Lenin and Philosophy and Other Essays*, London: New Left Books.

Andsager, J. (2005) "Seduction, Shock, and Sales: Research and Functions of Sex in Music Video," in T. Reichert and J. Lambiase (eds) *Sex in Consumer Culture: The Erotic Content of Media and Marketing* (pp31–50), New York, NY: Lawrence Erlbaum and Associates.

APA (2007) *Report of the APA Task Force on the Sexualization of Girls*, Washington, DC: American Psychological Association.

Archer, D., Iritani, B., Kimes, D. D., and Barrios, M. (1983) "Face-ism: Five Studies of Sex Difference in Facial Prominence," *Journal of Personality and Social Psychology*, 45, pp725–735.

Bandura, A. (1976) *Social Learning Theory*, Upper Saddle River, NJ: Prentice Hall.

Bendix, T. (2010) "Nicky Minaj Says She's Not Really Bisexual," AfterEllen.com, June 18, http://www.afterellen.com/blog/trishbendix/nicki-minaj-says-shes-not-bisexual.

Berger, J. (1972) *Ways of Seeing*, New York, NY: Penguin.

Boehlert, E. (1995) "The Modern Age," *Billboard*, 107(20), May 20, p97.

Butler, J. (1990) *Gender Trouble: Feminism and the Subversion of Identity*, London: Routledge.

Caputi, J. (2003) "Everyday Pornography," in G. Dines and J. M. Humez (eds) *Gender, Race, and Class in Media* (2nd ed.) (pp434–450), Thousand Oaks, CA: Sage.

Crain, R. (1997) "Viewpoint: Who Knows What Ads Lurk in the Hearts of Consumers? The Inner Mind Knows," *Advertising Age*, 68(23), June 9, p25.

Diamond, L. (2005) "'I'm Straight, but I Kissed a Girl': The Trouble with American Media Representations of Female–Female Sexuality," *Feminism and Psychology*, 15(1), pp104–110.

Elberse, A. (2008) "Should you Invest in the Long Tail?," *Harvard Business Review*, July/August, pp1–9.

Ellis, J. (2003) "Stars as Cinematic Phenomenon," in S. Redmond and S. Holmes (eds) *Stardom and Celebrity: A Reader* (pp90–97), Thousand Oaks, CA: Sage.

Fiske, J. (1997) *Reading the Popular*, London: Routledge.

Fortuijn, J. D., Horn, A., and Ostendorf, W. (2004) "'Gendered Spaces' in Urban and Rural Contexts: An Introduction," *GeoJournal*, 61(3), pp215–217.

Frederickson, B. L. and Roberts, T. A. (1997) "Objectification Theory: Toward Understanding Women's Lived Experiences and Mental Health Risks," *Psychology of Women Quarterly*, 21, pp173–206.

Frederickson, B. L., Roberts, T., Noll, S. M., Quinn, D. M., and Twenge, J. M. (1998) "That Swimsuit Becomes You: Sex Differences in Self-Objectification, Restrained Eating, and Math Performance," *Journal of Personality and Social Psychology*, 75(1), pp269–284.

French, M. (1985) *Beyond Power: On Women, Men, and Morals*, New York, NY: Ballantine Books.

Gamson, J. (1994) *Claims to Fame: Celebrity in Contemporary America*, Berkeley, California: University of California Press.

Gerbner, G. (1998) "Cultivation Analysis: An Overview," *Mass Communication and Society*, 1(3/4), pp175–194.

Gerbner, G., Gross, L., Morgan, M. and Signorelli, N. (2002) "Growing Up with Television: The Cultivation Perspective," in J. Bryant and D. Zillmann (eds) *Media Effects: Advances in Theory and Research* (pp43–68), Hillsdale, NJ: Lawrence Erlbaum Associates.

Glennie, A. (2012) "Madonna Sets a New Record for Most No. 1 Albums by Solo Singer with New Release," *MDNA: MailOnline*, April 1, http://www.dailymail.co.uk/tvshowbiz/article-2123764/Madonna-sets-new-record-No-1-albums-solo-singer-new-release-MDNA.html.

Gottlieb, J. (2011) "Singer Adele's Vocal Cord Surgery in Boston Called a 'Success'," *Boston Herald*, November 7, http://bostonherald.com/entertainment/music/general/view/2011_1107singer_adeles_vocal_cord_surgery_in_boston_called_a_success.

Gramsci, A. (1971) *Selections from Prison Notebooks* (Q. Hoare and G. Nowell–Smith, trans.), London: Lawrence and Wishart.

Greenberg, B. S., Mastro, D., and Brand, J. E. (2002) "Minorities and the Mass Media: Television into the 21st Century," in J. Bryant and D. Zillmann (eds) *Media Effects: Advances in Theory and Research* (pp333–351), New York: Routledge.

Gross, L. (2001) *Up from Invisibility: Lesbians, Gay Men, and the Media in America*, New York, NY: Columbia University Press.

Halberstam, J. (2010) "You Cannot Gaga Gaga," Blog post, March 17, http://bullybloggers.wordpress.com/2010/03/17/you-cannot-gaga-gaga-by-jack-halberstam/.

Hall, S. (1980) "Notes on Deconstructing the Popular," in R. Samuel (ed) *People's History and Socialist Theory* (pp227–249), London: Routledge.

Hall, S. (1993) "Encoding and Decoding," in S. During (ed) *The Cultural Studies Reader* (pp90–103), London: Routledge.

Hall, S. and Whannel, P. (1964) "The Young Audience," in S. Frith and A. Goodwin (eds) *On Record: Rock, Pop and the Written Word* (pp27–37), New York, NY: Routledge.

Heath, C. (1998) "Fiona Apple: The Caged Bird Sings," *Rolling Stone*, 778, January, pp30–36, 68.

Hesmondhalgh, D. (2002) *The Cultural Industries*, London: Sage.

Jessica G. (2008) "Tila Tequila: Good or Bad for Bisexual Women?," Blog post, September 4, http://jezebel.com/5045532/tila-tequila-good-or-bad-for-bisexual-women

Judd, A. (2012) "Ashley Judd Slaps Media in the Face for Speculation Over Her 'Puffy' Appearance," *The Daily Beast*, April 9, http://www.thedailybeast.com/articles/2012/04/09/ashley-judd-slaps-media-in-the-face-for-speculation-over-her-puffy-appearance.html, accessed April 10, 2012.

Junod, T. (2001) "The Devil in Greg Dark," *Esquire*, 135, February 12, pp128–135.

Kaplan, E. A. (1987) *Rocking Around the Clock: Music, Television, Post Modernism and Consumer Culture*, New York, NY: Routledge.

Kendall, E. (1962) "Success (?) of the Starmakers," *The New York Times*, September 30, pp37–40.

Kilbourne, J. (1999) *Can't Buy My Love*, New York, NY: Simon and Schuster.

Kilbourne, J. and Jhally, S. (directors) (2010) *Killing Us Softly 4*, DVD, Northampton, MA: Media Education Foundation.

Lapatine, S. (2008) "Juliana Hatfield Blogs from Eating Disorder Treatment Center," *Stereogum*, November 10, http://stereogum.com/34221/juliana_hatfield_blogs_from_eating_disorder_treatm/news/.

Lieb, K. (2007) *Pop Tarts and Body Parts: An Exploration of the Imaging and Brand Management of Female Popular Music Stars*, DPhil thesis, Syracuse University, Syracuse, NY, Umi/ProQuest, Microform 3281727.

Longhurst, R. (2000) "'Corporeographies' of Pregnancy: 'Bikini Babes'," *Environment and Planning D: Society and Space*, 18(4), pp453–472.

Martin, J. (undated) "Kelly Clarkson: 'I'm Over' People Scrutinizing My Weight," *Access Hollywood*, http://www.accesshollywood.com/kelly-clarkson-im-over-people-scrutinizing-my-weight_video_1368982, accessed April 5, 2012.

McCombs, M. E. and Shaw, D. L. (1972) "The Agenda-Setting Function of Mass Media," *Public Opinion Quarterly*, 36(2), pp176–187.

McCracken, G. (1989) "Who Is the Celebrity Endorser? Cultural Foundations of the Endorsement Process," *Journal of Consumer Research*, 16(3), pp310–321.

Morgan, M. (2002) "Growing Up with Television: The Cultivation Perspective," in M. Morgan (ed) *Against the Mainstream: The Selected Works of George Gerber* (pp193–213), New York, NY: Peter Lang.

MSN (2010) "Demi Lovato Cancels Tour, Checks into Rehab," *MSN Entertainment*, 1 November, http://music.msn.com/music/article.aspx?news=608954.

Mulvey, L. (1975) "Visual Pleasure and Narrative Cinema," in L. Braudy and M. Cohen (eds) *Film Theory and Criticism*, New York, NY: Oxford University Press.

NPR (2012) "Alabama Shakes: Full of 'Southern soul'," *NPR Music*, April 11, http://www.npr.org/2012/04/11/150445845/alabama-shakes-full-of-southern-soul.

Quinn, D. M., Kallen, R. W., and Cathey, C. (2006) "Body On My Mind: The Lingering Effect of State Self-Objectification," *Sex Roles*, 55(11/12), pp869–874.

Rose, G. (1993) *Feminism and Geography: The Limits of Geographical Knowledge*, Minneapolis, MN: University of Minnesota Press.

Safer, M. (2011) "The Many Meryls," Television series episode, in D. Browning (Producer), *60 Minutes*, December 18, New York, NY: CBS Broadcasting Inc.

Spain, D. (1992) *Gendered Spaces*, Chapel Hill, NC: University of North Carolina Press.

Szymanski, D. M. and Henning, S. L. (2007) "The Role of Self-Objectification in Women's Depression: A Test of Objectification Theory," *Sex Roles*, 56(1/2), pp45–53.

Van Munching, P. (2002) "The Devil's Adman," *Brandweek*, 43(41), November 11, p30.

West, C. and Zimmerman, D. H. (1987) "Doing Gender," *Gender and Society*, 1(2), pp125–151.

Wolf, N. (2002) *The Beauty Myth: How Images of Beauty Are Used Against Women*, New York, NY: Harper Perennial.

INDEX

Note: 'N' after a page number indicates a note; 'f' indicates a figure; 't' indicates a table.

Aaker, D.: and brands 17; and cultural resonance 23

Abdul, Paula: as brand 59, 61

accessibility: xviii; of artists in *temptress* phase 40, 58–61, 89, 102

AC/DC: and Bon Scott 167

Adams, Peter: xxi; on artists in *temptress* phase 106; on exoticism 115

Addiction: 123–5

Adele: *21* cover 116, 143, 172n3; as potential *career artist* 45–6; as *exotic* 114, 116; people to watch 166–7; as the *provocateur* 118;

Adorno, Theodor: and popularity 137–8; and production of popular culture 156

advertisers: and brand strength and brand equity 17; and celebrity brands xviii; and *Cultural Diamond* 53; and everyday pornography 122, 153; subconscious power of 163

age: as critical to artists' success 89, 101, 103; of Madonna 91, 156, 168; of male artists 94; youth as requirement for artists' success 95, 97, 113

Agron, Dianna: and good girls growing up 96

Aguilera, Christina: and "Beautiful" (video) 107, 171n23; brand management of 28–30; as career artist 42; comebacks of 64–5; *comeback/redemption* phase of 133–4; "Dirrty" (video) 121, 150–1, 172n11; as gay icon 129; lifecycle model of female artists 91; and *Maxim* 122, 172n11; and motherhood 122; and National Anthem 29, 170n22; as temptress 152; on *The Voice* (tv show) 159–60; *whore* phase of 119, 121–2

Ahlkvist, J. A.: and Will This Record Work for Us? xviii

Aiken, Clay: and popular culture 158

Alabama Shakes: and Brittany Howard as promising emerging artist 167–8; "Hold On" (TV performance) 173n21

Allen, Lily: as bad girl, not conforming to "*good girl*" type 99

Almighty Music Marketing 75

Althusser, Louis: and ISAs 145–6

Amazon 69, 74–5, 77–8

American Idol: 45, 59, 85, 157–8, 160, 171n16

Andsager, Julie: and feminine types in music videos 149–50, 152–3

Angelil, René: and protected status 127

appearance: importance of beauty and sex appeal for female artists 88, 107–8; thinness as requirement for artists' success 97, 102–3, 143, 154, 167; unimportance of, for male artists 94;

youth as requirement for artists' success 89, 101, 103, 113. *See also* sexuality

Apple 22, 69–70, 77–8. *See also* iTunes

Apple, Fiona: and "Criminal" (video) 99, 171n13; and eating disorders 154–156; as not conforming to *good girl* type 99–101, 171n14; and objectification 154–5

Archer, D.: and the male gaze 142–3

Armstrong, G.: and contemporary notions of brand 36

audiences: and agency of 7, 12–13, 20–1; and bi-directional brand meaning 56–7; and brand meaning as derived from 21; and critical theory view of 4; and popularity 138–9; and reaction to Lady Gaga's "Jo Calderone" 8, 170n10; as receivers of popular culture 3; and retail music sales 76–7; and women as 112

Austin Powers in Goldmember (movie): 98

authenticity: xx, 61–5

"Bad Romance" (Lady Gaga video): 1–2, 151, 169n4 (ch1)

Bandura, Albert: and social learning theory 140

"Beautiful" (Christina Aguilera video): 107, 171n23

"Beautiful Liar" (Beyoncé and Shakira video) 52, 170n3

beauty. *See* sexuality

Bedingfield, Natasha: as short-term brand 42

Belk, R. W.: and brands 24

Benatar, Pat: xvi; "You Better Run" (video) xvi, 169n4

Bendix, Trish: and pop stars and sexuality 147–8

Berger, John: and the male gaze 141

Berger, P. L.: and the social construction of the social world 6

Berlo, D. K.: and communication models 10–11

Beyoncé: and alternate identity of 56, 170n5; and "Beautiful Liar" (video) 52, 170n3; and brand extensions of 50, 52–3; as career artist 41t, 42; as exotic 114; as good girl 98–9; and "Hey Goldmember" (video) 98, 171n10; and *Sports Illustrated* 106, 151, 171n21; as temptress 106

Bieber, Justin: and brand strength 17; and gatekeeping 79; and gender differences 93

Billboard: and 1990s sales charts xvi; and Anthony Colombo xxi, 106; and Janet Billig-Rich xxi; Eric Boehlert 148; and charts measuring popularity of music 84; and Destiny's Child 98; and Fergie's *The Dutchess* 27; and major labels 71; and music consumers 76; and music industry gatekeepers 80; and physical CD sales 68–69, 75–76; and radio programming 84; and retail chain closures and sales losses in recent years 76; on Jill Sobule 148

Billig-Rich, Janet: on Adele 116; on Aguilera 134; on authenticity 63; on brand extension 54–5; on career artists vs. others 44–5; on lack of sex appeal as obstacle 107; on Lavigne 106; on Lisa Loeb 49; on Courtney Love 125

bisexuality: and Nicki Minaj 117; pop stars and sexuality 146–9

blockbuster model: 83–5

"Blown Away" (Carrie Underwood video) 103, 171n15

blues genre: 96–7

Blumer, Herbert: and symbolic interactionism and behaviorism 5

BMG Music Entertainment 71

Boehlert, Eric: on Jill Sobule and bisexuality 148

Borders: 75

boy bands 92–3, video montage of 171n5

brand equity 17–8, 23, 27

brand extensions 49–54, 62–3

brand meaning: and creators of 19; and customer attachment 18–19; Fournier on 19; as residing in and co-created by audiences 21

brand/brands: and *American Idol* vs. *The Voice* 160–1; and artists as managers of 15–16; and creation of, by celebrity firms 32–4; and Cultural Diamond framework 14–16; as cultural objects 14; and cultural resonance 22–4; definition of 36; financial value of 17–18; and gender issues 26; and multivocality of 24–5; and narrative constructions 23; and short-term nature of 37–9; and strength and equity of 17–18; and theoretical gaps regarding 36–9; and typology of, for female artists 40–3. *See also* person brands

Brion, Jon: and Fiona Apple 100

Brown, Chris: and facial prominence 143; and *F.A.M.E.* album cover 143, 173n7

Bruni, Frank: and temptress phase 96
Bullock, Anna Mae. *See* Turner, Tina
Butler, Judith: and gender performance
    139–41

"Can't Be Tamed" (Miley Cyrus video):
    108, 171n27
Caputi, J.: and everyday pornography 122,
    151–152
Cardoso, Lisa: biography xxi; and licensing
    and sponsorship 70–1
career artists: and definition of 42; and
    music industry view of 44–6; and
    typology of 40–1
Carey, Mariah: and brand extensions of 50;
    and *comeback/redemption* phase of 130–1;
    as *diva* 113; as *exiled* 126; as *good girl* 95;
    and motherhood 131–2; and *Playboy*
    106, 151, 171n20; as *protected* 126–7;
    sales of 42; as *temptress* 106, 151
Case, Neko: as indie star 41
celebrities, as *cultural objects*: 136
celebrity culture, and the study of: 12–13
celebrity endorsers: 25–6
celebrity firms: 32–4
"Celebrity Skin" (Hole video):171n12
Cher: xvi; and the *gay icon* 128–9
Christensen, C.: and technology in music
    business 32
Christman, E.: and digital music market
    68–9; labels 71–2; retail 76
Claims to Fame (Gamson): xviii
Clarkson, Kelly: as *career artist* 42, 45;
    as *the temptress* 102; and the
    objectification 154; 167
Clear Channel: 84
Coates, Norma: and gendering of rock
    music xx
Coca-Cola: 17
Cole, Paula: and Fiona Apple 100
Collaborations: 52–3
Colombo, Anthony: on *temptress* phase 106
comeback/redemption phase: 130–4
communication theory: 9–12
consumer culture theorists (CCTs): 18
consumers. *See* audiences
Cooley, Charles Horton: and symbolic
    interactionism 5
country music genre: 98
Cowell, Simon: and artist accessibility 59
Crain, Rance: and underrepresentation and
    sexualization of women 163
Cravens, K. S.: and brand value 17–18

creators, definition of: 2
"Criminal" (Fiona Apple video): 99, 171n13
critical theory: 4
Crow, Sheryl: and a *change of focus*:111–12
cultivation theory: 157–8
cultural consumption: 157
Cultural Diamond (Griswold): 2
Cultural Diamond framework: and artist
    brands 14–16; and *creators* as component
    part of 2, 3, 8, 11, 14, 16, 67–8, 76, 164;
    and *cultural objects* as component part of
    xix, 2, 3, 7, 14, 16, 53, 76, 88, 136–8, 144,
    and cultural resonance 22; and music
    industry 76; overview of 2–3, 3f; and
    popularity 138; and *receivers* as
    component part of 2, 3, 7, 9, 11, 16, 39,
    88, 135, 162, 164; and the *social world* as
    component part of xix, 2, 3, 6–9, 14–6,
    20–6, 37, 49, 53, 67, 74, 88, 111–2,
    118–21, 132, 137–8, 163–5; and view
    of audiences 20
cultural objects: brands as 14; celebrities as
    136; definition of 2; pop stars as 53, 138
cultural resonance: 22–4
Cyrus, Miley: and *Can't Be Tamed* album
    cover 109, 172n30; and "Can't Be
    Tamed" (video) 108, 171n27; as female
    pop star 64; as the *good girl* 95, 109; and
    Hannah Montana album 109, 172n29;
    and penis cake 108, 171n28; as the
    temptress 108–109

Dark, Gregory: and *good girls* 101–2;
    feminine types in music videos 150;
    and pornography 150
Davis, Clive: and the *diva* 113; and
    Whitney Houston 127–8
Davis, Frenchie: and challenging
    contemporary notions of pop stars 133,
    172n16
death: 38; and Amy Winehouse 99, 123–4;
    and Whitney Houston 127–8, 130
Destiny's Child 98; and "Emotion" (video)
    98, 171n9
Dickerson, James: xvii; and perfect formula
    for female artists
DiFranco, Ani: and road warrior 41
DioGuardi, Kara: and *Maxim* 107, 171n24;
    and songwriting 107; and *temptress* 107
Dion, Celine: and the *diva* 113; and
    protected status 126–7; and "Return to
    Las Vegas" (show) 126, 172n14; and
    self–imposed exile 126

"Dirrty" (Christina Aguilera video): 121, 150–1, 172n11

distribution: 77

diva phase: 113–14

Dreese, Mike: and retail 75

Dupri, Jermaine: and Mariah Carey 131

eating disorders: as part of "culture of anorexia" 103; and Fiona Apple 99, 154–5; and Juliana Hatfield 154; and Demi Lovato 154; and objectification theory 154–5, 164

Elaboration Likelihood Model: and audience processing of media messages 11

Elberse, Anita: and blockbuster model 83; and technological changes in entertainment distribution: 138

EMI Group PLC: 71–2

"Emotion" (Destiny's Child video): 98, 171n9

Erlewine, S. T.: and Katy Perry 109

Etheridge, Melissa: xx; and a *change of focus* 111–12

everyday pornography: 151–3. *See also* pornography and Caputi, Jane.

exotic phase: 114–18

"Express Yourself" (Madonna video): 150–1

Facebook: 72

facial prominence: 142–3

"Fame" (Lady Gaga perfume): 170n2

Fantasia: as short-term brand 42

Faulkner, R.: xviii

Fauxmosexuality: definition 147; and Nicki Minaj 147

female artists: and accessibility of 58–61; and brand-building process of 16–17; as *cultural object* 2; and the explicit sexuality of 106–7; and gender performance 140; and management and sales strategies for 43–4; and MTV's effect on the careers of xv; and opportunities available to, vs. male artists 8, 26–7; and organizing principles for managing 39–51; and the rise of, in the 1990s xvi–xvii; and sales of xvii; and sales typology for 40–3, 41t; and sex appeal as a critical marketing tool for xvii–xviii, 84–5, 164; and the sexualization of 92–4, 110, 152–3.

as *short–term person brands* 39, 46–9; *See also* appearance; and The *Lifecycle Model for Female Popular Music Stars*; pop stars; sexuality; sexualization; specific artists

feminist geography: and Rose, Longhurst, Spain, Fortuijn 161

"Fergalicious" (Fergie video): 142, 151, 169n5

Fergie: and the brand management of 27–8; and the "Fergalicious" (video) 142, 151, 169n5; and formulas for female artists' success xvii; and the male gaze 142

Ferris, Kerry: and popular culture studies 12

Film: 71, 141–2

Fiske, John: and brands 21; and popular culture 156–9

Florence + The Machine: xi; and licensing/song placement in television and film 51

Fournier, Susan: and brand extension 46; and brand meaning 17, 19; and managing person-brands 60; and multivocality of brands 24; and need for interdisciplinary thinking 47; and person-brand evolution 34–5; and person vs. product brands 39; and unintended brand meanings 21

Franklin, Aretha: and the *legend* 129

Frederickson, B. L.: and objectification 139, 153–4

French, M.: and power 151

Friedberger, Eleanor: and insignificant seller 41

Funny or Die (website): xvi

Gamson, J.: xviii

Gatekeepers: 78–84, 80t, 82f

gay icon phase: 128–9

gendered space: and popularity 139; and feminist geography 161; and construction and performance of gender: 161

gender issues: and brand construction of male vs. female artists 26; and femininity of pop music xx; and the male gaze 141–4; and opportunities available to female vs. male artists 8; Riley on 134; sexualization of male vs. female artists 92–4, 110; and weight loss of 103

gender performance 139–41

Gerbner, George: and cultural consumption 157–8

Germanotta, Stefani. *See* Lady Gaga

"Girlfriend" (Avril Lavigne video): 105, 171n18

girl groups: 98

Glee (tv show): 95–6, 171n8

Glickman, Simon: on artists' sexuality 93–4; on brand extension 53; on brand homogeneity 48; on Carey 131; on female artists 17; on Jones 115; on Lavigne 105; on Madonna 132; on sexuality as distraction 121

Goffman, Erving: and social roles, 5; and impression management, 5; *Cultural Diamond* 5; and Gaga 5–6

good girl phase: for blues and R&B genres 97–8; definition of 94–5, 110; and transition into adult roles 95–7

Gramsci, Antonio: and hegemony 144

Grant, John: and brand meaning 19

Grazian, D.: and critical theory 4

Green, Cee-Lo: and gender differences 92

Gregory, Raymond: and objectification 107–8

Griswold, Wendy: and the *Cultural Diamond* 2–3

Gross, Larry: and cultural consumption 158

Gross, Terry: and Alabama Shakes 167

Guilding, C.: and brand value 17–18

Halberstam, Judith (Jack): and gender 141

Hall, Stuart: and brands 35; and popularity 138; and cultural objects 146

Hanley, Kay: on applying artist learning to bands she manages 57–8; on applying artist learning to bands she manages 57–8; bio xxii; on brand and brand extension 49; brand meaning 56–7, 59, 65; on being a behind-the-scenes player 57; on brand differentiation 65; on "Dirrty" 121; unlikely extensions 59

Harvey, PJ: and indie star 41

Hatfield, Juliana: xxii; on blockbuster model 85; and eating disorders 154; and objectification 154

Heart: xv, 169n1

Heath, C.: and objectification 154–6

Hegemony: 144–6, 148

Henning, S. L.: and objectification 154

Herman, Dan: and short-term brands 37, 39, 46–7, 60

Herman, K.: and celebrity firms 34–5

Herman, Kerry: and *social world* 53

Hesmondhalgh, David: and cultural studies 159

Heteroflexibility: definition 147; and Katy Perry 147

"Hey Goldmember" (Beyoncé video): 98, 171n10

High Visibility (Rein et al): 13

Hill, Faith: and feminine types in music videos 150

Hill, Lauryn: and brands 42

Hinojosa, Jorge: bio xxii; on *career artist* 44; and brands 46; and role of labels 73, 78; and power of radio 73; and popularity 138; and popular culture 157

"Hit Me Baby One More Time" (Britney Spears video): 93, 171n6

"Hold On" (Alabama Shakes TV performance): 173n21

Hole: 99; and "Miss World" (video) 171n11; and "Celebrity Skin" (video) 171n12

Holt, Douglas: and brand consumption 21; and brand equity 23; and brand meaning 18; and brand myths 22; and brand narratives 23, 32; and context and culture 38; and cultural resonance 22; and Mountain Dew 23; and the multidisciplinary nature of branding 23–4

Homosexuality: 158

"Hot Legs" (Rod Stewart video): xvi; 169n3

hot mess phase: 122–6

Houston, Whitney: and brand extensions of 50, 53; as brand liability 63–4; as *diva* 113–14; and *good girl* persona of 28, 60–1, 95; as *legend* 130; as long-term brand/*career artist* 38; and *protected status* phase of 126–8

Howard, Brittany: and Alabama Shakes 167–8; "Hold On" (TV performance) 173n21

How Brands Become Icons (Holt): 32

Hung, Holly: bio xxii; on *comeback/redemption* 125; on rebirth as *good girl* 131–2; on licensing music to film 71; on *temptress phase*, Miley Cyrus and Katy Perry 109; on top selling artists, advocacy, and changing focus 112–113

"Hung Up" (Madonna video): 19, 170n18

hypodermic needle theory: and audience reception of media messages 9

identity: and brands as aids in defining 24; and "impression management" 5; and the "looking glass self" 5; and product symbolism 21–2; as a social process 6

ideological state apparatuses (ISAs): and their role in the *social world* 145–6

"I Kissed a Girl" (Katy Perry video): 146–8, 173n8

"I Kissed a Girl" (Sobule video): 148

"I'm a Slave 4 U" (Britney Spears video): 150–1, 173n10
"impression management": 5–6
income streams: and brand extensions 54; from licensing deals and sponsorship 70–1
Infinity: 84
The Innovator's Dilemma: (Christensen) 32
Interbrand: 18
ISAs: *See* ideological state apparatuses (ISAs)
iTunes: 69, 75, 77

Jackson, Janet: and feminist revolution of 1990s xvi; and gender 140; and wardrobe malfunction 121, 140, 172n10; as *the whore* 121
Jackson, Randy: and Paula Abdul 59
Jagger, Mick: and *the legend* 130; and *the temptress* 103; and Tina Turner 130
Jay-Z: and good girls 99
Jewel: and cultural resonance 23; and brands 63
Jhally, S.: and *the exotic* 114; and the male gaze 143–4; and everyday pornography 152–3; and gendered space: 162–3
J-Lo. *See* Lopez, Jennifer
Jones, Norah: and *Come Away with Me* album cover 115, 172n1; and *the exotic* 114–16; and *Not Too Late* album cover 115, 172n2; and *the temptress* 104
Judd, Ashley: and people to watch 165–6
Junod, Tom: and *the good girl* 102; and female types in music videos 150; and Gregory Dark 150
"Justify my Love" (Madonna video): 18, 170n16

Kaplan, E. Ann: and the male gaze 149
Keegan, Andrew: and *good girls* 96
Ke$ha: and the *hot mess*: 122–3
Kilbourne, Jean: and everyday pornography 152–3; and *the exotic* 114, and gendered space 162–3; and objectification of women in advertising 143–4
Killing Us Softly 4 (Kilbourne and Jhally): 152, 162–3
Knowles, Beyoncé. *See* Beyoncé
Kotarba, J.: and branding 13–14
Kotler, P.: and brands 36

labels. *See* record labels
Lady Gaga: and "Bad Romance" (video) 1–2, 151, 169n4 (ch1); before fame 118,
172n5; and *Born This Way* album cover 143, 173n4; and cultural resonance of 23; and "empowered deviance" 14–15; and "Fame" (perfume) 170n2; as *gay icon* 129; and gender performance 140–1; as "Jo Calderone" 7–9, 170n10; and "little monsters," relationship building, and brand resonance with audiences 20; and meat dress 6, 129, 170n7; and origin of brand 35; and outfits 1, 169n2 (ch 1); and product symbolism 22; as *provocateur* 118, 170n6; as pseudonym 56; and sales of xvii; and self-image management of 5–6; and social media platforms of 169n1 (ch1); as contemporary female pop star 1–2; and Twitter presence of 79; *A Very Gaga Thanksgiving* (tv show) 23, 170n21
Lambert, Adam: 158
Lang, Elizabeth: on brand images 47–8; on celebrity overexposure 43–4; on Cyrus 109; on Ke$ha 123; and Perry 109; on pornographic mentality 122; on Rimes 96–7; on risk management for brands 63–4; on sexualization of artists 92–3; on Spears 125; on Winehouse 123–4
Lauper, Cyndi: and MTV's effect on xvi
Lavigne, Avril: and *Blender* cover 104, 171n17as brand 48; and "Girlfriend" (video) 105, 171n18; and *Maxim* 106, 171n19; as temptress 104–6
Lazarsfeld, Paul: and communication theory 9
Lefsetz, Bob: and Taylor Swift 108; and *temptress* 108
legend phase: 91; 129–30
lesbianism: 146–7, 151
Lester, Paul: and Lady Gaga as *the provocateur* 118
Levine, Adam: and gender differences 92
Lewin, Kurt: and gatekeeping 79
licensing deals: 51–2, 70–1
Lifecycle Model for Female Popular Music Stars: and Aguilera's place in 91; and Beyoncé's place in 98–9; *change of focus* 91, 111–13; and *comeback/redemption* phase of 91, 130–4; and *diva* phase of 91, 113–14; and *exotic* phase of 91, 114–18; and *gay icon* phase of 91, 128–9; and *good girl* phase of 91, 94–102; and *hot mess* phase of 91, 122–6; and *legend* phase of 91, 129–30; and Madonna's place in 91; and origins of 88; an overview of 90–1, 90f; and *protected*

status phase of 91, 126–8; and *provocateur* phase of 91, 118–19; and Rimes's place in 96–7; and *self-imposed exile* phase of 91, 126; and *temptress* phase of 91, 96–7; and *whore* phase of 91, 119–22

"Like a Virgin" (Madonna video): 18, 170n13

"Like I Love You" (Justin Timberlake video): 92, 171n2

Lilith Fair 111

Lil Wayne: and collaborations 52

Loeb, Lisa: and brands 49, 54

"London Bridge" (video): 142

"looking glass self": 5

Lopez, Jennifer: and collaborations 52

Lovato, Demi: and objectification 154

Love, Courtney: as good girl 99, 101; as hot mess 122, 125; on Winehouse 125, 172n13

Luckmann, T.: and cultural symbols 6

Madonna: and agency of 168; and brand of "sexual playfulness" 15, 18–19; and Britney Spears 19, 52, 170n19; as career artist 42; and *comeback/redemption* phase 132–3; and "Express Yourself" (video) 150–1; as *gay icon* 128; and "Hung Up" (video) 19, 170n18; and "Justify My Love" (video) 18, 170n16; as *legend* 129; and *Lifecycle Model of Female Popular Music Stars* 91; and "Like A Virgin" (video) 18, 170n13;and "Material Girl" (video) 18, 151, 170n15; and motherhood 91; and MTV's effect on the career of xv; and "Music" (video) 19, 170n17; and Nicki Minaj 53; and "Papa Don't Preach" (video) 18, 170n14; and sales of xvii; and Super Bowl performance 156, 173n20

magazine covers: 161

magic bullet theory: 9

mainstreaming: and television 158

male artists: and opportunities available to, vs. female artists 8, 26–7; and sexualization of, vs. female artists 92–4, 110

male gaze: and Adele 143; and effects of 143–4; and "Fergalicious" video 142; and Mulvey 141–2; and music industry context 139; and patterned representations of the 164; and sexually experimenting for the benefit of the 146–7; and Streep 142; 146, 149,

Maroon 5: 92; and "Moves Like Jagger" (video) 92, 171n3; and "Payphone" (video) 92, 171n4

Martinez, Vicci: and representation of gay artists on television 158

"Material Girl" (Madonna video): 18, 151, 170n15

McClary, Susan: xvi–xvii and reception of female pop stars as novel or unexpected

McClellan, Beverly: and non-traditional looking pop stars 133; and representation of gay artists and otherwise non-traditional artists on television 158, 172n16

McCracken, Grant: and celebrity endorsers 25; and cultural meaning 138

McLachlan, Sarah: as *change of focus* 111–12

Mead, George Herbert: and symbolic interactionism 5–6

Meatloaf: and gender difference 94

media. *See* social media platforms; technology

media literacy: 144, 170n12

Melville, Douglas: on Adele 116–17; on celebrity marketing 47; on celebrity overexposure 59; on lack of sex appeal as career obstacle 108; on sexualization of male vs. female artists 94; on Shakira 54–5; on unmarketability of older female artists 101

M.I.A.: and "Paper Planes" (video) 119, 172n6; as the *provocateur* 119; on popular culture 156; and Super Bowl performance 119, 172n7

Michele, Lea: *as good girl* 96; in *GQ* 171n8

Minaj, Nicki: and bisexuality 147–8; collaborations of 52–3; as *exotic* 117, 172n4; and the stated and presumed sexuality of 117–18; and *Pink Friday* (album cover) 143, 173n5; as *temptress* 117

Minnelli, Liza: as legend 129

"Miss World" (Hole video): 171n11

mobile phones: 74

Mojo, LLC: 71

Monteith, Cory: and good girls 96

Moon, Dawn: and sexuality 147

Moore, Alecia. *See* Pink

Morgan, Michael: and cultural consumption 158

Morin, Edgar: and *cultural objects* 138

Morris, Jamie: bio xxii; on *good girls*, geography, and religion 97–8 motherhood: and Aguilera 122; for Carey 131–2; and expectations of 125; and Madonna 91

Mottola, Tommy: and *protected status* 127

Mountain Dew: and cultural branding 23

"Moves Like Jagger" (Maroon 5 video): 92, 171n3

mp3.com: and consumer expectations 77

MTV: and female artists 88; and Fiona Apple 121; and Gaga 7; and legendary artists 91; and Kay Hanley 57; and the male gaze 149; and Tina Turner 130; and video types for women 150; as a cultural force xv–xvi; as a booster of brands 16; as a social reference point 12

Multivocality: and use in developing brand meaning while targeting 24–5, 160

Mulvey, Laura: and male gaze 141–2

Murray, Lars: bio xxiii; on labels 72; on radio 73; on influence of social media 72

"Music" (Madonna video): 19, 170n17

music industry: and blockbuster model 83–5; and distribution of music 77; and gatekeeping 78–84, 80t, 82f; and hegemony 144–6; and independent labels 80–1; and non-musical factors in sales 77–8; and powerful women in 163; and radio 73–4, 83–4; and recent changes to dynamics of 67–8; and record label consolidation 71–3; and retail outlets for 74–7; and sales of CDs vs. digital music 68–9; and structure of 68–70

Musicland Holding Corp.: 75

music stores: 74–7

Nakia: and being an openly gay contestant on *The Voice* 158

Names: and branding 55–6

Napster: and changing gatekeepers 67; and consumer expectations 77; and music industry revolution 32

narratives. *See* personal narratives

Negus, Keith: and blockbuster model 83; and portfolio management 83

Newbury Comics: and music retail 75

The New Marketing Manifesto (Grant): 19

"noise": as disrupting messages 9

Obama, Barack: and Twitter success 79

Objectification: of women and impact on self 153–4; and theory 154; and illegality of 107; and men 143; and Ashley Judd 166

objectification theory: tenets and effects 153–6

"Papa Don't Preach" (Madonna video): 18, 170n14

"Paper Planes" (M.I.A. video): 119, 172n6

Part of Me (documentary): 153

Patrick, Shannon: and brands 46

"Payphone" (Maroon 5 video): 92, 171n4

Perry, Katy: "I Kissed a Girl": as hetero-normative 146–8; (video) 146, 173n8; *Part of Me* (documentary) 153; *Teenage Dream* cover 143, 173n6; as *temptress* 108–9; and Twitter presence of 79

Perry, Linda: and 4 Non-Blondes 107, 171n22; and songwriting 107; and selling songs 107

personal narratives: 23–4, 89

person brands: and evolution of 34–5; and female pop stars as 39; and maintenance considerations for 40; versus product brands 16–17, 39; and strategies for managing 55–65

Pink: as brand 56

Pit Bull: and collaborations 52

pop stars: as *cultural objects* 53, 138; and definition of xix–xx; and sexuality 146–8. *See also* brands; female artists

popular culture: and critical theory 4; and Fiske on 156; and production of 156–61; and studies of 12–13; and symbolic interactionism 4–5

popularity: and Adorno 137–9; and *Billboard* 84; and standardization 137–9; and desperation 29; and diversification 48, 53; and music company effect on 138; and social construction of 25

pornography: in everyday life 122, in the music industry 150–3

portfolio management: and Keith Negus, 50, 83

post–modern gaze: and E. Ann Kaplan 149; and music videos 149

product symbolism: and self-concept 21–2; and brands as used to form identity 21–2

protected status phase: 91, 126–8

provocateur phase: 91, 118–19, 170n6

psychographics: 47

Puma: 70–1

Pussycat Dolls: 120, 122

Queen Latifah: as *change of focus* 111–12

Quinn, D. M.: and objectification 154

R&B genre: 96–7
Radio: 73–4, 83–4
rap artists: 52–3, 92
Real Networks: 77
Receivers: 2–3. *See also* audiences
record labels: 71–3, 80–1
Rein, I. J.: 13
retail outlets: 74–7
reverse gender display: 8
Rhapsody: 77
"Right There" (Nicole Scherzinger video): 120, 172n9
Rihanna: and gatekeeping 79
Riley, Tim: bio xxiii; on adolescent societal mode of assessing and objectifying women 135; on brands 43–4, 62; on Britney Spears 62; on good girls 97; on the *legend* 130, 132–4; on Madonna 132–3; on Mick Jagger and Tina Turner 130; on short-term brands 43–4; on Tina Turner, Whitney Houston, and church 97
Rimes, LeAnn: as *good girl* 95–7
Rindova, V. P.: and celebrity endorsers 25; and celebrity firms 32–4
Roberts, T. A.: and objectification 139, 153–4
Robson, Wade: and brands 61
Rose, G.: and feminist geographers 161

Sade: as brand 42
sales: of CDs vs. digital music 68–9; non-musical factors in 77–8
Scherzinger, Nicole: and "Right There" (video) 120, 172n9; as *the whore* 120, 122
Schroeder, Jonathan: and artist brands 15, 21
self-imposed exile phase: 126
self-objectification: 153–4
sexuality: and everyday pornography 151–3; and career limitations of "unsexy" performers 107–8; and Hanley on 65; and limited societal definitions of 162; as marketing tool for female artists xvii–xviii, 84–5, 164; and pop stars 146–8; as requirement for female artists' success 89, 159, 162; and weight loss 102–3
sexualization: definition of 152; of "good girls" 95–8; Judd on 166; of male vs. female artists 92–4; and *whore* phase 119
"Sexy Back" (Justin Timberlake video): 92, 171n1 (ch 4)

Shakira: and "Beautiful Liar" (video): 52, 170n3; as *career artist* 42; and collaborations of 52; as *exotic* 114; and Twitter presence of 79; and "Waka Waka" (video) 54, 170n4
Shankar, Geethali. *See* Jones, Norah
Sheffield, Rob: and *the diva* 133
Shelton, Blake: and paternalism 159; and *The Voice* 159
Shoemaker, P. J.: and gatekeeping 79
Short-term brands: and gaps in marketing theory and definition of 36, 39;
Short-term person brand: and definition 38–40; and management of 39, 46–9; and predictability/unpredictability of 46, 62; and typology 40–3; and updating brands 66
Signorelli, Nancy: and cultural consumption 158
Simon, Carly: xvi
Sobule, Jill: and bisexuality 148
social constructionism: 170n8
social media platforms: 72–3, 79, 169n1 (ch1)
social world: 2, 7
Solomon, Michael: and culture symbols 6; and product symbolism 21
Sony Music Entertainment: 71–2
Spears, Britney: as artificial construction 61–2; as children's entertainer 93, 171n7; and "Hit Me Baby One More Time" (video) 93, 171n6; and *hot mess* phase of 124–5; and "I'm a Slave 4 U" (video) 150–1, 173n10; and Madonna 52; and motherhood 125; and sales of 42; sexualization of 30, 93; and Twitter presence of 79; *whore* phase of 119–20
Spektor, Regina: as indie star 41
Stefani, Gwen: *as temptress* 104
Stewart, Martha: as brand 34–5, 46
Stewart, Rod: xvi; "Hot Legs" (video) 169n3
Strawberries: 75
Streep, Meryl: and celebrity endorsers 25–6; and gender differences in celebrity assessment 142; and the male gaze 142
Streisand, Barbra: as brand 42–3; as *diva* 113; and *The Essential...* album cover 172n15; as *gay icon* 128–9; and sales 42
Sullivan, Andrew: and consumer empowerment and sense-making 12–13
Super Bowl (2012): 156
"Sweetheart" (song): and Mariah Carey and Jermaine Dupri 131

Swift, Taylor: as adolescent 108; and appearance 129; as glamorous 106; as good girl 95; and *Red* album cover 108, 171n26; and relationship management 72; *as temptress* 108; and Twitter success 79; and *Vogue* 108, 171n25

symbolic interactionism theory: 4–5

symbolism. *See* product symbolism

Szymanski, D. M.: and objectification 154

technology: and music distribution 77; and popularity 138; and radio 73–4

television use: 158

temptress phase: Beyoncé's movement into 98–9; Cyrus's place in 108–9; definition of 102, 110; Lavigne's movement into 104–6; Perry's place in 109; Rimes's movement into 96–7; Swift's place in 108; Underwood's movement into 103

Thompson, Stephen: on artists as *gay icons* 128–9; on Clarkson 45; on Jones 115; on Madonna 132; on Perry 109; on personal disclosures 60–1; on Pussycat Dolls 120; on sex appeal as marketing tool 103–4; on sexualization of boy bands 93; on Underwood as archetypal country

Thomson, David: and the *gay icon* 128

Timberlake, Justin: as children's entertainer 93, 171n7; and female brands 61; and gender differences 92; and "Like I Love You" (video) 92, 171n2; and "Sexy Back" (video) 92, 171n1 (ch 4)

"Total Eclipse of the Heart" (Bonnie Tyler video): xvi; parody 169n2

Tower Records: 75

Tunstall, KT: and brand 42

Turner, Ike: and *the legend* 129–30

Turner, Tina: cultural resonance of 23; as legend 129–30; MTV's effect on career of xv; as *protected* 130

Twain, Shania: as *career artist* 42; as part of 90s boom xvi

Twitter: 72, 79

two-step flow theory: 10

Tyler, Bonnie: xvi; "Total Eclipse of the Heart" (video) xvi; (parody) 169n2

Underwood, Carrie: and "Blown Away" (video) 103, 171n15; and the *good girl* 98; and the *temptress* 102–3

Universal Music Group: 71–2

Unwelcome and Unlawful: Sexual Harassment in the American Workplace (Gregory) 107–8

uses and gratifications theory: 11–12

Van Etten, Sharon: and brand type 41

Van Munching, Phillip: and Aguilera's brand implosion 29; and brands 29; and need for female artist to "show the goods" 29

Vannini, P.: and the branding process 13–14

videos: and feminine types in 149–51; as gendered space 161; and post-modern gaze of 149

Vivendi Universal: 71

The Voice (tv show): and brand-within-a-brand structure of 60; and Christina Aguilera's humanity and likeability on 30; 133; and compassionate contest show 160; and representation of minority contestants on television 157–61; and top-rated new show 133

"Waka Waka": (Shakira video) 54, 170n4

Wal-Mart: 75

Walters, Barry: and brands 61

Warner Music Group: 71–2

weight: of Adele 143; of Clarkson 154, 167; and marketing of female artists 102–3; of Rimes 97

West, C.: and gender 8, 139–40

Whannel, P.: and popularity 138

whore phase: 91, 119–22

Willis, Bruce: as celebrity endorser 25–6

"Will this Record Work for Us": (Ahlkvist and Faulkner) xviii

Wilson, Ann: 169n1

Wilson, Nancy: 169n1

Winehouse, Amy: and *good girls* 99; and hot mess 122–5; and untimely death of 99, 123–4

Wipperfurth, A.: and brand meaning 18; and brand managers 25

women. *See* female artists; pop stars

X Factor (tv show): 125

"You Better Run": (Pat Benatar video) xvi; 169n4

YouTube: 72

Zimmerman, D. H.: and doing gender 8, 139–40

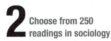